DATE DUE

NOV 2 3 1993	
DEC 0 4 1993	
DEC 2 3 1993	
NOV 1 4 1995	
APR 1 8 1996	
DEC 0 4 1996	

BRODART   Cat. No. 23-221

THE WAR CORRESPONDENTS

THE
AMERICAN
CIVIL WAR

THE WAR CORRESPONDENTS

THE
AMERICAN
CIVIL WAR

IAN F. W. BECKETT

ALAN SUTTON

First published in the United Kingdom in 1993
Alan Sutton Publishing Ltd · Phoenix Mill · Far Thrupp · Stroud · Gloucestershire

First published in the United States of America in 1993
Alan Sutton Publishing Inc · 83 Washington Street · Dover · NH 03820

British Library Cataloguing in Publication Data

Beckett, I.F.W.
The War Correspondents: The American Civil War
I. Title
973.7

ISBN 0-7509-0044-X

Library of Congress Cataloging in Publication Data applied for

Typeset in 10/12 Times.
Typesetting and origination by
Alan Sutton Publishing Limited.
Printed in Great Britain by
The Bath Press, Avon.

CONTENTS

ACKNOWLEDGEMENTS

The author acknowledges his grateful thanks to Miss Simpson and the staff of the Ministry of Defence Library; Ian Oliver and James Deffet of the Graphic Arts Department of the US Naval War College, Newport, Rhode Island; the staff of *The Times* Archive of News International PLC; and the staff of the US Army Military History Institute at Carlisle, Pennsylvania.

Photographs and illustrations are reproduced by kind permission of the following: the Massachusetts Commandery, Military Order of the Loyal Legion Collection at the US Army Military History Institute, pp. 9, 11, 16, 21, 25, 26, 27, 28, 33, 35, 37, 40, 48, 49, 51, 57, 58, 61, 63, 68, 71, 74, 79, 80, 82, 87, 89, 100, 105, 107, 109, 117, 119, 123, 127, 131, 136, 138, 139, 143, 144, 145, 146, 149, 150, 156, 159, 171, 174, 176, 177, 178, 180, 182; the US Army Military Institute Collection, pp. 12, 50, 60, 76, 86, 140, 173; the Mansell Collection, p. 134; P. Parish, *The American Civil War* (Eyre Methuen, 1975), maps, pp. 45, 92; the photograph of Francis Lawley (p. 82) is reproduced by permission of Birmingham Library Services.

INTRODUCTION

When William Howard Russell, the newly arrived war correspondent of *The Times*, was first introduced to Abraham Lincoln in Washington in March 1861, the President remarked: '*The London Times* is one of the greatest powers in the world – in fact, I don't know anything which has much more power – except perhaps the Mississippi.' Similarly, the black political activist, Frederick Douglass, remarked that Americans 'watched eagerly to see what *The London Times* had to say'. When Russell subsequently went south to visit those states which had seceded from the Union, the well-known Southern diarist, Mary Chestnut, was also to record in July 1861 that 'People here care a great deal for what Russell says because he represents *The Times* and *The London Times* reflects the sentiments of the English people.'

Indeed, the 'Thunderer' of Printing House Square was frequently regarded as an authentic mouthpiece of the British government and, although such was far from the case, it could be said broadly to represent the views of the social, economic and political establishment. As such, its editorials and coverage of events would likely be seen as significant by foreign governments and it was little wonder that Russell was assiduously courted by prominent figures both in the North and South. In addition, of course, Russell himself had essentially created the craft of war correspondent and won an international reputation for his reports from the Crimean War, those reports contributing to the fall of Lord Aberdeen's government in February 1855.

While the use of propaganda was hardly new, the power of a mass circulation press – the circulation of *The Times* appears to have varied between 68,000 and 108,000 from 1861 to 1865 – was clearly becoming an increasingly important factor in the waging of modern warfare and one of which both politicians and soldiers would need to be aware. Indeed, it might well be argued that the lack of official censorship in the Confederacy, compared with what was at least attempted – however unsuccessfully – in the North, did the South's political leadership few favours. At the international level, however, the press had an even greater potential to do harm to the relationship between states if, in the way in which its editorial content or reportage was slanted, it contributed to popular pressures on government to take certain courses of action. As it happened, the stance that was to be taken by *The Times* during the course of the American Civil War was to complicate greatly the task of the British government, led by Lord Palmerston from June 1859 until his death in October 1865.

While Britain and the United States had fought twice – apart from the independence struggle between 1775 and 1783 there had also been the war of 1812 to 1814 – there were still the ties of common heritage and, above all, those of economics. Indeed, between 1815 and 1860 Britain and the United States were each other's best customers. Britain, of course, imported cotton from the South but also took Northern agricultural produce such as wheat and other grains, while she exported manufactured goods and, especially, capital to the United States, the latter assisting in the development of

American railroads. Such economic realities had tempered diplomatic disputes so that, for example, agreement had been reached in 1846 to fix the boundary between the Oregon territory and Canada at the 49th parallel while, four years later, the Clayton–Bulwer treaty saw Britain and the United States both renounce territorial ambitions in Central America and agree to jointly promote a canal across the Panamanian isthmus.

Nevertheless, there was reflected in the attitude of *The Times* a latent distrust among many establishment Englishmen of the potential power of the United States and of its overtly democratic system. In that regard it was understandable if some saw in the outbreak of the American Civil War both the expectation of a weakening of that power potential and also proof of the instability of the American federal political system. Moreover, by contrast with the Lincoln administration, which appeared to have protectionist aspirations and did, in fact, go ahead with the introduction of new tariffs under the provisions of the Morrill Tariff Act in February 1861, the Confederacy espoused the principle of free trade. Britain, and indeed *The Times*, opposed the institution of slavery but the abolition of slavery was not an avowed aim of the North until the autumn of 1862. Consequently there was no crisis of conscience in seeing the survival of the Confederacy as being in Britain's interests and, once war had begun, *The Times* assuredly did look to those interests.

In reality, however, British public opinion was deeply divided over the war and the traditional interpretation of a British aristocratic identification with the Confederacy and of a working-class identification with the North has been discredited, for all that the South was generally depicted as a rural arcadia populated by a landowning society of English descent and the North as an urbanized bestial immigrant society – the stereotypes will be apparent in some of the reports reproduced in this volume. Conservative opinion did, indeed, tend to favour the South but the North was by no means without its supporters among the aristocracy, the Duke of Argyll being a prominent champion of the Union. Moreover, while radical and provincial middle-class opinion appeared to favour the North, it was actually the leading radical, John A. Roebuck, who was to bring forward an unsuccessful motion in the House of Commons for the recognition of the Confederacy in June 1863, while W.E. Gladstone was not alone in finding it difficult to judge between the merits of freedom of trade and of self-determination for the South on the one hand against emancipation on the other.

Similarly, while there were those British working men who identified emancipation with their own struggle for improved labour conditions, there was considerable support for the South among Lancashire textile workers, whose livelihood was most affected by the imposition of the Northern blockade on the South in April 1861. As it happened, there was a considerable surplus of cotton in Britain at the time the war began and over-production was a more direct cause of the distress in the textile districts than the imposition of a blockade. Moreover, the cotton glut actually negated the Confederacy's own suspension of cotton exports in an attempt to encourage British intervention. Thus, economic distress related to the war was not immediate, and in any case alternative sources of cotton had been found by its latter stages. Then again, other British industries benefited from supplying the wartime requirements of both North and South and this tended to reinforce the desire to maintain a strict neutrality. Indeed, a political leadership as pragmatic as that presided over by Palmerston was unlikely to be drawn into intervention until such time as the issue of Southern independence was not in doubt since there was little for Britain to gain and much to lose. Thus the British government firmly declared its neutrality in May 1861 and, in so doing, received the full support of *The Times*.

It should be said, of course, that there was no expectation that the South could be brought back into the Union by force of arms, and this view persisted for some considerable time. This was certainly the case in the offices of *The Times*, whose American-based correspondents, as will be seen, continued to display the same faith in the ability of the Confederacy to win its independence almost until the very moment when the South collapsed. However, since the South's 'King Cotton' diplomacy was not going to stimulate intervention, it would have required sustained Confederate battlefield success to shake the resolve of the British government's leadership as a whole to maintain its neutrality. In this regard the Confederate defeat at Antietam in September 1862, which was immediately followed by Lincoln's emancipation proclamation, ended any realistic expectations of intervention on behalf of the South since it occurred at the very moment when British recognition was seriously being considered. Thereafter, Britain was rather more concerned by events in Europe such as the Polish revolt against Russia in 1863 and the war fought by Austria and Prussia against Denmark in the following year.

That did not mean that the relationship between Britain and the Union would be free of tensions, especially since Britain's declaration of neutrality and its implied endorsement of the Confederacy was so greatly resented in the North. Thus disputes continued to arise, and it was in their reaction to these that the British and American press posed the greatest threat to the control being exercised over events by their respective governments. The affair of the British mail steamer, *Trent*, from which two Confederate emissaries to Europe were removed apparently by the unilateral rather than officially approved action of a Union naval officer in December 1861, certainly did result in hasty British preparations for the defence of Canada.

The defence of Canada generally remained a problem especially when the imposition of conscription in the North made Canada an attractive refuge for those seeking to evade service, while Confederate agents also saw it as a useful base for raids against the North as in that on the Vermont town of St Albans in October 1864.

Other British vessels were also to be detained and, perhaps understandably, such seizures aroused the ire of *The Times* although the British government's attitude was rather more ambivalent, since a maritime power such as Britain would actually benefit in the long term from any general international recognition of the principle of blockade on the high seas. It had been the British imposition of blockade in the prosecution of its war against Napoleonic France that had been the principal issue in bringing the United States to war against her in 1812, and there was a certain irony in the Union's sudden willingness in 1861 to accept the Declaration of Paris of 1856 recognizing and regulating blockade when the United States had previously declined to do so. Another issue was to be the construction of Confederate commerce raiders and warships in Britain, notably that of the *Alabama*, which sailed from Birkenhead in March 1862, and the so-called Laird rams, which Britain detained in the same port in September 1863.

Given such difficulties, the continuing hostility of *The Times* to the North or, for that matter, the equal hostility of the *New York Herald* to Britain did little to assist Anglo-

American relations during the war or after the North had secured victory in April 1865. Indeed, there was to be a sustained contemporary critique of *The Times* in 1865 by Leslie Stephen, the author and editor. Pointing out that the newspaper was indeed likely to be seen as an indicator of British attitudes in the United States, Stephen attacked *The Times* on a variety of grounds. There was, for example, its poor record as a 'prophet' of the war's outcome: 'Like a man in a dark room, it knocked its head straight against the wall, without even putting out its hands to save itself.' There was the apparent continuing expectation that a military dictator was about to emerge in the North, the constant emphasis upon the North's supposed reliance upon immigrants for its armies, the frequent interpretation of what turned out to be Northern victories as defeats, the inconsistencies in the paper's apparent editorial policy, its moral condemnation of the North and, in particular, its ambivalent attitude to the issue of slavery and emancipation. The result in Stephen's view was 'a very serious mischief', from 'pouring out a ceaseless flood of scurrilous abuse' for all that it was 'couched, indeed, in decent language'.

Stephen was essentially correct in his depiction of the attitudes prevalent in the columns of *The Times* and was later acknowledged to be so even in the relevant volume of the paper's official history, published in 1939. However, he perhaps ignored the fact that there was a degree of consistency in the opposition to British intervention and in the concern that British interests were of paramount importance, even if editorial judgement was distinctly lacking in displaying such partiality to the South at the same time as espousing neutrality. Moreover, there was at least a degree of moderating balance to the editorials in the frequent contributions of William Vernon Harcourt, under the pseudonym of '*Historicus*'. Yet in the last analysis *The Times* failed the challenge presented by the war between 1861 and 1865 in a way which damaged its own image and that of Britain.

Part of the problem was the relative ignorance of the United States at Printing House Square, only its editor, John T. Delane, and one of its senior editorial staff, Robert Lowe, having visited the country and both very briefly. Neither appears to have enjoyed an experience which only reinforced existing prejudices, while the manager of *The Times*, Mowbray Morris, was of West Indies planter stock and blamed Britain's own abolition of slavery for the loss of his family's fortune. It has also been suggested that the sheer volume of conflicting material flowing into London from the United States during the war was beyond the capacity of Delane and his staff to interpret correctly.

Much depended, therefore, upon the quality of the correspondents in the field and, for varying reasons, *The Times* was not to be well served in this respect. No one could doubt Russell's general objectivity and his sympathies were with the North rather than the South. Thus, although Russell was clearly charmed by the attentions he received in the Confederacy, the leading Confederate propagandist in England, Henry Hotze, believed that Russell's depiction of the South did not materially assist his efforts to win European recognition. Ironically, however, it was Russell's very objectivity in graphically describing the Union rout at the first battle of Manassas/Bull Run in July 1861 which so antagonized Northern opinion that Russell was subsequently prevented from accompanying the Union army in the so-called Peninsular campaign in April 1862. As a result, Russell chose to leave America. Similarly, another correspondent of *The Times*, Antonio Gallenga, sent out in 1863, also returned to Britain prematurely when he, too, was effectively barred from accompanying Union forces in the West. The paper's experienced New York correspondent at the start of the war, J.C. Bancroft Davis, was an American sympathetic to the North. He grew increasingly frustrated with the editorial policy in London, however, and resigned in December 1861.

With the departure of Bancroft Davis and of Russell, the responsibility for reporting from the war fell to Charles Mackay, who replaced the former in February 1862, and Francis Lawley, who began reporting from the Confederacy in September of the same year. Neither were without experience as journalists but both were passionate support- ers of the South. Accordingly, they simply reinforced the proclivities of the London office and Mackay in particular was to earn the opprobium of Stephen for 'one long effort, lasting for three years, to shut his own eyes and the eyes of his countrymen to the existence of any heroic qualities in the people amongst whom he lived'. Certainly, as will become apparent, Mackay had his clear prejudices and he remained fairly firmly tied to New York with many of his reports dwelling on local city politics or on com- mercial matters. Moreover, just as Russell had been increasingly denied any special access to policy makers after the Bull Run dispatch, Mackay was totally frozen out from such circles. He was to be dismissed by Mowbray Morris on 21 April 1865, by which time it was rather too late to make amends for the way in which the coverage of the war by *The Times* had become perceived in the now victorious North. Yet if his prejudices and limitations are understood and accepted, Mackay can still be a valued guide to contemporary perceptions of events and his descriptive writing is frequently very atmospheric.

If Mackay exaggerated opposition to the Lincoln administration in the North, Lawley generally ignored opposition to the Confederacy in the South and his praise for Southern generalship in Virginia knew few bounds. He travelled quite widely in the South, however, and his access to the Southern military leadership often makes him a valuable witness to events – and he has been widely accepted as such by historians. If his style did not match that of Russell it was still often highly memorable, as when he chose to depict what he described as 'the unchronicled incidents of battles – the unconsidered trifles which await picking up and collecting'.

What follows is essentially a narrative of the Civil War through the eyes of these five correspondents of *The Times* – Bancroft Davis, Russell, Gallenga, Mackay and Lawley – with occasional reference to some additional (but invariably unnamed) occasional correspondents. Their reports were not the sole coverage of American events in the newspaper since heavy use was also made of extracts from American newspapers and of items of news received from the latest steamer to dock at Liverpool or some other British or Irish port. Indeed, their reports invariably appeared some time after the events they described and, in the case of Lawley in particular, a month or more could elapse before his articles breached the Northern blockade. In addition, the comment of the newspaper on the war embraced its own editorials and leaders, articles by outsiders such as those by Harcourt and, of course, the letters from the reading public.

Nevertheless, what was to a degree relatively considered reportage makes for a better narrative framework than any attempt to include the full range of the contents of *The Times* over this period and, for the latter, readers are referred to Hugh Brogan's selec- tion published in 1975, in which only limited use could be made of the dispatches of the various correspondents. Other than the Brogan selection, only one other publication has offered any body of extracts from *The Times*, namely W.M. Stanley Hoole's selection from the reports of Francis Lawley, published in a limited edition of 450 copies in 1964. In this case only very short extracts – often just a few sentences – were reproduced from any single article, of which over eighty were printed from the hundred or so Lawley sent back to London.

The chosen way of representing Lawley's work in the Hoole volume is understandable given the sheer length of some of these dispatches – the eight written between 29 April and 19 May 1863, for example, covering the Chancellorsville campaign, total 15,000 words alone. Much the same could be said for the reports of the others. Inevitably selection has been equally difficult for this edition but has been made both on the basis of those articles which carry forward the narrative and those which illustrate or illuminate particular aspects of the war. An attempt has been made to convey not just the military and naval operations but also the way in which the war affected societies and politics in the North and South. As in the case of those other books which have utilized extracts from the reports, it has not been feasible to reproduce the whole of such lengthy articles. However, a sufficiently long extract has been selected in each case to attempt to convey the general flavour of the report, and the whole of a particular section has been reproduced. Material added by this editor to clarify a reference to an individual or an event is placed in square parentheses while the linking narrative places contemporary reports in historical context and current historical perception.

1861

During the 1840s and 1850s the United States was a rapidly growing country both in terms of its population, which increased from about 17 million in 1840 to almost 32 million by 1860, but also in size. Texas, which had won its independence from Mexico in 1836, joined the union in 1845 while the United States' own war against Mexico in 1845–6 resulted in the acquisition of California and the territories of Utah and New Mexico. The original thirteen colonies of the eastern seaboard had been joined by a further twenty states while the Washington, Nebraska and Kansas territories had also been established in the 1850s. As the new territories opened so there was the further westward shift of population assisted by the expansion of mass communication, especially more than 30,000 miles of railway track that was laid down by 1860. In the east there was also increasing urbanization and industrialization.

However, amid such growth and change the southern states appeared increasingly as an almost separate culture and certainly had what has been described as a distinct sectional identity. The South was not the slave-owning aristocracy of popular imagination, since only approximately a quarter of its 1.5 million heads of families owned any slaves at all, and not much more than 40 per cent of these possessed more than five slaves. Nevertheless, for all that there was a large non-slave-owning middle class in the South, the planter interest did exercise effective political power and it was undeniable that it was the 'peculiar institution' of slavery which most clearly differentiated the South from the remainder of the United States. By 1860 there were some 3.5 million slaves in the eleven southern states of Alabama, Arkansas, Florida, Georgia, Louisiana, Mississippi, North Carolina, South Carolina, Tennessee, Texas and Virginia with a further 450,000 in the so-called 'border' states of Delaware, Kentucky, Maryland and Missouri. Slavery had continued to exist when many had once assumed that it would simply wither away, because of the growth in demand for cotton in both the North and Europe at the beginning of the nineteenth century. Fast becoming a staple crop upon which the whole southern economy was dependent, cotton not only provided a new rationale for slave labour but also inhibited wider economic growth – even though a boom in cotton prices brought much prosperity in the 1850s.

Symbolic of the divergence between northern and southern culture, therefore, slavery became the principal political issue in the 1840s and 1850s. Despite the emergence of an abolitionist movement in the 1830s, the issue was not abolition itself but whether or not slavery would expand into the new territories. In turn the whole political balance within the Union was of particular concern, for as each new state was admitted so it acquired two members in the Senate, implying for the South the possibility that it could be increasingly out-voted in what it regarded as its special interests, and raising the spectre of federal intervention. A state's rights within a federal system and the ability or otherwise of a state to withdraw or secede from the union thus also became a very real issue. In 1850 a measure of compromise was reached whereby California was admitted to the union as a free state, but the Utah and New Mexico territories were established without commitment either way on the future of slavery within them. The organization of the Kansas and Nebraska territories in 1854, however, resulted in such bitter sectional conflict when delegating to the settlers the future status of slavery there, that it split the Whig party which had emerged as the main rival to the Democratic Party in the 1830s. From one section of the Whigs developed a new Republican Party firmly opposed to any extension of slavery.

Violence between 'free staters' and pro-slavers in Kansas added to the increasing tensions, as did the decision of the Supreme Court in 1857 that Dred Scott, a Missouri slave formerly resident with his master in Illinois and the then territory of Wisconsin, could not claim freedom on the basis of such residence and, further, that Congress had no power to prevent the establishment of slavery in any territory. The raid by the militant abolitionist, John Brown, on the federal arsenal at Harper's Ferry in October 1859 increased southern alarm, and many in the South came to believe it a natural consequence of Republican activity for all that Brown had no actual link with the party. Moreover, slavery had also effectively divided the Democratic Party, whose current incumbent in the White House, President James Buchanan was not standing for re-election in the presidential elections due in November 1860. Unable to agree on a candidate, the Democrats ended with northerners nominating Stephen Douglas and southerners John Breckinridge to contest against the Republican candidate, Abraham Lincoln, who had himself emerged as something of a compromise, and the candidate from a new Constitutional Union Party, John Bell. With the anti-republican groups so split, Lincoln gained a clear majority of the votes available in the electoral college, although he won only 40 per cent of the popular vote. More significantly, Lincoln decisively won the northern states and, in the process, realized the deepest fears of the South concerning a Republican administration, which would take office in March 1861. Almost immediately the question of secession came once more to the forefront of debate.

The *Times* correspondent in New York since 1854 and the third incumbent of the position since its establishment in 1849, was a lawyer and future distinguished American diplomat and judge, J.C. Bancroft Davis (1822–1907). As the son of a prominent anti-slavery Whig, Bancroft Davis was no friend of the South and, in the past, had often been exasperated by what he saw as Southern demands. He could see little alternative to secession when he wrote on 19 December 1860, his report appearing on 3 January 1861:

I do not see how secession is now to be avoided. In making this statement, however, it is important to define what secession is. It is easier to say what it is not than what it is. It is not order and good government. It is not submission to the law, and accepting a President elected in the manner provided by the Constitution and the laws. It is not a regard for the rights of others. It is nothing, in fact, which law-abiding Englishmen are taught to respect and observe. On the other hand, the

Abraham Lincoln

first step of secession, the paper separation, which is all that is yet meant by the word, is not necessarily a dissolution of the Federal Government. The National Constitution and the traditions and forms of the National Government may yet remain for the States which are willing to submit to law and observe its forms. For these Mr Lincoln will still remain the President, chosen in the regular constitutional way. Nor does it even imply necessarily a dissolution of the Federal Union, as, after the seceding States have voted themselves out of the Union, they may be brought back in two ways – either by negotiation or by force, provided, in the first case, the negotiators are willing to concede all that the rebellious States demand; or, in the other alternative, that the remaining States are strong enough and sufficiently united to authorize a resort to force. With the exception of four, or, at most, six of the cotton States, there is, in my opinion, no preference in the South for disunion; and if the other Southern States temporarily secede – which from my information I am inclined to think will be the case – it will be because they are forced into it, and because they hope to induce negotiations which, prolonged, may result in re-establishing the Union. That several of the cotton States will secede in the course of the next month I have little doubt. They believe that they can force the border States to follow them; and it is the general opinion at Washington, among those best able to judge, that unless immediate concessions are made by the North the border States will be forced to follow, and that the reconstruction of the Federation on a modified basis will be thus assured. Thus, in the eyes of such politicians, the union of the entire Slave States in the movement, so far from implying an ultimate dissolution of the Union, will ensure its speedy reunion, with such guarantees as will ensure its continuance. Some politicians aim at the absolute expulsion, in any event, of contumacious anti-slavery New England; but those who are now countenancing a united co-operative Southern action look to an early reconstruction of the Union in some form. They forget that it is easier to destroy than to create, and they are willing to hazard the destruction of a noble Confederation, under which the nation has prospered beyond example in history, the rule of which has been a gentle one, almost unfelt at home, and the flag of which is respected abroad to the most remote corner of the globe, – they are willing to hazard this, and plunge the country possibly in a civil war, for the chance of uniting the Slave States, and gaining a further political advantage for property in slaves. In the present excited state of the public mind it is absolutely impossible to predict even the immediate future. It is subject at any moment to be directed into the course of violence by the will of passionate men, or by the chances of an accident.

In fact South Carolina, which had come close to secession over the federal imposition of tariffs in the so-called nullification crisis of 1832–3, passed a secession ordinance through a special convention of its legislature on the day after Bancroft Davis penned his report. Similar moves were triggered in other states so that by 1 February 1861 Mississippi, Florida, Alabama, Georgia, Louisiana and Texas had all followed suit. Immediate attention in South Carolina, however, focused on federal property in the state, not least the coastal and harbour protection forts in Charleston harbour. President Buchanan was clearly anxious to avoid provocation but events were precipi-

Robert Anderson

tated by the action of the federal commander of the small garrison at Fort Moultrie, Major Robert Anderson, ironically a Kentuckian who had been a slave owner. Bancroft Davis's account of the growing confrontation at Charleston was written on 1 January 1861 and appeared in print on 17 January:

The opportunities for a peaceful solution of the difficulties between the North and the South are rapidly passing away. The attitude of South Carolina, unfortunately sustained by other planting states, leaves no ground that Northern statesmen can, with any respect for themselves, or any regard for sound principles of government, stand upon. Not only have they left the Union without waiting for a discussion of the terms upon which the separation may take place, which, to say the least, would have been civil to the other States, but they have by an armed force taken possession of all the Federal forts in Charleston harbour, except the one in actual occupation of Federal troops, of the Post-office and Customs-house, and of an arsenal containing 70,000 stand of arms. The channel of this harbour is defended by three forts – Fort Moultrie at the north; another fort, the name of which I do not now remember, at the south [Fort Johnson]; and Fort Sumter, midway between the two in the water. To the south of this latter fort are flats – to the north of it and between it and Fort Moultrie is the channel. Until Wednesday last [26 December] the whole of the little force in charge of Major Anderson was in Fort Moultrie. During the night he transported his whole force, ammunition and provisions to Fort Sumter, spiked the guns of Fort Moultrie, and burnt their carriages. The move, as a strategy, was masterly, for the new position is accessible only by water, is mounted with the heaviest and most approved modern guns,

commands both of the other forts, so as to make them untenable, can be held by
the little force under Major Anderson's command, and, what may become important if war breaks out, commands the city of Charleston.

Ultimately Buchanan resolved to reinforce Anderson, but using an unarmed
merchantman, *Star of the West*, which was turned back by fire from South Carolina
batteries on 9 January. Anderson declined to open fire himself without definite orders
and, for all intents and purposes, there matters rested while the Buchanan administration served out its last weeks of office. However, as Lincoln made his way from Illinois
to Washington for his inauguration, representatives of the seceding states met at
Montgomery in Alabama on 4 February to draft a new constitution and establish a provisional government for the Confederate States of America, the choice for provisional
president falling on a former Secretary of War, Jefferson Davis of Mississippi. As
Bancroft reported on 19 February in a dispatch printed on 4 March:

While Mr Lincoln is making his triumphal procession towards Washington,
Mr Jefferson Davis, the President elect of the Southern Confederacy, is
doing the same thing towards Montgomery. He, too, is carried in special trains; he,
too, meets crowds of enthusiastic admirers, and he, too, has to make speeches. He
has also made his inaugural address, which I enclose, it being too long to embody
entire in this letter, although of sufficient public interest to merit publication. He
repudiates entirely reunion, except on the basis of the new Constitution, but
invites accession from the Northern States. The Southern amendments he calls
explanatory of the well-known intent of the framers of the Constitution of the

The inauguration of Jefferson Davis at
Montgomery

United States. In this he is mistaken, for, if anything is clear, it is that the framers of that Constitution thought that they were constructing a national Government, not a Confederation of States without power in the central Government to retain a member wishing to retire. If that be the meaning of the Constitution of the United States, it is the greatest sham in history. The new Southern Government is now fairly installed, without giving the people it assumes to govern an opportunity to say whether they wish it or not, and has invested itself with the war-making power. The hundreds of thousands of dollars spent by South Carolina in preparations for attacking Fort Sumter are now, fortunately for peace, of no use until the new Government chooses to direct the force they have gathered together; or until South Carolina, dissatisfied at delay, secedes again.

Lincoln's inauguration took place on 4 March and, on the very next day, he was confronted with a dispatch from Anderson indicating that Fort Sumter could not hold out unless resupplied. A similar situation also existed in respect of the federal garrison at Fort Pickens in Florida. Lincoln decided to reinforce Pickens on 12 March although, in fact, this had still not been effected in early April due to the delay in the transmission of the instructions and the reservations of the local commanders. The decision to resupply Sumter was finally taken on 4 April with the expedition sailing from New York four days later, but with the clearly stated intention that fire would not be opened unless the Confederate authorities who had assumed responsibility at Charleston did so first.

As the final crisis approached, the most celebrated of war correspondents, William Howard Russell (1820–1907), was arriving to represent *The Times*. His reputation for ever established by his reports from the Crimean War of 1854–6, the Irish-born Russell reached New York on 14 March and made his way to Washington where he met Lincoln and his Cabinet. Like Bancroft Davis, Russell was broadly sympathetic to the North but, as he reported in a dispatch of 29 March printed on 16 April, he would view matters from a detached perspective:

It is difficult for one who has arrived so recently in this country and who has been subjected to such a variety of statements to come to any very definite conclusion in reference to the great questions which agitate it. But as far as I can I shall form my opinions from what I see, and not from what I hear, and as I shall proceed South in a few days there is a probability of my being able to ascertain what is the real state of affairs in that direction. As far as I can judge – my conclusion, let it be understood, being drawn from the prevailing opinions of others – 'the South will never go back into the Union.' On the same day I heard a gentleman of position among the Southern party say, 'No concession, no compromise, nothing that can be done or suggested shall induce us to join any Confederation of which the New England States are members;' and by another gentleman, well known as one of the ablest of the Abolitionists, I was told, 'If I could bring back the Southern States by holding up my little finger I should consider it criminal to do so.' The friends of the Union sometimes endeavour to disguise their sorrow and their humiliation at the prospect presented by the Great Republic under the garb of pride in the peculiar excellence of institutions which have permitted such a revolution as Secession without the loss of one drop of blood. But concession averts bloodshed. If I give up my purse to the footpad who presents a pistol at my head I satisfy all his demands, and he must be a sanguinary miscreant if he pulls trigger afterwards. The policeman has, surely, no business to boast of the peculiar excellence, in such a transaction, of the state of things which allows the transfer to take place without bloodshed. A Government may be so elastic as, like an overstrained india-rubber band, to have no compressive force whatever, and that very quality is claimed for the Federal Government as excellence by some eminent men whom I have met, and who maintained the thesis, that the United States Government has no right whatever to assert its authority by force over the people of any State whatever; that, based on the consent of all, it ceases to exist wherever there is dissent, – a doctrine which no one need analyse who understands what are the real uses and ends of Government. The friends of the existing Administration, on the whole, regard the Secession as a temporary aberration, which a 'masterly inactivity', the effects of time, inherent weakness, and a strong reaction, of which they flatter themselves they see many proofs in the Southern States, will correct. 'Let us,' they say, 'deal with this matter in our own way. Do not interfere. A recognition of Secession would be an interference amounting to hostility. In good time the violent men down South will come to their senses, and the treason will die out.' They ignore the difficulties which European States may feel in refusing to recognize the principles on which the United States were founded when they find them embodied in a new Confederation, which, so far as we know, may be to all intents and purposes constituted in an entire independence, and present itself to the world with claims to recognition to which England, at least, having regard to precedents of de facto Governments, could only present an illogical refusal. The hopes of other sections of the Northerners are founded on the want of capital in the Slave States; on the pressure which will come upon them when they have to guard their own frontiers against the wild tribes who have been hitherto repelled at the expense of the whole Union by the Federal troops; on the exigencies of trade, which will compel them to deal with the North, and thereby to enter into friendly relations and ultimate re-alliance. But most impartial people, at least in New York, are of opinion that the South has shaken the dust off her feet, and will never enter the portals of the Union again. She is confident in her own destiny. She feels strong enough to stand alone. She believes her mission is one of extension and conquest – her leaders are men of singular political ability and undaunted resolution. She has but to stretch forth her hand, as she believes, and the Gulf becomes an American lake closed by Cuba. The reality of these visions the South is ready to test, and she would not now forego the trial, which may, indeed, be the work of years, but which she will certainly make. All the considerations which can be urged against her resolves are as nothing in the way of her passionate will, and the world may soon see under its eyes the conflict of two Republics founded on the same principles, but subjected to influences that produce repulsion as great as exists in two bodies charged with the same electricity. If ever the explosion come it will be tremendous in its results, and distant Europe must feel the shock.

Despite the contacts he had made with the Northern leadership, Russell could obtain little inside information of value and decided to travel south, particularly as hostilities appeared imminent. Indeed, as Russell travelled, the Confederate authorities resolved to demand the surrender of Anderson's garrison at Sumter before it could be resupplied. Anderson rejected the ultimatum on 10 April and at 4.30 a.m. on 12 April 1861 Confederate batteries opened fire on Fort Sumter. After thirty-three hours of bombardment, Anderson capitulated on 14 April. On the following day Lincoln issued a proclamation to raise 75,000 men to serve for ninety days to suppress armed insurrection in the South. Virginia voted to secede on 17 April and Lincoln proclaimed a blockade of the southern coasts two days later. That same day, Bancroft Davis reported from New York in a dispatch printed on 6 May:

It is just 86 years to-day since the first shot was fired in the War of American Independence at Lexington, in Massachusetts, at break of day on the warm morning of a prematurely summerish day. On the anniversary of that day we hear by telegraph of the first blood – and that, by a singular coincidence, the blood of Massachusetts men [the only casualty at Sumter, resulting from the bursting of a gun during a last salute to the fort's flag before it was hauled down] – shed in the new war, which has been commenced by those who seek to subvert all that was accomplished in the struggle for Independence. The great civil war that everybody had regarded as an improbability is now fairly inaugurated, – blood has been shed, sectional animosities have been aroused, – Virginia has seceded, or will do so soon in the van of the Border Slave States, – there is every probability that Kentucky, Tennessee, Arkansas, and North Carolina will follow, – Maryland is trembling poised between her allegiance to the stars and stripes and her sympathy for slavery, and everything now promises a war between the consolidated Slave States and the American Government – a war for the extension of African slavery and the annihilation of constitutional Government, except as subservient to that institution.

The events of the past week have moved on so rapidly that I have thought you would perhaps desire a stray letter between the regular Cunard packets. It is but a week to-day since, in a time of peace which the Administration at Washington were bent on continuing, [Brigadier-] General [Pierre G.T.] Beauregard opened his attack upon Fort Sumter. Within the week Fort Sumter has been evacuated, its garrison transferred to New York, its very existence forgotten in the rapidity of the march of events. A little contest in the harbour of Charleston has grown into a great civil war. The effect of the news in New York of the attack upon the fort is as unexpected as it is overwhelming. I confess that I was not prepared for it; for, knowing the demoralization of the party leaders – political demoralization, I mean, not personal or moral – I did not suppose that the popular heart was beating so strong for the national flag and the national Government. So it is, however; and the result has taken everybody by surprise.

The proclamation of Mr Lincoln, announcing a state of war, and calling upon the remaining States to contribute their quotas towards the defence of the flag and the recovery of the forts, has aroused the national pride and touched the national heart in every Northern State, while, with an equal rapidity, it has carried the

Pierre Beauregard

Southern Border States towards the rebels. From the moment the blow was struck all party differences vanished here, and so strong was the public indignation against the rebels that it became dangerous for a man to avow Southern sympathies. This feeling had begun to show itself before my last letter. But on the following day the manifestation was much more enthusiastic. Then the first troops from the East arrived on their way to Washington, and it was also known that our 7th Regiment, the pride and the pet of New York, whose ranks are made up of the sons of her first merchants, leading lawyers, and best statesmen, was to be the first called from this town to the defence of the capital. It was a bright sunshiny April day, with one of those clear crystal American atmospheres that every one who has ever been in America will remember. The town had broken out into an eruption of the star-spangled banner. It floated from every hotel, from every bank, from every insurance-office. It was draped in festoons across the streets, the shipping in the harbour was alive with the gaiety of its colours, it was carried in miniature on the headstall or saddle of every omnibus horse and drayhorse in the crowded Broadway, and its colours were seen on the rosettes of the private carriages. Without seeing it, it is, I fear, impossible to conceive how the loyalty of this people to their flag had suddenly and spontaneously gushed out. The Massachusetts regiment had hardly left the ferry, when it was announced that the *Baltic* was at her dock, with Major Anderson and his command. The crowd gathered at once at the dock, and the scene of the reception is described as enthusiastic in the extreme. Later in the day, as I was passing the hotel where the Major is quartered, I saw a crowd going in and coming out; many of them working men, apparently returning from their day's work. I fell into the queue to see what was to be seen, and soon found myself shaking hands with a short, thin, weather-beaten man with a bronzed face and a keen black eye, and in a military frockcoat, that I knew at once to be Major Anderson, and then was hurried on to make way for the next aspirant for a shake. Even ladies, walking in the avenue, seeing the crowd, joined in the line to see the hero, for the scandalous reports against his loyalty found no response here, and are now completely set at rest by the official accounts, which show he did everything that could be done to maintain himself, and finally evacuated without a surrender.

Sumter had fallen while Russell was at sea en route for Norfolk in Virginia where he entrained for Charleston. From there he sent back on 21 April his description of Sumter, printed on 14 May:

At a distance the fort bears some resemblance to Fort Paul at Sebastopol. It is a truncated pentagon, with three faces armed – that which is towards Morris Island being considered safe from attack, as the work was only intended to resist an approach from the sea. It is said to have cost altogether more than 200,000 pounds sterling. The walls are of solid brick and concrete masonry, built close to the edge of the water, 60 feet high, and from eight to 12 feet in thickness, and carry three tiers of guns on the north, east, and west exterior sides. Its weakest point is on the south side, where the masonry is not protected by any flank fire to sweep the wharf. The work is designed for an armament of 140 pieces of ordnance of all calibres. Two tiers are under bomb-proof casemates, and the third or upper tier is *en barbette*; the lower tiers intended for 42-pounder paixhan guns; the second tier for eight and ten-inch columbiads, for throwing solid or hollow shot, and the upper tier for mortars or guns. But only 75 are now mounted. Eleven paixhan guns are among that number, nine of them commanding Fort Moultrie. Some of the columbiads are not mounted. Four of the 32-pounder barbette guns are on pivot carriages, and others have a sweep of 180 degrees. The walls are pierced everywhere for musketry. The magazine contains several hundred barrels of gunpowder, and a supply of shot, powder, and shells. The garrison was amply supplied with water from artificial wells. The war garrison of the fort ought to be at least 600 men, but only 79 were within its walls, with the labourers – 109, all told – at the time of the attack.

The walls of the fort are dented on all sides by shot marks, but in no instance was any approach made to a breach, and the greatest damage, at one of the angles on the south face, did not extend more than two feet into the masonry, which is of very fine brick. The parapet is, of course, damaged, but the casemate embrasures are uninjured. On landing at the wharf we perceived that the granite copings had suffered more than the brickwork, and that the stone had split up and splintered where it was struck. The ingenuity of the defenders was evident here. They had no mortar with which to fasten up the stone slabs they had adapted as blinds to the windows of the unprotected south side, but Major Anderson, or his subordinate, Captain Foster, had closed the slabs in with lead, which he procured from some water piping, and had rendered them proof against escalade, which he was prepared also to resent by extensive mines laid under the wharf and landing-place, to be fired by friction tubes and lines laid inside the work. He had also prepared a number of shells for the same purpose, to act as hand grenades, with friction tubes and lanyards, when hurled down from the parapet on his assailants. The entrance to the fort was blocked up by masses of masonry, which had been thrown down from the walls of the burnt barracks and officers' quarters along the south side. A number of men were engaged in digging up the mines at the wharf, and others were busied in completing the ruin of the tottering walls, which were still so hot that it was necessary to keep a hose of water playing on part of the brickwork. To an uninitiated eye it would seem as if the fort was untenable, but, in reality, in spite of the destruction done to it, a stout garrison, properly supplied, would have been in no danger from anything, except the explosion of the magazine, of which the copper door was jammed by the heat at the time of the surrender. Exclusive of the burning of the quarters and the intense heat, there was no reason for a properly handled and sufficient force to surrender the place. It is needless to say Major Anderson had neither one nor the other. He was in all respects most miserably equipped. His guns were without screws, scales, or tangents, so that his elevations were managed by rude wedges of deal, and his scales marked in chalk on the breech of the guns, and his distances and bearings scratched in the same way on the side of the embrasures. He had not a single fuse for his shells, and he tried in vain to improvise them by filling pieces of bored-out pine with caked gunpowder. His cartridges were out, and he was compelled to detail some of his few men to make them out of shirts, stockings, and jackets. He had not a single mortar, and he was compelled to the desperate expedient of planting long guns in the ground at an angle of 45 degrees, for which he could find no shell, as he had no fuses which could be fired with safety. He had no sheers to mount his guns, and chance alone enabled him to do so by drifting some large logs down with the tide against Sumter. Finally, he had not even one engine to put out a fire in quarters. I walked carefully over the parade and could detect the marks of only seven shells in the ground, but Major Whiting told me the orders were to burst the shells over the parapet so as to frustrate any attempt to work the barbette guns. Two of these were injured by shot, and one was overturned, apparently by its own recoil, but there was no injury done inside any of the casemates to the guns or works. The shell splinters had all disappeared, carried off, I am told, as 'trophies'.

Russell was also able to verify the deep animosities within the new Confederacy, writing a further dispatch from South Carolina on 30 April which, when it appeared on 28 May, gave a southern perspective on the North:

Assuredly the New England demon who has been persecuting the South till its intolerable cruelty and insolence forced her, in a spasm of agony, to rend her chains asunder. The New Englander must have something to persecute, and as he has hunted down all his Indians, burnt all his witches, and persecuted all his opponents to death, he invented Abolitionism as the sole resource left to him for the gratification of his favoured passion. Next to this motive principle is his desire to make money dishonestly, trickily, meanly, and shabbily. He has acted on it in all his relations with the South, and has cheated and plundered her in all his dealings by villainous tariffs. If one objects that the South must have been a party to this, because her boast is that her statesmen have ruled the Government of the country, you are told that the South yielded out of pure good-nature. Now, however, she will have free trade, and will open the coasting trade to foreign nations, and shut out from it the hated Yankees, who so long monopolized and made their fortunes by it. Under all the varied burdens and miseries to which she was subjected, the South held fast to her sheet anchor. South Carolina was the mooring ground in which it found the surest hold. The doctrine of State Rights was her salvation, and the fiercer the storm raged against her – the more stoutly demagogy, immigrant preponderance, and the blasts of universal suffrage bore down on her, threatening to sweep away the vested interests of the South in her right to govern the States – the greater was her confidence and the more resolutely she held on her cable. The North attracted 'hordes of ignorant Germans and Irish', and the scum of Europe, while the South repelled them. The industry, the capital of the North increased with enormous rapidity, under the influence of cheap labour and manufacturing ingenuity and enterprise, in the villages which swelled into towns, and the towns which became cities, under the unenvious eye of the South. She, on the contrary, toiled on slowly, clearing forests and draining swamps to find new cotton-grounds and rice-fields, for the employment of her only industry and for the development of her only capital – 'involuntary labour'. The tide of immigration waxed stronger, and by degrees she saw the districts into which she claimed the right to introduce that capital closed against her, and occupied by free labour. The doctrine of squatter 'sovereignty', and the force of hostile tariffs, which placed a heavy duty on the very articles which the South most required, completed the measure of injuries to which she was subjected, and the spirit of discontent found vent in fiery debate, in personal insults, and in acrimonious speaking and writing, which increased in intensity in proportion as the Abolition movement, and the contest between the Federal principle and State Rights, became more vehement.

Passing on through Georgia into Alabama, Russell made his way to the provisional Confederate capital at Montgomery. He had found the South Carolina planter society very welcoming but in Montgomery from which he wrote on 6 May he was confronted by the realities of 'involuntary labour':

To-day I visited the Capitol where the Provisional Congress is sitting. On leaving the hotel, which is like a small Willard's [the principal hotel in Washington], so far as the crowd in the hall is concerned, my attention was attracted to a group of people to whom a man was holding forth in energetic sentences. The day was hot, but I pushed near to the spot, for I like to hear a stump speech or to pick up a stray morsel of divinity in the *via sacra* of strange cities, and it appeared as though the speaker was delivering an oration or sermon. The crowd was small. Three or four idle men in rough, homespun, makeshift uniforms leant against the iron rails enclosing a small pond of foul, green-looking water, surrounded by brickwork which decorates the space in front of the Exchange Hotel. The speaker stood on an empty deal packing-case. A man in a cart was lis-

tening with a lack lustre eye to the address. Some three or four others, in a sort of
vehicle which might either be a hearse or a piano van, had also drawn up for the
benefit of the address. Five or six men in long black coats and high hats, some
whittling sticks, and chewing tobacco, and discharging streams of discoloured
saliva, completed the group. 'N-i-ne h-hun-nerd and fifty dollars! Only nine
h-hun-nerd and fifty dollars offered for him,' exclaimed the man in the tone of
injured dignity, remonstrance, and surprise which can be insinuated by all true
auctioneers into the dryest numerical statements. 'Will no one make any advance
on nine hunnerd and fifty dollars?' A man near me opened his mouth, spat, and
said, 'Twenty-five.' 'Only nine hunnerd and seventy-five dollars offered for him.
Why at's radaklous – only nine hunnerd and seventy-five dollars! Will no one,'
etc. Beside the orator auctioneer stood a stout young man of five-and-twenty years
of age, with a bundle in his hand. He was a muscular fellow, broad-shouldered,
narrow-flanked, but rather small in stature; he had on a broad, greasy, old wide-
awake, a blue jacket, a coarse cotton shirt, loose and rather ragged trowsers, and
broken shoes. The expression of his face was heavy and sad, but it was by no
means disagreeable, in spite of his thick lips, broad nostrils, and high cheek-bones.
On his head was wool instead of hair; his whiskers were little flocculent black
tufts, and his skin was as dark as that of the late Mr Dyce Sombro or of Sir Jung
Bahadoor himself. I am neither sentimentalist nor Black Republican, nor negro
worshipper, but I confess the sight caused a strange thrill through my heart. I tried
in vain to make myself familiar with the fact that I could, for the sum of $975,
become as absolutely the owner of that mass of blood, bones, sinew, flesh, and
brains as of the horse which stood by my side. There was no sophistry which
could persuade me the man was not a man – he was, indeed, by no means my
brother, but assuredly he was a fellow-creature. I have seen slave-markets in the
East, but somehow or other the Orientalism of the scene cast a colouring over the
nature of the sales there which deprived them of the disagreeable harshness and
matter-of-fact character of the transaction before me. For the Turk, or Smyrniote,
or Egyptian to buy and sell slaves seemed rather suited to the eternal fitness of
things than otherwise. The turbaned, shawled, loose-trowsered, pipe-smoking
merchants speaking an unknown tongue looked as if they were engaged in a legitimate business. One knew that their slaves would not be condemned to any very
hard labour, and that they would be in some sort the inmates of the family and
members of it. Here it grated on my ear to listen to the familiar tones of the
English tongue as the medium by which the transfer was effected, and it was
painful to see decent-looking men in European garb engaged in the work before
me. Perhaps these impressions may wear off, for I meet many English people who
are the most strenuous advocates of the slave system, although it is true that their
perceptions may be quickened to recognize its beauties by their participation in
the profits. The negro was sold to one of the bystanders, and walked off with his
bundle God knows where. 'Niggers is cheap' was the only remark of the
bystanders.

On the following day Russell went to meet the Confederate government, this account
like the former being carried in *The Times* on 30 May:

The offices of the Government are contained under one roof in a large red brick building of unfaced masonry, which looks like a handsome first-class warehouse. On the first landing is a square hall, surrounded by doors on which legible inscriptions are fixed to indicate the offices of 'The President', 'The Secretary of War', 'The Attorney-General', 'The Secretary of State', of 'The Cabinet', etc., and on a landing above are situated the offices of the other members of the Government. The building is surmounted by the flag of the Confederate States. There is no sentry at the doors, and access is free to all, but there are notices on the doors warning visitors that they can only be received during certain hours. The President was engaged with some gentlemen when I was presented to him, but he received me with much kindliness of manner, and when they had left entered into conversation with me for some time on general matters. Mr Davis is a man of slight, sinewy figure, rather over the middle height, and of erect, soldierlike bearing. He is about 55 years of age [actually a month short of 53]; his features are regular and well-defined, but the face is thin and marked on cheek and brow with many wrinkles, and is rather careworn and haggard. One eye is apparently blind, the other is dark, piercing, and intelligent. He was dressed very plainly in a light gray summer suit. In the course of conversation he gave an order for the Secretary of War to furnish me with a letter as a kind of passport in case of my falling in with the soldiers of any military posts who might be indisposed to let me pass freely, merely observing that I had been enough within the lines of camps to know what was my duty on such occasions. I subsequently was presented to Mr [LeRoy P.] Walker, the Secretary-at-War, who promised to furnish me with the needful documents before I left Montgomery. In his room were General Beauregard and

Jefferson Davis

several officers, engaged over plans and maps, apparently in a little council of war, which was, perhaps, not without reference to the intelligence that the United States troops were marching on Norfolk Navy-yard, and had actually occupied Alexandria [in Virginia]. On leaving the Secretary I proceeded to the room of the Attorney-General, Mr [Judah P.] Benjamin, a very intelligent and able man, whom I found busied in preparations connected with the issue of letters of marque [for privateering]. Everything in the offices looked like earnest work and business.

It was not necessarily a foregone conclusion that every southern state would secede and there were often substantial minorities which opposed secession as in Virginia where, although voters ratified the secession decision on 23 May, there was sufficient opposition for what was to become the new state of West Virginia to break away and remain with the United States. Nevertheless, on the day Russell witnessed the slave auction, Arkansas seceded to be followed by Tennessee concluding an alliance with the Confederacy on the day Russell met the Confederate Cabinet. North Carolina was also to secede on 20 May. Maryland, Missouri and Kentucky were effectively divided with Kentucky even initially declaring its neutrality on the day North Carolina seceded, although both Missouri and Kentucky were theoretically admitted to the Confederacy in November and December 1861 respectively.

As both sides prepared for war, Britain declared her own neutrality on 13 May 1861, thereby unofficially recognizing the Confederacy as a belligerent. Bancroft Davis reported from New York on 28 May on the reaction, his dispatch being printed on 12 June:

I shall fail in my duties as a faithful correspondent if I longer neglect to speak of the growing and, so far as I can judge, deep-seated feeling of regret in the popular mind at the manner in which England has received the news of the war. This sentiment began to manifest itself about a month since, when the public first thought that it perceived manifestations of a change in English public sentiment towards the South, and it has steadily increased with each day. I hear from all classes and all sides bitter complaints against the Government – more bitter and more heartfelt than the passionate outbreaks which you will find in the newspapers – complaints that the Government hastened, on the first news of war, to give to the rebels the support even of a proclamation of neutrality, recognizing them as entitled to equal countenance and consideration with this Government, which has long been on such friendly terms with the people of England. Why, it is asked by such persons, does the British Government meet the United States, contending with persons in rebellion to extend the domain of Slavery, with a different and harsher policy than it had for Austria contending with Hungary? [Hungarian revolt, 1848–9] What has the United States done that England should welcome its disintegration? Why, then, has the British Cabinet made such hot haste to give a status to rebels here? As I have already said, this feeling is deep-seated, widespread, and threatening. I can only speak, from my own knowledge, of the feeling in the city of New York; but I hear the same accounts from all parts of the interior. I can speak positively about New York, that the public mind is, however unjustly, rapidly becoming possessed of the idea that England sympathizes with Southern

Slavery in its attacks upon the institutions of this country; and that, under this apprehension or misapprehension, the good and kindly feeling which three generations of peaceful and friendly relations have created are vanishing away. Indeed, whatever may be the fate of the rebellion, whether successful or a failure, and no matter what may be hereafter said in England when the relative strength of the two parties is better known, I fear that it will be long before the hearty admiration – one might almost say affection – for England that existed throughout the North two months since will be restored.

Bancroft Davis clearly appreciated the disparity in strengths between the North and the South, the latter having a white population of only 5.5 million compared to the 20 million inhabitants of the North. Thus, while the number of volunteers answering Lincoln's call reached some 500,000 by the end of 1861, the South faced manpower deficiencies from the beginning and was compelled to introduce conscription in April 1862. The South had only 9,000 miles of railway track compared to over 21,000 miles in the North and that in the South was often only single track, poorly maintained and of widely different gauges. Of the million tons of pig iron and 2.5 million tons of iron ore produced in the United States in 1860 only 36,790 and 76,000 tons respectively had been produced in the South and most of its existing industrial plant was in those parts of Tennessee and Kentucky which were never effectively under Confederate control. In these circumstances the secession of Virginia with its Tredegar Iron Works at Richmond was of enormous importance.

Initially, however, neither side could expect much from the large number of volunteers flocking to the colours in response to Lincoln's proclamation and his subsequent call in May 1861 for 42,000 volunteers to replace those ninety-day men whose terms of enlistment were expiring, or to the Confederacy's call for 100,000 men in March 1861. The regular army as it existed in 1861 was only 16,000 strong with about 1,100 officers, of whom almost 300 immediately resigned to join the Confederacy. Both sides therefore lacked sufficient trained personnel and appointments among state militia and volunteer units were often subject to local political interference. Travelling up the Mississippi, Russell encountered such state forces and commanders on both sides. On 20 June, for example, he wrote from Cairo, Illinois on his earlier visit to a Confederate encampment at Randolph Point, some 60 miles above Memphis. They were Tennessee forces under the command of a former lawyer, Gideon Pillow, who enjoyed the rank of Major-General in the Provisional Army of Tennessee:

For five weeks the Tennessee under General Pillow, who is at the head of the forces of the State, have been working at a series of curious entrenchments, which are supposed to represent an intrenched camp, and which look like an assemblage of mud beaver dams. In a word, they are so complicated that they would prove exceedingly troublesome to the troops engaged in their defence, and it would require very steady, experienced regulars to man them so as to give proper support to each other. The maze of breastworks, of flanking parapets, of parapets for field-pieces, is over-done. Several of them might prove useful to an attacking force. In some places the wood was cut down in front so as to form a formidable natural abattis; but generally here, as in the batteries below, timber and brushwood were left uncut up to easy musket shot of the works, so as to screen an advance of riflemen, and to expose the defending force to considerable annoyance. In small camps of 15 to 20 tents each the Tennessee troops were scattered, for health's sake, over the plateau, and on the level ground a few companies were engaged at drill. The men were dressed and looked like labouring people – small farmers, mechanics, with some small, undersized lads. The majority were in their shirt sleeves, and the awkwardness with which they handled their weapons, showed that, however good they might be as shots, they were by no means proficients in manual exercise. Indeed, they could not be, as they had been only five weeks in the service of the State, called out in anticipation of the Secession Vote, and since then they have been employed by General Pillow on his fortifications. They have complained more than once of their hard work, particularly when it was accompanied by hard fare, and one end of General Pillow's visit was to inform them that they would soon be relieved from their labours by negroes and hired labourers. Their tents, small ridge-poles, are very bad, but suited, perhaps, to the transport. Each contains six men. I could get no accurate account of their rations even from the Quarter Master General, and Commissary-General there was none present; but I was told they had a 'sufficiency – from half a pound to one pound of meat, of bread, of sugar, coffee, and rice daily'. Neither spirits nor tobacco is served out to these terrible chewers and not unaccomplished drinkers. Their pay 'will be' the same as in the United States Army or the Confederate State's Army – probably paid in the circulating medium of the latter. Seven or eight hundred men were formed into line for inspection. There were few of the soldiers in any kind of uniform, and such uniforms as I saw were in very bad taste and consisted of gaudy facings and stripes on very strange garments. They were armed with old-pattern percussion muskets, and their ammunition pouches were of diverse sorts. Shoes often bad, knapsacks scarce, head-pieces of every kind of shape – badges worked on the front or sides, tinsel in much request. Every man had a tin water-flask and a blanket. The General addressed the men, who were in line two deep (many of them unmistakable Irishmen), and said what generals usually say on such occasions – compliments for the past, encouragement for the future. 'When the hour of danger comes I will be with you.' They did not seem to care much whether he was or was not; and, indeed, General Pillow in a round hat, dusty black frock coat, and ordinary 'unstriped' trowsers, did not look like one who could give any great material accession to the physical means of resistance, although he is a very energetic man. The Major-General, in fact, is an attorney-at-law, or has been so, and was partner with Mr [James K.] Polk [President of the United States, 1844–8], who, probably from some of the reasons which determine the actions of partners to each other, sent Mr Pillow to the Mexican War [as Brigadier-General of Volunteers], where he nearly lost him, owing to severe wounds received in action. The General has made his intrenchments as if he was framing an indictment. There is not a flaw for an enemy to get through, but he has bound up his own men in exorable lines also. At one of the works a proof of the freedom of 'citizen soldiery' was afforded in a little liberty on the part of one of the privates. The men had lined the parapet, and had listened to the pleasant assurances of their commander that they would knock off the shovel and hoe very soon, and be replaced by the eternal gentlemen of colour. 'Three cheers for General Pillow', were called for, and were responded to by the whooping and screeching sounds that pass muster in this part of the world for cheers. As they ended a stentorian voice shouted out, 'Who cares for General Pillow?' and, as no one answered, it might be unfairly inferred that gallant officer was not the object of the favour or solicitude of his troops; probably a temporary unpopularity connected with hard work found expression in the daring question.

In fact, Russell's assessment of Pillow was not far wrong for, as a Brigadier-General in the Confederate Army, Pillow deserted his command at Fort Donelson in February 1862 in the company of his immediate superior and fellow amateur soldier, John B. Floyd, leaving the conduct of the surrender negotiations to the West Point-trained Simon Bolivar Buckner. Pillow briefly commanded in the field once more at Murfreesboro/Stone's River in January 1863 but accusations of cowardice then led to his permanent assignment to administrative duties.

On the day after filing his dispatch on Pillow, Russell also recounted his visit to another amateur soldier but, this time, on the Union side, the reports appearing in *The Times* on 20 and 21 June respectively. Ironically this amateur, Brigadier-General Benjamin M. Prentiss of Illinois, was to have his military career blighted by a far from unsuccessful holding action on the first day of the Battle of Shiloh in April 1862, resulting in his capture with much of his division of the Union Army of Tennessee, but which actually bought invaluable time for the Union forces. When Russell met Prentiss he was at Camp Defiance near Cairo, attempting to block both the Ohio and Mississippi rivers with his Illinois forces of predominantly German, Polish and Hungarian immigrants:

Simon Buckner

Benjamin Prentiss

In the evening, as I was walking up and down the levée after a day of exhausting heat, an extraordinary tumult attracted my attention, and on running to the hotel whence the noise proceeded I discovered a whole regiment drawn up two deep without arms, and shouting out in chorus, 'Water! water! water!' The officers were powerless, but presently General Prentiss came round the corner, and mounting on a railing proceeded to address the soldiery in energetic terms, but in substance his remonstrance would have been considered, in the French or English army, as much a breach of discipline as the act it had censured. These men had broken out of barracks after hours, forced their officers and the sentries, and came up shouting to the headquarters of their General to complain of a deficiency of water. The General addressed them as 'Gentlemen'. It was not his fault they wanted water. It was their officers who were to blame, not he. He would see they had water, and would punish the contractor, but they must not come disturbing him by their outcries at night. Their conduct was demeaning to themselves, and to their comrades. Having rated the 'Gentlemen' soundly, he ordered them back to their quarters. They gave three cheers for the General, and returned in regular line of march with their officers. The fact was that the men on returning from a hot and thirsty drill found the water-barrels which ought to have been filled by the contractor empty, and not for the first time, and so they took the quartermaster's business into their own hands. Their officers did not wish to be very strict, and why? The term of the men's voluntary service is nearly over, they have not yet been enrolled for the service of the State; therefore, if they were aggrieved they might be disposed to disband and not renew their engagements and so the officers would be left without any regiment to offer the State. But they went off in an orderly

manner, and General Prentiss, though much annoyed by the occurrence, understands volunteers better than we do. There is no doubt but that the quartermaster's
department is in a bad condition in both armies. Mr Forstall has proposed to the
Southern authorities to hang any contractor who may be detected cheating. There
would probably be few contractors left if the process were carried into effect in the
North. The medical department is better in the Northern than in the Southern
armies. But even here there is not an ambulance, a cacolet, or a mule litter. When
[Lieutenant-] General [Winfield] Scott [General-in-Chief of the Union Army]
made his first requisition for troops and money, or rather when he gave in his estimate of the probable requirements to carry on the war, I hear the Ministry laughed
at his demands. They would be very glad now to condone for the original figures.
Little do they, North or South, know what war must cost in money, life, in misery.
Already they are suffering, but it is but a tithe of what is to come, for the life and
the misery have not been expended and felt. In the Memphis papers two days ago
I saw a notification that draughts would be issued by the magistrates to families
left in distress by the departure of their heads and supports to the seat of war. In
the Cairo papers to-day I observe an appeal to the authorities to do something to
aid the citizens reduced to pauperism by the utter stagnation of trade.

Russell returned to Washington on 3 July, his return hastened by the imminent
advance of the Union Army commanded by Major-General Irvin McDowell towards
Richmond in Virginia whence the Confederate capital had been transferred from
Montgomery on 21 May. Rather than advance on Richmond, Winfield Scott had proposed his so-called 'Anaconda Plan' to blockade the South both by sea and by seizing
control of the Mississippi, but increasing public pressure compelled Scott to direct

Irvin McDowell

McDowell to attack the advanced Confederate forces at Manassas Junction/Bull Run in Virginia. On 12 July Russell described both Lincoln and Scott for his readers as they reviewed New York regiments passing in review, his dispatch appearing on 29 July:

What a change since the heir of England [Edward, Prince of Wales on his official visit of October 1860] stood there by the side of one who may prove to be the last President of the United States – united, at least, as a voluntary entirety! The feeble courtliness of Mr Buchanan is replaced by the straightforward purpose and energy of Mr Lincoln, on whose broad shoulders has fallen the grievous legacy of his predecessor's vacillation and errors; and the letters, dispatches, and messages which nurtured civil war are succeeded by speeches to armed legions who are about to end it by conquest or in defeat. It is probable the English public are already familiar with the lines of the sallow, long, and strongly marked face of the present President, which to me is indicative of shrewdness, honesty, and some love of humour; the eyes are deeply set, dark, not very bright, but penetrating and kindly; the tall lank body, set on long loose legs, with powerful arms swinging by his sides, is inclined with a slight stoop forwards, and in his movements, if there be not much grace, there is no lack of vigour. Beside him, towering over the crowd and topping even the President, stands General Scott, the veteran, but for whom it is not too much to say, in spite of heaven-born warriors and citizen soldiers in civil life, just as Cabinets exist in the Militia and Volunteer regiments, the President would probably not be there at all. The bold leonine front of the man, the massive head and broad forehead, the full fine eye, the mouth broad and distinctly cut, and the square resolute chin arrest attention and recall the types

Winfield Scott

of some better known commanders; but Americans are justly proud of one who in a military career extending beyond half a century has been uniformly successful, and who has not been less fortunate in any diplomatic or political functions he has undertaken to discharge. The Virginians, who burnt the house in which he was born lest it should see the birth of another traitor, and who changed the name of a county in their State called after him to that of Davis, will not do him any harm with posterity. His look and manner indicate that his mind is still vigorous, though the snows of 76 winters have wreathed their honours round his brow; but when the towerlike frame and great torso are set in motion there is a feebleness in gait and a want of power in the limbs which show that age and wounds and hard labour have taken their hostages and securities.

McDowell's force of some 35,000 men moved on 16 July 1861, the intention being to launch a flank attack on the 20,000 Confederates at Manassas commanded by Beauregard. It was essential, however, that a further 11,000 Confederate troops in the Shenandoah valley to the west commanded by Brigadier-General Joseph E. Johnston should be prevented from reinforcing Beauregard, and some 15,000 Union troops at Harper's Ferry under Robert Patterson were supposed to occupy Johnston's attention. In the event, Johnston easily evaded Patterson and, in the first significant use of the railway in actual war, brought the first of his forces to join Beauregard on 19 July. An often confused battle occurred on 21 July with McDowell's flanking movement initially pressing the Confederates back on Henry House Hill where Confederate Brigadier-General, Thomas J. Jackson, earned the nickname of 'Stonewall'. As further Confederate troops arrived from the Shenandoah the Union army broke and fled back over the Bull Run, becoming intermingled with the many civilians who had come out from Washington to view the battle. On the following day Russell, who had been among the spectators, set down his experiences in what became one of his most celebrated and controversial dispatches, the text appearing in *The Times* on 6 August:

On our left front a gap in the lowest chain of the hills showed the gap of Manassas, and to the left and nearer to us lay the 'Junction' of the same name, where the Alexandria Railway unites with the rail from the west of Virginia, and continues the route by rails of various denominations to Richmond. The scene was so peaceful a man might well doubt the evidence of one sense that a great contest was being played out below in bloodshed, or imagine, as Mr [William H.] Seward [Lincoln's Secretary of State, who had been his principal rival for the Republican presidential nomination] sometimes does, that it was a delusion when he wakes in the morning and finds there is civil war upon him. But the cannon spoke out loudly from the green bushes, and the plains below were mottled, so to speak, by puffs of smoke and by white rings from bursting shells and capricious howitzers. It was no review that was going on beneath us. The shells gave proof enough of that, though the rush of the shot could not be heard at the distance. Clouds of dust came up in regular lines through the tree-tops where infantry were acting, and now and then their wavering mists of light blue smoke curled up, and the splutter of musketry broke through the booming of the guns. With the glass I could detect now and then the flash of arms through the dust

clouds in the open, but no one could tell to which side the troops who were moving belonged, and I could only judge from the smoke whether the guns were fired
towards or away from the hill. It was evident that the dust in the distance on our
right extended beyond that which rose from the Federalists. The view towards the
left, as I have said, was interrupted, but the firing was rather more heavy there
than on the front or right flank, and a glade was pointed out in the forest as the
beginning of Bull's or Poole's Run, on the other side of which the Confederates
were hid in force, though they had not made any specific reply to the shells
thrown into their cover early in the morning. There seemed to be a continuous
line, which was held by the enemy, from which came steady solid firing against
what might be supposed to be heads of columns stationed at various points or
advancing against them. It was necessary to feed the horses and give them some
rest after a hot drive of some 26 or 27 miles, or I would have proceeded at once to
the front. As I was watching the faces of Senators and Congressmen, I thought I
had heard or read of such a scene as this – but there was much more to come. The
soldiers who followed each shot with remarks in English or German were not as
eager as men generally are in watching a fight. Once, as a cloud of thick smoke
ascended from the trees, a man shouted out 'That's good; we've taken another battery; there goes the magazine.' But it looked like and I believe was the explosion
of a caisson. In the midst of our little reconnaissance Mr [Frank] Vizetelly, who
has been living and, indeed, marching with one of the regiments as artist of the
Illustrated London News, came up and told us the action had been commenced in
splendid style by the Federalists, who had advanced steadily, driving the
Confederates before them – a part of the plan, as I firmly believe, to bring them
under the range of their guns. He believed the advantages on the Federalist side
were decided, though won with hard fighting, and he had just come up to
Centreville to look after something to eat and drink, and to procure little neces-
saries, in case of need, for his comrades. His walk very probably saved his life.
Having seen all that could be discerned through our glasses, my friend and myself
had made a feast of our sandwiches in the shade of the buggy; my horse was eat-
ing and resting, and I was forced to give him half an hour or more before I mounted, and meantime tried to make out the plan of battle, but all was obscure and
dark. Suddenly up rode an officer, with a crowd of soldiers after him, from the village. 'We've whipped them on all points!' he shouted, 'We've taken their batteries, and they're all retreating!' Such an uproar as followed. The spectators and the
men cheered again and again, amid cries of 'Bravo!' 'Bully for us!' 'Didn't I tell
you so?' and guttural 'hochs' from the Deutschland folk and loud 'hurroos' from
the Irish. Soon afterwards my horse was brought up to the hill, and my friend and
the gentleman I have already mentioned [Vizetelly] set out to walk towards the
front – the latter to rejoin his regiment if possible, the former to get a closer view
of the proceedings. As I turned down into the narrow road, or lane, already mentioned, there was a forward movement among the large four-wheeled tilt waggons,
which raised a good deal of dust. My attention was particularly called to this by
the occurrence of a few minutes afterwards. I had met my friends on the road, and
after a few words rode forward at a long trot as well as I could past the waggons
and through the dust, when suddenly there arose a tumult in front of me at a small

bridge across the road, and then I perceived the drivers of a set of waggons with the horses turned towards me, who were endeavouring to force their way against the stream of vehicles setting in the other direction. By the side of the new set of waggons there were a number of commissariat men and soldiers, whom at first sight I took to be the baggage guard. They looked excited and alarmed, and were running by the side of the horses – in front the dust quite obscured the view. At the bridge the currents met in wild disorder. 'Turn back! Retreat!' shouted the men from the front, 'We're whipped, we're whipped!' They cursed and tugged at the horses' heads, and struggled with frenzy to get past. Running by me on foot was a man with the shoulder-straps of an officer. 'Pray what is the matter, Sir?' 'It means we're pretty badly whipped, and that's a fact,' he blurted out in puffs, and continued his career. I observed that he carried no sword. The teamsters of the advancing waggons now caught up the cry. 'Turn back – turn your horses' was the shout up the whole line, and, backing, plunging, rearing, and kicking, the horses which had been proceeding down the road reversed front and went off towards Centreville. Those behind them went madly rushing on, the drivers being quite indifferent whether glory or disgrace led the way, provided they could find it. In the midst of this extraordinary spectacle an officer, escorted by some dragoons, rode through the ruck with a light cart in charge. Another officer on foot, with his sword under his arm, ran up against me. 'What is all this about?' 'Why we're pretty badly whipped. We're all in retreat. There's General Tyler there badly wounded.' And on he ran. There came yet another, who said, 'We're beaten on all points. The whole army is in retreat.' Still there was no flight of troops, no retreat of an army, no reason for all this precipitation. True, there were many men in uniform flying towards the rear, but it did not appear as if they were beyond the proportions of a large baggage escort. I got my horse up into the field out of the road, and went on rapidly towards the front. Soon I met soldiers who were coming through the corn, mostly without arms; and presently I saw firelocks, cooking tins, knapsacks, and greatcoats on the ground, and observed that the confusion and speed of the baggage-carts became greater, and that many of them were crowded with men, or were followed by others, who clung to them. The ambulances were crowded with soldiers, but it did not look as if there were many wounded. Negro servants on led horses dashed frantically past; men in uniform, whom it were a disgrace to the profession of arms to call 'soldiers', swarmed by on mules, chargers, and even draught horses, which had been cut out of carts or waggons, and went on with harness clinging to their heels, as frightened as their riders. Men literally screamed with rage and fright when their way was blocked up. On I rode, asking all 'What is all this about?' and now and then, but rarely, receiving the answer, 'We're whipped;' or, 'We're repulsed.' Faces black and dusty, tongues out in the heat, eyes staring – it was a most wonderful sight.

Russell did not reach Washington until 11 p.m., the roads clogged by the wreckage of McDowell's army although the actual loss on both sides had been small: about 2,000 Confederate casualties and 1,600 Union casualties exclusive of some 1,200 taken prisoner. Indeed, victory had disorganized the Confederates to the same extent that defeat had disorganized the Union forces and there was no effective pursuit, particularly as rain began to fall the following morning. Nevertheless, the psychological impact of the first major encounter of the war was considerable, Bancroft Davis reporting on the reactions in New York on 23 July in a dispatch published alongside that of Russell on 6 August:

The morning papers had been issued in the usual 'sensation' style, with half a column of the largest type, giving the details of a supposed victory over General Beauregard, and nine-tenths of New York, not taking the trouble to read those details with care, believed it. About 11 o'clock came the first news of defeat in the form of a telegram from Washington, to the effect that General M'Dowell was retreating on Washington in good order. By common consent all business was suspended. Men gathered in crowds about the various newspaper offices, and as fast as news was received from Washington 'extras' were issued and short condensed bulletins were posted. I cannot picture in any of the ordinary language applicable to individual feeling the deep sense of public loss and wrong that followed. It was not that many or most of the readers had lost a friend or acquaintance in some of the many New York regiments that were more than decimated in the fight. These feelings, however natural, seemed forgotten in the greater public loss – the loss, according to the first accounts, which have since been much modified, of General M'Dowell's command and his artillery – the demoralization of the fine army that had moved from Washington a few days before, and that had fought so gallantly only the day before. Yet, even when estimating the loss at these gigantic proportions, there was no disposition to submit to the greater loss of the free institutions and liberties of this country by yielding to an armed conspiracy for their overthrow. The Anglo-Saxon love of freedom and of settled free government and detestation of slavery and of military despotism came out all the stronger for the reverse. Not a man among the multitude that congregated about the corners of the streets and stood patiently at the newspaper offices for hours thought of yielding or dreamt of peace; or, if he did, he kept his thoughts and dreams to himself. On the contrary, all talked resolutely, but sadly of the necessity for renewed effort. The military enthusiasm, which was beginning to flag under the great drain upon it, was excited anew. The 7th Regiment, which was mustered out of service a month since, met at their armoury as soon as they could be got together, and are now ready for fresh service if wanted. Several of the fire companies took steps to fill up the ranks of the Fire Zouaves, sadly thinned by the battle. A new regiment, nearly ready, was filled up and sent on by the next train to Washington, and the several recruiting stations, which have been doing a poorish business for a few weeks, became again the scenes of active work. While all felt saddened and humiliated by a defeat which was believed yesterday to be much more damaging than it turns out to be, the resolution to persist in defence of the institutions of the country grew stronger with the necessity. The free North is not so unworthy of its descent as to yield to the first reverse.

With the Union defeat clearly prolonging hostilities, Lincoln called for an army of a million men enlisted for three years and entrusted command of what was to be called the Army of the Potomac to the thirty-four-year-old Major-General George B.

McClellan, who had enjoyed some early successes against Confederate forces in what was to become West Virginia. An excellent administrator but also extremely cautious, McClellan anticipated that it would be many months before he was ready to undertake active operations. Consequently attention was drawn to campaigning elsewhere. One such campaign was the extension of the Union Navy's blockade of the southern coasts, beginning with the closure of Hatteras inlet in North Carolina by an amphibious force in which the military forces were commanded by the Massachusetts politician, Major-General Benjamin F. Butler. Russell reported on Butler's progress on 2 September, the dispatch being printed on 16 September:

The news from Cape Hatteras, which was received here [Washington] yesterday, caused great exultation. It is described, of course, as a 'grand battle'. It is certainly a great success, and it has been achieved so easily that the original design of the expedition has been abandoned, and, instead of blocking up the entrance and destroying the passages, General Butler and Commodore Stringham arrived at the much more sound conclusion to occupy the works which they found ready built to their hands, which course offers the advantages stated in the general dispatch, and must prove of the most serious inconvenience to the enemy, and a terror and dismay to North Carolina. I doubt not the influence of this coup will be felt at Richmond and Manassas, and it may probably induce the Confederates to risk an attack on Washington, or a march into Maryland. It must certainly lead to a diffusion of part of their forces to watch the rivers and cities of North Carolina. It will be observed that the Confederate account of the surrender of the forts ascribes

William Seward

the result to want of ammunition; and, on looking over the inventory of the captured material, it certainly appears as if they had only ten 32 lb shell, and no round
shot at all. They were hammered at from more than two miles with [Rear
Admiral, former head of the Ordnance Bureau and artillery inventor John A.]
Dahlgren's 10-inch shell (15-inch fuzes), and had very little chance indeed in an
open work without casemates, while their retreat was cut off by the fire of the
ships along the spit and by the landing of the troops on the beach. It is very doubtful whether the President or the politicians of the extreme Republican party will
approve the capitulation, inasmuch as the officers and men surrendered on condition that they were 'to be treated as prisoners of war'. Ergo, they are not rebels or
to be treated as rebels. Again, and perhaps more important, the articles of capitulation are signed by 'S[amuel] Barron, flag officer, C.S. Navy, commanding naval
forces, Virginia and North Carolina,' although General Butler in his report
observes he was determined 'not even to give an official title to the officer in command of the rebels!' Strange, indeed! In that same document, and immediately
before that very statement, there is not only the articles of capitulation insuring for
officers and men the treatment due – not to 'rebels', but – to 'prisoners of war',
but after the words 'Benj. F. Butler, Major-General U.S.A., commanding', comes
the style and title of Flag-officer Barron, of C.S. Navy.

It would not be the only occasion on which Butler was involved in controversy. As it
happened, the Union campaign in Missouri was one of even greater controversy when
the commander of the Union Department of the West, the former Governor of
California and unsuccessful Republican candidate for the presidency in 1856, Major-
General John C. Fremont, on his own authority issued a proclamation of martial law on
30 August 1861 which *inter alia* freed slaves of Confederate supporters. Reporting
from Washington on 6 September in a dispatch appearing on 23 September, Russell
sensed the embarrassment of the administration:

The mass of the South are fighting for a Union of their own, to which they have
insensibly transferred their loyalty, and their national feeling, which unquestionably is great, in the old flag, and believe they are fighting against an alien
enemy – one Abraham Lincoln, who is aided and abetted by the powers of darkness and their Yankee co-efficient. And yet I have reason to believe Mr Lincoln is
one of the most moderate men in the section of his own Cabinet which looks to
internal politics, and that in the present distracting discussions he generally
inclines to the view that the North is not making a war against slavery, and that the
result of her success need not be the liberation of the Negro. Mr [Montgomery]
Blair [Postmaster-General], who is a downright dour Covenanter of the American
sort, and with whom the Southern slaveholders are sons of Belial – 'a sword of the
Lord and Gideon' man, who could smite Philistines hip and thigh from the rising
to the going down of the sun – and several hours after – with a grim satisfaction in
being a chosen instrument – I speak, of course, metaphorically, and not physically
– has a great influence, derived from the clearness of his head, his persistency, and
the rigidity of his principles, among his party; but his doctrines would most likely
end in confining the United States to the original New England settlements or in

John C. Fremont

establishing a dictatorship resting on bayonets. What prelacy, Popery, and monarchy were to the men of the first Covenant, Southern rights, slaveholding included, are to Mr Blair. Nor are they less so to Mr [Salmon P.] Chase [Secretary of the Treasury], who possesses, after all, the largest and most solid brain in the Cabinet, but who had no objection at one time to let the South go if it liked, believing that the system on which it was founded must be in the end, and that not distantly, the means of inflicting a punishment and vengeance on the seceding States far more terrible than any either the army or navy of the North could execute. It may readily, then, be imagined how General Fremont's proclamation increases the difficulty and augments the animosities which exist in the sections of the Cabinet. Lest it might be supposed that the law confiscating slaves who had been employed by their masters against the United States in any way, which Congress passed at the last moment [6 August], and which the President signed so reluctantly, has been taken by General Fremont as his authority for the edict he has put forth, it may be as well to point out that he goes so far beyond the terms of the statute as to liberate slaves of masters who are in rebellion against the Government, and so far as his district extends, therefore, he would, if successful, liberate nearly all the slaves, because there can be but little doubt that a vast number of the masters in the South are in rebellion against the Government of the United States. To the Democrats of the North, who are at this instant talking of 'guarantees' for the South and the revision of the Constitution in the same breath in which they speak of the vigorous prosecution of the war for the Union and denounce secession as revolution, the doctrine, founded as it is on the undefined powers of martial law, must be particularly objectionable. It may be a bold stroke of General Fremont to attach to himself a coherent mass of the Republicans, or it may be a simple act of war without any *arrière pensée*. At all events, it is embarrassing. The Commander of the Forces of the West is an ambitious, bold, and enterprising man, but it will surprise me to find he proves a very great man. He is profuse in expenditure, energetic in action, and speculative in plans, but still I doubt whether he can effect all that is expected of him with the materials at his disposal.

In fact, Russell's assessment of Montgomery Blair was wrong since he was conservative on the issue of slavery and was eventually forced to resign in 1864 in order for the radicals within the Republican party to accept Lincoln's renomination. As for Fremont, when he declined to modify his proclamation he was dismissed in October 1861, although he was to return briefly to field command in a disastrous campaign against 'Stonewall' Jackson in the Shenandoah in 1862. Once more effectively dismissed, he eventually resigned from the army in June 1864, declining to run as a radical Republican candidate for the presidency later that year.

One who would contest the 1864 presidential election was McClellan, whose Democratic sympathies almost certainly added to his caution in risking his army in battle. McClellan, who was to replace Scott as General-in-Chief in November 1861, was already seen by some as a quasi-Napoleon figure, a strong 'man on horseback' when Russell reported his impressions of the young general on 7 October 1861, his report appearing on 22 October:

W hen I had the pleasure of conversing with General M'Clellan for the first time he asked me several questions, with evident interest and friendly curiosity – not unusual on the part of Generals in reference to their antagonists – respecting General Beauregard [whom Russell had met at both Charleston and Montgomery]. In his case there was all the more reason for such inquiries, in the fact that they were old fellow students and class mates [not so, as Beauregard had graduated from West Point in 1838, eight years before McClellan although both had served with the engineers and in the Mexican War]. To my mind there is something of resemblance between the men. Both are below the middle height. They are both squarely built, and famed for muscular power since their college days. Beauregard, indeed, is lean and thin-ribbed; M'Clellan is full and round, with a Napoleonic tendency to embonpoint, subdued by incessant exercise. Beauregard sleeps little; M'Clellan's temperament requires a full share of rest; both are spare and Spartan in diet, studious, quiet. Beauregard is rather saturnine, and, if not melancholic, is of a grim gaiety; M'Clellan is genial even in his reserve. The density of the hair, the squareness of the jaw, the firmness and regularity of the teeth, and the outlines of the features are points of similarity in both, which would be more striking if Beauregard were not of the true Louisianian Creole tint while M'Clellan is fair-complexioned. Beauregard has a dark, dull student's eye, the dullness of which arises, however, from its formation, for it is full of fire, and its glances are quick and searching. M'Clellan has a deep clear eye, into which you can look far and deep, while you feel it searches far and deep into you. Beauregard has something of pretension in his manner – not hauteur, but a folding-armed, meditative sort of air, which seems to say, 'Don't disturb me; I'm

George B. McClellan

thinking of military movements.' M'Clellan seems to be always at leisure; but you feel at the same time you ought not to intrude too much upon him, even when you seek in vain for the grounds of that impression in anything that he is doing or saying. Beauregard is more subtle, crafty, and astute; M'Clellan is more comprehensive, more learned, more impressionable. Beauregard is a thorough soldier; M'Clellan may prove he is a great general. The former only looks to military consequences, and disregards popular manifestations; the latter respects the opinions of the outer world, and sees political as well as military results in what he orders. They are both the creatures of accident, so far as their present positions are concerned. It remains to be seen if either can control the current of events, and if in either the artilleryman or the cavalry officer of the old United States' army [as indicated earlier, both were actually engineers] there is the stuff around which history is moulded, such as that of which the artilleryman of Brienne [Napoleon] or the leader of the Ironsides [Cromwell] was made.

While Russell had only told the truth as he had seen it concerning the Union rout at Manassas/Bull Run, there had been undoubted anger in the Lincoln administration at the wide publicity accorded the dispatch and, indeed, there was even to be a petition from Philadelphia in September 1861 urging that Russell be expelled. In a sense Russell was also taking the blame for the attitude of *The Times* for, while both Russell and Bancroft Davis were sympathetic to the North, this was, of course, by no means the case in the editorial offices of Printing House Square, where, as indicated in the introduction, the outbreak of hostilities had brought about a calculation of Britain's interests which had led to increasing criticism of the North and its policies. Bancroft Davis was increasingly disillusioned by his employers and this as much as his ill health influenced his decision to tender his resignation as New York correspondent in December 1861. Rightly or wrongly, *The Times* was also frequently seen as reflecting official British policy. As indicated earlier, Britain's declaration of neutrality had not been well received in the North and it was recognized that there was substantial support for the Southern cause in Britain. It was somewhat unfortunate, then, that two Confederate envoys, John Slidell and James Mason, being sent to Europe to seek British and French recognition for the South were intercepted and detained by Captain Charles Wilkes of USS *San Jacinto* on 8 November on the high seas off Cuba, while travelling in the British steamer *Trent*. As Russell knew when writing from Washington on 19 November in a dispatch published on 3 December, Wilkes's action was of the utmost seriousness for relations between Britain and the North:

The news from America by this mail will need no introduction to public notice – it is deeply and painfully interesting, and nothing that I can say is required to fix upon it every thought of the nation. Presuming that the intelligence has reached London (either by the West India mail or by the *City of Washington*, which left New York on Saturday) before the arrival of this letter, I shall at once proceed to a brief history of this extraordinary and unprecedented occurrence, of which full details can be had from the American papers, and from the passengers of the *Trent*. If I use words such as 'outrage' or 'insult' in the remarks I shall have to make, they will be merely the expressions most suited to characterize such an unusual display of force towards an allied and friendly Power, and are not intended to prejudge the issues which are raised in this country in reference to the absolute right of the United States to make that display and to use that force in accordance with international law. It appears that the United States' second-class screw steamer *San Jacinto*, of 13 guns, Captain Wilkes, on her way back from the coast of Africa to reinforce the blockading fleet, put into Havannah for coal, and while there Captain Wilkes heard that Mr Slidell and Mr Mason, the Commissioners from the Confederate States to France and England, had engaged passengers on board the Royal West India mail steamer *Trent* at Havannah, and would sail for England on the 7th inst. He immediately resolved to seize upon them, and for that purpose lay out in the Bahama Channel, where he met the *Trent* on the 8th of November, and brought her to by firing round shot across her bows. This is believed to have occurred in Spanish waters. A boat loaded with marines was sent on board the *Trent*, under the command of Lieutenant Fairfax, who informed the captain that he had come to arrest Mr Mason and Mr Slidell, his passengers. Mr Mason was on deck at the time, and Mr Slidell came up from his cabin almost immediately. In one account it is said the captain refused to show his passenger list or give any information to Lieutenant Fairfax, and that the latter recognized Mr Mason from previous acquaintance, and it is added that the latter appealed to the captain for protection, and asked if he would permit such an insult to his flag, to which appeal that gentleman made an inaudible reply. It may be inferred that he remonstrated against the seizure, as it is known he made a protest to Lieutenant Fairfax against the act before the latter left the ship with his prisoners. The gentlemen, on being informed of their danger, went below to their cabins, but Lieutenant Fairfax followed them, and declared he would remove them by force if necessary. Mr Mason and Mr Slidell declared they would only yield to force, and the marines, who had gone below with the officer, then took them by the shoulders, which was a sufficient display of force for the purpose, and the prisoners then took leave of their families, who were induced, by the express wish of husband and father, to proceed on their way to Europe in the *Trent*, after a scene which is described as inexpressibly affecting. Mr Eustis, who was acting as secretary to Mr Slidell, and Mr M'Farland, who was accompanying Mr Mason in the same capacity, were also arrested, and were transferred, with their baggage and papers, to the *San Jacinto*, where they drew up a formal protest against their arrest, and delivered it to Captain Wilkes for his Government. The *Trent* then resumed her voyage, taking with her Mrs Slidell, her daughters and sons, and Mrs Eustis and her two children. The husband of the latter lady was member of Congress for Louisiana, and is an able and amiable man; he is in delicate health, and was proceeding to Europe as much to enjoy quiet and procure medical treatment as to engage in politics. His wife is the only child, I believe, of Mr Corcoran, the opulent banker of Washington. Of Mr Mason and Mr Slidell and their mission enough has been said already. They are now in Fort Warren, and the whole country rings with joy at the news that enemies so skilful, so energetic, so accomplished should by this unexpected stroke of daring be placed in the power of the United States when it seemed that their mission must inevitably have prospered. But they have ceased to be 'rebels'. Their forms expand in their dungeon. Instead of being the disloyal citizens of the rebellious provinces of the United States, which they were when they entered the British packet, they are the recognized 'ambassadors of a belligerent and independent nationality'! For thus is the violence avenged, and thus, at the very moment of its commission, are the authors of the outrage hoisted by their own petard. Joy at the news, then astonishment, then a general inquiry, 'What will England say?'

While the British reaction was awaited, Russell also reported on 29 November – it was printed on 13 December – on one of the many Germans fighting with the Union Armies, the colourful Brigadier-General Louis Blenker, who had arrived in the United States as an exile from the 1848 revolution in his homeland:

The 'Blenker' difficulty has not yet been arranged. This officer first came into notice here in consequence of the way in which he covered the retreat of the Federal army from Bull's Run with his Germans; but he is a soldier of some experience, having served in the Bavarian army, and having been in the employment of King Otho in Greece, where he was engaged with the disaffected tribes in the mountains and saw active service. His soldiers have had several privileges granted to them; among others the boon of lager beer, which is sold in their camps, but is forbidden to the less fortunate warriors of other nationalities. It is alleged against them that in consequence of this, or in compliance, perhaps, with the dictates of a more fiery patriotism than exists in the heart of the New Englander, the Blenkerites are rather unruly, and are certainly destructive in their tastes. The way in which they dismantle a 'secest' house, tear down fences, obliterate gardens, and 'chaw

Louis Blenker

up' farms is perfectly marvellous. It is not to be expected that they should understand the distinctions between Unionist and Disunionist, as they do not speak
English. Every act of devastation is laid to the Blenker men. Now, licence and
lager beer have powerful attractions for the wilder spirits, and the result is that the
German camps are favourite places of resort for those soldiers who can get there.
Sometimes they do not get away so easily, nor are they always in a state to merit
the approbation of their officers on their return. All the Germans desire to reach
this haven of the blessed, and General Blenker has been applied to by numbers of
his countrymen to procure their exchange into regiments in his division. The other
day he sent a private letter intended solely for General M'Clellan's eye in reference to this exchange. Now, the Commander-in-Chief, whatever be his other
attributes, does not possess that quality which distinguished Napoleon, the Duke
of Wellington, or old Fritz [Frederick the Great], – he is not famous for answering
letters, nor does he, I am told, regulate his own correspondence. Perhaps he has
too much of it. But, at all events, General Blenker's letter, though specially directed to General M'Clellan, was not delivered to him, but was opened and read by
[Brigadier-] General [Randolph B.] Marcy, the father-in-law of the General who is
the Chief of the Staff, and who has the rigid notions of an old soldier respecting
the rules of correspondence between the chief of an army and his subordinates. He
replied to the letter in a manner which General Blenker considered personally
offensive, and a correspondence ensued in which the resignation of that officer
was tendered. But the Germans were not to be deprived of their commander so
easily; a ferment arose in the camps when they heard of it, and the authorities, in
much doubt and difficulty, temporized with the angry Teuton, who will be fol-

lowed in his retirement, if it takes place, by the Prince [Felix] of Salm-Salm [the son of a Prussian nobleman serving on Blenker's staff, who was to be killed fighting with the Prussian forces in the Franco-Prussian War in August 1870], by General Sabel [unidentified], and a host of officers, and who would be followed by many more of his command if they could get 13 dollars a month, food, and clothing as readily elsewhere. General Blenker has been disappointed by his omission from the list of officers who are to command corps d'armee. It has been determined, I believe, decisively to divide the army [of the Potomac] into three corps – one to be commanded by M'Dowell, the others by [Major-General Fitz John] Porter and [Major-General William B.] Franklin; and, as Blenker has been passed over, it is proposed to form a separate corps of Germans to mollify him; but serious objections exist to this course on the part of the American Generals, supported by a few of the civilians. This German element is coming to the front. As one of their leaders said to me, 'We have crushed the native American party already; we have put it to the sword. But when the war is over we will not be content with a negative position; we must have a fair share in the country which we have fought for and saved.'

For the moment, however, it was naturally the *Trent* affair which was of most concern. Not perhaps unexpectedly the British Cabinet demanded the release of Mason and Slidell, and began preparations for possible war against the North, reinforcements being gathered for immediate transportation to Canada. An ultimatum was agreed in London on 1 December 1861 although its actual language was somewhat modified by the intervention of the Prince Consort in what was to prove virtually his last act before his death on 14 December. Moreover, while the ultimatum was dispatched aboard the steamer, *Europa*, on 2 December with the demand for an apology and the release of the envoys within seven days of its receipt, the British ambassador, Lord Lyons, was instructed to make only Lincoln and Seward aware of the terms and to delay its formal presentation to the Lincoln administration. Russell's dispatch of 16 December published on 8 January 1862 recorded the news that the *Europa* had reached Halifax in Nova Scotia:

Last night the news came that the *Europa* had arrived at Halifax, bearing a Queen's messenger with dispatches for Lord Lyons, and it was added that the British Government had come to the decision to demand the surrender of Messrs Mason and Slidell, and, further, that Lord Lyons, in case of refusal, was ordered to leave Washington. There were some doubts expressed in reference to the authenticity of these statements, but those who believed them to be true discussed the probable course of the United States Government and the conduct of the British Ministry with warmth and excitement. So far as I can hear, there was no disposition evinced in any quarter to yield to the demand, which, indeed, has been long canvassed as a result likely to follow the act of Captain Wilkes. The members of the Cabinet, the President, the Generals, or at least General M'Clellan, have all been prepared for the question, and last night they could only repeat the arguments for and against the compliance with or refusal of the proposition to be made by our Government. There is now, however, a feeling of bitter mortification here that, at the moment when victory seemed inclining in their favour, and when the current was setting in against the Confederate States, the statesmen of the North must either receive a tremendous check or submit to the performance of an act which they, right or wrong, consider an extreme humiliation. The anger of the Democracy of America would be directed against their own Ministers, unless the latter could divert it upon the English people. It is probable that the reports of the intentions of our Government are exaggerated both as to the mode and substance of the representations and demands attributed to them. The calmer-minded see only one course to pursue, if they would wish to preserve the Union and to conquer the South, and that is to yield up Slidell and Mason, and then to solace themselves by a vow of eternal hostility to Great Britain, and the promise to their hearts of future revenge upon her in some moment of weakness or difficulty. The more violent are quite ready to meet all the world in arms, and they solace themselves too with the thought that Great Britain would be presented to the world as the patron and protector of slavery if she raised the blockade of Southern ports, and entered into direct relations with the Slave States for the supply of cotton. Nor are they without a hope of actual reunion springing out of a war with England, believing in the hostility of the South to the British rather than in their attachment to the Union. That, however, is admitted as a remoter consequence of war.

Following his instructions, Lyons did not formally hand over the ultimatum until 23 December, by which time Lincoln and his colleagues had had sufficient time to ponder the consequences of not complying with the British demands – not least the fact that the North was reliant upon India for its saltpetre supplies. On Christmas Day the Lincoln administration resolved to release Mason and Slidell on the grounds that Wilkes had acted without instructions, though without apologizing. Thus the crisis was defused and Seward even subsequently offered to allow British reinforcements to Canada to cross Maine rather than use the ice-bound St Lawrence river. Russell reported the American decision on 27 December, his dispatch appearing on 10 January 1862:

Omitting all matters of detail till next post, I hasten to announce that the Government of the United States has acceded to the demand of Great Britain and has consented to surrender Mr Mason, Mr Slidell, and their secretaries. This morning Mr Seward sent Lord Lyons a request that his Lordship would call at the State Department, and in the interview which took place Mr Seward handed the British Minister an exceedingly voluminous note, which will no doubt see the light some day in England, and informed him at the same time that the captives were at his Lordship's disposal. Let us take this act as the expression of the conviction in the minds of the American Government that they were wrong in retaining their prisoners, and that the seizure was an outrage, nor let us, till we know the nature of the dispatch, attribute any other motives to them than the desire to do what is right. The effect in this country, when it is known, will be exceedingly great, for such a dish of humble pie cannot be taken into stomachs without a great deal of nausea. Do not imagine that the real intelligence and worth of the people will disapprove the act. The men I allude to are the writers in the 'sensation' press, and the bunkum orators, as well as the more violent Abolitionists, who by insult-

ing meances and intemperate pledges have bound themselves to oppose the concession, no matter how just it might prove to be. Doubtless, Mr Seward in the
elaborate dispatch he has written will seek to show that Great Britain has laid
down some new principle in this transaction, and in swelling periods will endeavour to demonstrate that by yielding the prisoners the United States has gained
some great point for herself and the world in general from Great Britain, which
can never again take political offenders from neutral ships. Let it be so. The case
is memorable enough and clear enough to serve as a precedent. No one can doubt
but that the relations of both countries would have been much more satisfactory if
the Government of Washington had restored the prisoners as soon as it heard of
the capture, and if all the irritating writing and speaking here, and the expense,
anxiety, and sense of indignity to which we were exposed in Great Britain, had
been obviated. I fear that the wrath to come will be greater than anything yet experienced by us, and that a terrible future is in store for Great Britain, at the indefi-
nite time when so many great things are to come to pass. The Government here,
which has thus far got over its external dangers, will now have to face a tremendous ordeal. The sense of justice or right or even necessity cannot prevail over the
cherished love of doing what they like among the masses. The Union can get more
than half a million of men to fight for her, at considerable expense it is true, but
moved in the main, let us admit, by love for the Union; but she could, I am
assured, raise a million to fight against England. That is, the hate of Great Britain
is at least twice as strong as the love of the Union among many millions of
Americans. They will be disappointed this time. If Mason and Slidell be surrendered without any extravagant threats in the press, or without any indignation
meetings, we may hope that friendly relations will be preserved for years to come,
as it will be a token that in a crisis the sound sense, patriotism, and desire to do
what is demanded by justice and right predominate in the United States over the
violence of popular passion. Let us stand by and see if it will be so, and let us be
thankful meantime that we are spared the war which would have been forced on
us in vindication of our honour had the Government here been deaf to the voice of
reason.

In reality, for all its drama, the *Trent* affair was more a public than a diplomatic crisis since both governments wished to avoid war and would not be swayed by popular
indignation. Indeed, the British government was now likely to be even more cautious
over its relations with the Confederacy and, ironically, Mason and Slidell did more to
gain the South recognition while held in the North than they were to achieve while free
to travel the capitals of Europe.

1862

As the new year dawned there was little immediate prospect of the Army of the Potomac advancing south. Russell reported on the difficulties from Washington on 23 January, in a dispatch printed on 13 February:

As the condition of the roads and of the country in Virginia continues as bad as ever, it is likely that no movement of the army of the Potomac will take place until winter is over, unless the General is bold enough to trust to a bridge of frost, which may break when he is in the middle of it, and leave him floundering in a sea of mud. Indeed, some of the journals are already preparing the public mind for a prolonged inactivity of the standing army of the Potomac; but they are in ignorance of the views of the authorities, or they may be used, as the telegraph was the other day by the military officials in the West (at least, with their sanction), to delude the people by erroneous statements of movements being accomplished which have never taken place. If the enemy were deceived by such *ruses de guerre*, the officers would not deserve so much censure. It is possible that the Military Committee [presumably either of the House of Representatives or the Senate] may have been satisfied by the promises of action to come, or it may be that the General does really intend to throw the Confederates off their guard, and make a dash at them one of these fine frosty days. The thing could be done – just done, by moving the whole force off suddenly, making a forced march so as to arrive in front of the enemy's lines by daybreak, and by a concerted plan, under fire of the numerous field artillery, breaking his line in the centre or overwhelming it on either flank. Such marches as that from the camps on the line from the front at Alexandria round by the Chain-bridge to the position at Centreville have often been made, and have ended in successful battles. To make such an effort now it would be necessary to have a hard frost and a certainty of its duration for a day or two, and there should also be some reasonable certainty of success in the attack. Without being very sickly, the army is by no means in health. In one division of less than 8,000 men more than 700 were sick, and it may be taken as a fair average that 10 per cent of the army are not fit for fighting – a ratio of little consequence here to what it would be in an army in motion, inasmuch as they could all be sent into the city hospitals or those at the north side of the river. The drill of many of the regiments has improved within the last two months; battalion and brigade drills and field days have been sedulously and daily attended to, and the result, when I left Washington, was an obvious improvement in the appearance of the

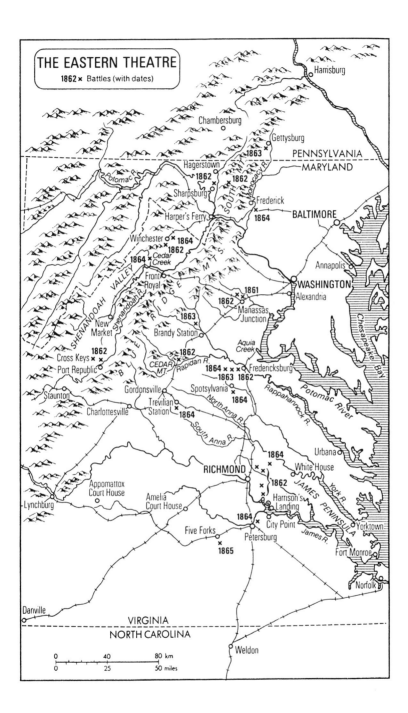

THE EASTERN THEATRE

1862 × Battles (with dates)

Harrisburg

Chambersburg

Gettysburg
1863

PENNSYLVANIA
MARYLAND

Hagerstown
1862   1862
Sharpsburg
Frederick
Harper's Ferry
1864   BALTIMORE

Winchester × 1864
1862
1864 × Cedar
Creek
Annapolis

Front
Royal
1861
WASHINGTON
1862   Alexandria
Manassas
Junction

New
Market
1863
Brandy Station
Aquia
Creek

Cross Keys × 1862
Port Republic
CEDAR
MT.   Rapidan R.
1862
1864 × × Fredericksburg
1863 1862

Gordonsville   Spotsylvania
1864
Staunton
Trevilian
Charlottesville   Station 1864

Urbana

1864
RICHMOND   × ×   White House
× 1862   JAMES PENINSULA
Appomattox
Court House
Amelia
Court House
Harrison's
Landing
Yorktown
Lynchburg
1864 × City Point
Five Forks   Petersburg
× 1865   Fort Monroe

Norfolk

Danville
VIRGINIA
NORTH CAROLINA

0   40   80 km
0   25   50 miles

Weldon

troops on the parade-ground, and in all their movements under arms. Discipline was becoming better, and the hand of command was gradually hardening, contracting, and closing its fingers on the yielding body. The recent bad weather, however, caused an increase of sickness and a relaxation of drills and parades, and it also materially affects the transport animals, many hundreds of which are in a miserable condition. It would have saved a great deal of money to have set to work two or three months ago, and, with the amount of labour and material at the disposal of the authorities in the willing arms of the troops and in the stone and timber of the country, to have repaired, drained, bridged, and relaid the roads through which the teams are now struggling to the death with the forage and supplies of the army. But, then, such works would have excited a suspicion that 'something was not going to be done immediately'. When I left Washington for a short time, the coming event of difficulties with the roads had cast its shadow before. But even then we could get about and cross the river, and visit our friends in camp without inconvenience beyond splashed boots and cold rides home at night. General M'Clellan's reputation satisfies the soldiers that they are judiciously handled, and they do not appear – or, at least, they did not – to find fault with the immobility to which they have been condemned. The people here are not quite so well pleased.

With so little occurring in the East, Russell visited Canada in February 1862. However, by the time he had returned there had been a significant Union advance in the West. Control of the western rivers had been an essential component of the 'Anaconda Plan' but it was only in February 1862 that activity seriously began in Major-General Henry W. Halleck's Department of Missouri and Brigadier-General Don Carlos Buell's Department of Ohio, primarily delayed by the fact that command in the West was divided between them and that both were cautious by nature. Finally, under pressure from his more active subordinates Brigadier-General Ulysses S. Grant and Commodore Andrew H. Foote, Halleck authorized an advance to the Confederate Fort Henry on the Tennessee. Having secured the surrender of Fort Henry on 6 February, Grant and Foote then took their troops and gunboats to Fort Donelson on the Cumberland, Grant by the overland route and Foote by retracing his steps down the Tennessee and then up the Cumberland. The commander of all Confederate forces west of the Allegheny mountains was the well-regarded General Albert Sidney Johnston, endeavouring to cover a massive 500-mile front with only some 70,000 men. In fact, Johnston had generally neglected the Tennessee and Cumberland rivers since the Mississippi was erroneously regarded as more vital to the Confederacy's interests. Kentucky, too, was seen as especially important to the Confederacy despite the vital industrial resources of Nashville on the Cumberland and, accordingly, Johnston had his two largest troop concentrations at Bowling Green opposite Buell in eastern Kentucky and Columbus on the Mississippi in western Kentucky opposite Halleck's main force. The Union advance on Fort Henry neatly split Johnston's two forces, compelling him to abandon eastern Kentucky and retreat from Bowling Green to Nashville. Initially he intended only to keep a small delaying force at Fort Donelson but then changed his mind and reinforced it to a strength of some twelve thousand men under the command, it will be recalled, of John B. Floyd and Gideon Pillow. In fact when Foote and Grant attacked on 14 February 1862, Confederate batteries savaged Foote's gunboats and a breakout attempt by the much outnumbered Confederate forces came very close to success on the following day, until Pillow lost his nerve and called it off. Surrender followed on 16 February but not before Floyd and Pillow had escaped. Johnston had lost a third of the forces he had originally had at Bowling Green and, confronted with an advance by both Buell and the new Army of the Mississippi that Halleck had entrusted to the command of Brigadier-General John Pope, he abandoned both Columbus and Nashville, thereby losing all Kentucky and much of Tennessee – although Confederate forts remained on the Mississippi itself as Russell reported on 1 March in a dispatch appearing on 20 March:

The flag of truce sent down *en espion* to Columbus reports today that the Confederates are evacuating the position, destroying their winter quarters, burning their stores, and removing their guns, except those in the water batteries. Let there be no outcry made about this use of the flag of truce, which has been perverted on both sides. There is no want of instances where it has been similarly employed in recent wars in Europe. There is a railway from Columbus, which is on the left bank of the Mississippi, below Cairo, to Memphis, whence there are railroad communications with the whole of the Southern and Western States; but the Confederates were exposed to complete isolation by the recent successes of their enemy on their flank and rear on the Cumberland and Tennessee rivers. It is scarcely credible that they will be guilty of the folly of falling back on 'Island No. 10', which lies above Memphis, in the Mississippi. If they do, a dose of Dahlgren shot and mortar shells will but induce them to repeat the capitulation of Donnelson [*sic*]. There was a strongly situated intrenched camp on the bluffs, some hours' journey above Memphis, when I was there, where they could better make a stand, but their river positions are exposed to be taken in reverse, and they will not like to put themselves under two fires. The Mississippi expedition [Pope] is now moving down the river, and the land forces are said to be in motion also; nor do the Federals hesitate to express their conviction that they will be in New Orleans in a very short time after they have overcome the resistance to be expected near Memphis. That city was poorly defended by parapets of cotton bales and some heavy batteries when I was there, and any attempt to protect it would lead to the destruction of the place by the fire of the iron-plated gunboats. These latter are considered a great success. Foote's flagship was struck 61 times at Donnelson, and the iron mail suffered little, though the woodwork was knocked to pieces. The news which has just arrived that the Confederates are surrounded by Buell's forces at Murfreesborough is most important, if true, but granting that there is a railroad from Nashville, which has fallen into the hands of the Federals, to that place, it must be by virtue of great strategical and marching powers that General Buell has got round his enemy so completely as to be able to demand their unconditional surrender. Undoubtedly, the possession of that place would be a heavy blow to the Confederates. It would apparently throw the whole of the railroad into their hands down to the junction with the Memphis line, cutting off communication with Virginia, North Carolina, and the Eastern Slave States, except by a most circuitous route. It is not easy to perceive how Beauregard, who is down with them, can extricate the Confederates if these reports be correct.

Don Carlos Buell

In reality Buell had not been able to trap further Confederate forces since, with the assistance of Beauregard who had arrived in the West just before the fall of Donelson, Johnston managed to concentrate his forces once more on Corinth, Mississippi with the addition of a further 15,000 reinforcements rushed up from the deep south. Russell also underestimated the damage done to Foote's gunboats although the appearance of such armour-plated craft was undoubtedly significant, following on from the use of armoured floating batteries during the Crimean War. Within a few weeks, too, Russell was reporting on the first clash of iron-clad warships in battle, the Confederate *Merrimac* or *Virginia*, which had emerged from Norfolk to destroy or damage three conventional wooden battleships on 9 February, being confronted with the Union *Monitor* two days later. Russell did not witness the battle and his account on 11 March, published on 27 March, drew on that in the *Baltimore American*, but he went on to describe the extraordinary *Monitor* designed by John Ericsson:

> The latter was intended to operate against the Confederate batteries on the Potomac, and arrived at Fortress Monroe [at Hampton Roads, Virginia] by chance just in time to render the most vital service. Her iron deck is not two feet above the water, but on going below she is found to be fitted up with as much lux- ury as a yacht, and to be comfortable and commodious; all that is to be dreaded is her 'turning turtle' in a seaway. Her construction is complicated and ingenious – one vessel inside another. The sides of the vessel are formed of plate iron, half an inch thick, outside of which is white oak 26 inches thick, outside of this again is rolled iron armour five inches thick. The deck is supported by heavy braced oak beams, upon which is laid planking seven inches thick, covered with rolled plate

iron one inch thick. The turret consists of a rolled plate iron skeleton, one inch thick, to which are riveted two thicknesses, of one inch each, of rolled iron plates. Outside of this again are six plates of rolled iron, all firmly bolted together with nuts inside, so that if a plate is started it can be at once tightened again. The top is covered with a bomb-proof roof perforated with holes. The lower part of the gun carriages consists of solid wrought-iron beams. These are planed perfectly true, and are placed parallel in the turret, both of the guns pointing in the same direction. The ports through the side of the tunnel are only large enough to permit the muzzle of the gun to be thrust through. Inside of them are wrought-iron pendulums, which close them against the enemy as soon as the gun recoils. She is armed with two of the largest Dahlgren guns, made to revolve by a pair of steam-engines placed beneath the deck, the guns are trained by bearings on deck, visible through side-sights. The turret is, in fact, one of Cowper Cole's cupolas slightly modified. The lower vessel is of iron, one half inch thick, and made in the usual manner. She carries her machinery, coal, etc., aft, and forward the officers' quarters, ammunition and stores. The two partitions of the vessel are separated by a wrought-iron bulkhead. The officers' quarters are very roomy and handsome, and are ventilated and lighted by openings from the deck. Her machinery consists of two horizontal tubular boilers, containing 3,000 square feet of fire surface, and two horizontal condensing engines of 40-inch diameter of cylinders and 22-inch stroke of piston.

The clash between the *Monitor* and the *Merrimac*

The propeller is 9 feet in diameter and 16 feet stroke. It has four blades. For the better ventilation of the vessel there are two fan-blowers, drawing air down through bomb-proof gratings in the deck. Though not exactly intended for a sea vessel, she can proceed to sea or to any point along the coast without fears of the least injury. She carries generally three months' provisions, and is supplied with a condensing apparatus for supplying fresh water. As an evidence of the rapidity with which this vessel has been completed, we may state that her keel was laid on the 25th of October, 1861, and steam was first applied on the 31st of December in the same year. She was launched on the 30th of January last. The blowers got out of order on her voyage [from New York] and the crew suffered a little in consequence before she arrived at Monroe.

By comparison the *Virginia*, raised on the sunken but salvaged hull of the *Merrimac* – Confederate forces having taken the Norfolk Navy-yard in April 1861 – was almost conventional although its appearance was equally strange. The clash between the two was effectively a draw and neither vessel was risked again. Subsequently the *Merrimac*

Union naval officers on the *Monitor*, July 1862

Manassas Junction after its abandonment by the Confederates in March 1862

was scuttled when Norfolk was taken by Union forces in May 1862, and the *Monitor* was lost while on tow in a storm off Cape Hatteras in December 1862. Nevertheless, the battle off Hampton Roads had changed the face of naval warfare although Britain and, to a lesser extent, France were already well advanced in the construction of sea-going ironclad fleets.

The ultimate fate of the *Merrimac* resulted from McClellan finally advancing towards Richmond, though not in the way originally anticipated by most observers. Initially McClellan proposed an amphibious landing at the mouth of the Rappahannock behind the forward Confederate defences at Manassas. When Joseph Johnston withdrew his forces south of the Rappahannock in early March, however, McClellan proposed landing instead at Fortress Monroe and advancing up the peninsula between the York and James rivers to strike at Richmond from the east. In the meantime there was some comment when it was discovered that the Confederate positions at Manassas had not been as strong as McClellan had claimed. Another aspect of the Confederate abandonment of Manassas was described by the newly arrived New York correspondent of *The Times* in succession to Bancroft Davis, the Scots-born Charles Mackay (1814-89), a minor poet and song-writer who had also had considerable newspaper experience on the *Morning Chronicle* and as editor of the *Glasgow Argus, Illustrated London News* and *London Review*. He had even written a two volume work on the United States, *Life and Liberty in America*, published in 1859. Written on 1 April, his report appeared on 17 April 1862:

Broadway, which as every traveller in America knows, is one of the finest streets in the world for the purposes of military or other processions, is devoted almost every day in the week to some display that tends to keep alive the military ardour of the people, and to impress the minds of the youthful generation with the pomp and circumstance of glorious war. From the roofs of its multitudinous stores and hotels – glittering in white marble, or massively sombre in iron, or brown-stone, or granite – hundreds of star-spangled banners float and flaunt by day and by night, and the roll of the drum and the music of military bands are continually heard as volunteers, both infantry and cavalry, march up or down the spacious thoroughfare on their way to or from the seat of war. Since the abandonment of Manassas by the Confederates, and the occupation of that historic ground by the Federal troops, these displays have been more than usually frequent; and funeral processions, of a length and splendour that would have rejoiced the hearts of M. Ledru Rollin and the other members of the French Provisional Government of 1848, have paraded the long and beautiful street, and called forth the teeming crowds of New York to gaze and wonder. On Saturday last the bodies of Colonel Slocum, Major Ballow and Captain Towers, three Rhode Island officers of the 27th Regiment who fell at Bull Run, lay in state at the Astor-house. They were disinterred by their friends on the battlefield, where they were found buried, it is said, with their faces downwards. If this was intended as a mark of indignity, as alleged, these New England compatriots made ample amends to their insulted remains, and gave them a funeral in which all New York participated. The long procession passed through a portion of Broadway and the Bowery, the band playing the 'Dead March' in *Saul*, and the flags floating half-mast high from every public and most of the private buildings in the city, including the churches; and thence took the steamboats through Long Island Sound to the burial place provided for the deceased heroes in their native State of Rhode Island. The field of Bull Run continues to be explored for the discovery of the remains of officers who fell in that struggle, and who were hurriedly or ignominiously buried by the enemy, so that New York will soon have opportunities of paying many similar tributes of respect to the memory of deceased defenders of the Union; opportunities of which, according to the present temper of its people, it will not be slow to avail itself. The whole moral atmosphere is warlike. The people have eaten of the insane root of military glory that takes the reason captive, and clamours for large doses of the stimulant. If the inevitable bill that must be paid for indulgence in the luxury do not act as a sedative the worse for the fortunes and happiness of this Republic.

Ironically, within five days of Mackay writing his dispatch both Union and Confederate supporters were to be shocked by the 20,000 total casualties arising from the counterblow of Albert Sidney Johnston and Beauregard against Grant and Buell, whom Halleck (now placed in overall command in the West) had ordered to concentrate at Pittsburg Landing north of Corinth. Striking Grant around the church of Shiloh on 6 April 1862, Johnston and Beauregard drove the Union forces back on Pittsburg Landing although the stand of Prentiss enabled Grant to reorganize on Pittsburg Landing itself. With Buell's arrival next day, the Union forces counter-attacked and forced Beauregard to retreat, Johnston having bled to death from a bullet severing the artery in his leg on the first afternoon. Subsequently Beauregard withdrew from Corinth at the end of May. In a dispatch of 9 April appearing in *The Times* on 23 April, Russell recounted both the battle at Shiloh and the Confederate loss of 'Island No. 10' on the Mississippi to Pope's forces on 8 April, which led to the fall of Memphis in early June:

The news of two great events is carried to Europe by this mail. One might have been, and, indeed, was anticipated as exceedingly probable, and affords another instance of the want of capacity in choosing defensive positions and in estimating the value of the enemy's means, which has been illustrated by several similar actions on the part of the Confederates. Island No. 10 has surrendered, with either the whole or a large part of its garrison, and the rout of the covering army, with a heavy loss in guns and prisoners. The other is, if the confused and hurried reports which have been received up to the departure of the steamer are to be depended upon in the main, a battle of colossal dimensions, commenced by an attack of the Confederates from Corinth on the Federal army at Pittsburg, and ending in their repulse after a prodigious, if not fabulous slaughter on both sides.

With McClellan's army landing on the peninsula on 4 April, events from the point of view of the Confederacy had apparently taken a further turn for the worse. Russell had intended to join McClellan's peninsular campaign but it was at this point that the controversy over the Bull Run dispatch was revived. Lincoln's Secretary at War, Edwin M. Stanton, refused to allow Russell to accompany the Army of the Potomac. On 3 April Russell penned his last dispatch from America, the piece being printed on 24 April:

Before I proceed to write the last letter, in all probability, which I shall have occasion to date from the United States of America, it will be necessary to state the circumstances under which I am compelled to abandon the post to which I have been so long faithful, under an ordeal the severity of which can be known to none but myself. While there was a chance of my being useful in correcting the exaggerations and misstatements which were sent across the Atlantic, I endured the hostility that had been engendered against me, and I did not despair of the American people in the Northern States eventually doing justice to the integrity of my motives, particularly if fortune should give me an opportunity of recording a victory, instead of detailing the incidents and the close of a defeat. Although I had extenuated much, I was conscious I had never set down aught in malice concerning them. I bore the attacks made upon me in silence, which I shall not qualify by any adjective, and from time to time my patience was rewarded by unexpected marks of sympathy and by tokens of friendship and goodwill which I shall always cherish. But now a power is brought to bear against me which I cannot resist nor evade. The Government of the United States of America not merely refuses me permission to accompany its armies in the field; it not only gives me orders not to do so, but the Secretary at War, if not with the original sanction, at least without the dissent of the President, prevents the General in command of the Army of the Potomac receiving me in his camp, after he had invited me to attend the progress of his army; and, through me, treats the officer who was but a few weeks ago the idol of statesmen, journalists, and people, as he is yet the favourite of his army, with marked discourtesy. The guest of General M'Clellan is forbidden to embark on board the ship on which he had received a passage, by his express authority, and is removed by the express directions of Mr Stanton from under the charge of the officer of the General's Staff [Brigadier-General Van Vliet, McClellan's Quartermaster-General] to whom he had been consigned.

Refused permission to board the steamer, *Canonicus*, Russell simply chose to leave the United States altogether without actually consulting his employers in London. Effectively it left coverage of events solely in the hands of Mackay, whose strongly pro-Southern views inevitably alienated the Northern establishment and whose identity as the correspondent of *The Times* became known at an early stage. An unknown 'Occasional Correspondent' sent a few dispatches from Washington immediately after Russell's departure, such writers not being formally employed by *The Times* but usually sub-contracted by the official correspondent. Whoever he was, he lacked Russell's mastery of words and it was Mackay in New York who attempted to follow events in both the East and the West. In terms of the latter, there was yet further Union success when Commodore David Farragut and Benjamin Butler took New Orleans on 1 May 1862, its defences stripped of manpower and gunboats for the campaigns in Tennessee. Mackay reported the city's fall on 2 May, his dispatch appearing on 16 May:

A ll doubt of the capture of New Orleans has been at an end for the last two days. Corroborations of the fact, though contradictory as to the details, had arrived from so many quarters, that the natural incredulity of an often-deceived public had yielded to the accumulation of evidence even before the receipt this morning of the official correspondence between Commodore Farragut, the Federal Commander of the Mississippi flotilla, and Mr Monroe, the Mayor of the city. When the news first arrived the wonder was not so much that New Orleans should have fallen, but that the Southern Generals, Engineers, and captains of iron-clad rams and gunboats should not have made better use of their time and opportunities in preparing for the defence of so important a place, and that two days were more than sufficient to accomplish against the commercial emporium of the South what 20 days failed to accomplish against Island No. 10 in the comparatively unimportant regions of the middle Mississippi. The catastrophe is a startling one, and has been quite as unexpected to the North as it must have been to the South. It is evident from the correspondence between the Commodore and the Mayor, that the General in command of the Confederate forces had left the city with his whole army, as soon as he found it to be untenable. Though the correspondence gives no details, and no official reports have yet been received by the Federal Government, it seems, as far as any clue to the truth can be obtained through the maze of imperfect and conflicting testimony which has reached this city, principally through the medium of Southern newspapers brought within the Federal lines before Yorktown [on the peninsula] by runaway negroes and deserters, that the means of attaining this great victory were as simple as they were extraordinary. Either two or a larger number of ironclads (some accounts say as many as 13 but not all iron-

David Farragut

clad) [in fact it *was* thirteen] succeeded in forcing their way past Forts Jackson and St Philip, through a terrific yet harmless storm of shot and grape [one Federal sloop was sunk by ramming and three others failed to get past the forts in this action on 24 April]. This impedimenta surmounted, they steamed leisurely up to New Orleans, anchored in midstream, and threatened either to shell the city or cut the levée and lay it under water in case of resistance. The iron-clad vessel *Louisiana*, constructed after the fashion of the *Merrimac*, and on the support of which for attack or defence the Confederates appear to have largely calculated [in fact, while taking part in the defence with its guns, the *Louisiana* did not have working engines], was either captured or destroyed by Commodore Farragut's superior force, while the *Mississippi*, a second vessel of the same kind, was scuttled to prevent her falling into the hands of the Federals. In these circumstances, the city lying wholly at the mercy of the flotilla, which was riding unassailable on the swollen river, several feet above the level of the streets, [Major-] General Mansfield Lovell resolved to save his army, if he could save nothing else, and took his departure, with his whole force, by the Jackson Railway, to Camp Moore, 78 miles distant on the road to Memphis. The Mayor, thus left without naval or military aid, yielded, like a wise man, to inevitable necessity as soon as he was summoned to surrender. But, in placing the city at the mercy, or under the protection, of the conqueror, he refused to hoist the Stars and Stripes on the public buildings, or to give any orders to that effect to his subordinates.

Subsequently Farragut's flotilla ranged as far up the Mississippi as Vicksburg but this proved too hard a nut to crack. With McClellan justifying his continuing caution in approaching Confederate defensive works at Yorktown partly by Lincoln's retention of an additional 50,000 men under McDowell to cover Washington, where there was much disquiet at the success of 'Stonewall' Jackson in worsting a succession of Union commanders in the Shenandoah valley, Mackay's attention was drawn to the political activities of Union generals Hunter and Butler. Major-General David Hunter was commanding the Department of the South comprising those coastal areas of Florida, Georgia and South Carolina occupied by Union forces in continuing amphibious operations when, like Fremont in the previous year and whom he had actually briefly replaced as commander of the Department of the West, he took it upon himself to abolish slavery in his command on 9 May. Mackay's report of 20 May was printed on 3 June:

As was anticipated by every one, the President has lost no time in disavowing the extraordinary order of General David Hunter, setting free the slaves of Georgia, South Carolina, and Florida. Mr Lincoln did not wait to have official cognizance of the document, but, taking its authenticity for granted, and setting it forth in his own proclamation, he has solemnly repudiated it, and re-stated clearly and emphatically his policy and intentions on the whole subject of negro slavery. The President did not stir in the matter a moment too soon. The hours and even the minutes were precious, and were turned to hostile account through all the Border States, and wherever else a suspicion was possible that the Government had suddenly changed its policy and become a convert to the views of Mr Wendell Phillips and the Ultra-Abolitionists. That the repudiation, prompt and decisive as it is, will allay the excitement which the order caused throughout the South is not to be expected, for the Southern leaders and editors have taken care to give the utmost possible publicity to a document that was so well calculated to strengthen the existing hostility to the North, and will take equal pains to prevent Mr Lincoln's explanation from reaching the people. The Democratic and Pro-Slavery party are not satisfied with the mere reprimand which the proclamation conveys, and call for General Hunter's removal. But as the General has friends in the Cabinet, and is supposed to be sheltered under the broad aegis of Mr Secretary Stanton, to whom the President defers in military matters, it is possible that he will be allowed to retain his post. But even in that case, in a country where the private soldier does not renounce his politics in consenting to fight for the Government, it will be for General Hunter to decide whether the rank and file share his opinions or those of the President. In either case, a very high-minded officer would solve the difficulty by resigning his command; and as such a course would gratify the Abolitionists as much as it would the Pro-Slavery and Democratic party, though for very different reasons, there is a general expectation that a new appointment to the military department of Georgia, South Carolina, and Florida will be immediately placed at the disposal of the Government.

In fact Hunter, who also angered Southerners by raising the lst South Carolina Coloured Infantry, did not lose his command until failing to take Charleston later in 1862 and he was to be recalled to field command in the Shenandoah in 1864. Meanwhile 'Butcher' Butler or 'The Beast' as he was also to become known, was arousing controversy for his direction of occupation policies in New Orleans, perhaps his most notorious order being that on 15 May, in which he proclaimed that any woman insulting the occupying troops 'shall be regarded and held liable to be treated as a woman of the town plying her avocation'. Mackay reported on Butler's order, which was to cause particular indignation in Britain, on 30 May, his dispatch appearing on 13 June:

The proclamation was so unmanly as well as so unsoldierlike as to be incredible. Nobody in New York believed in its authenticity. It was said to be a fabrication of General Beauregard for the purpose of inflaming the Southern mind still further against the North; and one New York journal, bitterly hostile to the South, declared that if General Butler had really issued such a document he was a disgrace to the army, and should immediately be dismissed. But the proclamation is now admitted to be true, and is likely to be more prejudicial to the Northern arms than a defeat in a pitched battle. The people of New Orleans are subdued by superior force, but they do not acknowledge the Northern Government. They offer it passive resistance in default of any other; and the women, high and low, rich and poor, not only wave Secession flags from their windows, and wear Secession ribands in their bonnets, and teach their little children to revile the 'Yankees', but when they pass a Federal soldier or officer in the streets they move out of his way with expressions of disgust in their faces, if not on their tongues, as if there was contamination in his touch or presence. They resort to all the manoeuvres of woman's malice – and how great that can be if aroused, either in love or war, needs not be told – to prove to the Federal armies how odious they are to the South, and that the ultimate subjection of such a people is impossible. General Butler would have done well to treat this display of feminine spite with indifference, if he could not treat it with good-humour. He might even have gone so far as to say that if women mixed themselves in public affairs like men, they would be treated with the severity of the sex they assumed, and locked up for the night in the guard-house, to teach them the impropriety of playing with edged tools; but

Benjamin Butler

when he went so far as to say that women insulting the soldiers of the United States by word, or look, or gesture should be treated as 'harlots plying their vocation in the streets', he outraged all decency and humanity, and committed an error as a General only exceeded in amount by his breach of good manners as a gentleman. The offending and offensive document has been publicly read in every camp and in every church of the South, and will not only cover the name of General Butler with obloquy, but will go far to supplement the half-rations of the Southern armies by a glow of indignation far more warming to their hatred than a full allowance of whisky, or any Southern stimulant that fires the blood and inflames the passions of an excitable and proud people.

While McClellan's advance up the peninsula was far from rapid, it was sufficiently threatening to Richmond for Jefferson Davis to demand an almost equally reticent Joseph Johnston to attack the Union forces. Accordingly Johnston attacked that portion of McClellan's army south of the Chickahominy river on 31 May around Seven Pines/Fair Oaks. In an inconclusive two days' fighting, Johnston himself was wounded and was replaced by the Confederate President's military adviser, in command of what was now to be known as the Army of Northern Virginia. Writing on 10 June in a dispatch printed on 23 June, Mackay reflected an early impression conveyed by

(Mortar) Battery No. 4 of McClellan's army before Yorktown, May 1862

Johnston's successor to observers which was not to be sustained for long, the President's adviser being none other than General Robert E. Lee:

From a proclamation to the 'Army of Richmond', signed by Mr Jefferson Davis, and dated on the Monday after the battle, thanking it for its gallantry and good conduct, it appears that the Southern President was present at the battle of Fair Oaks, or Seven Pines as it is sometimes called, but was not in command. The post of honour was held by an older, but perhaps not better soldier [in fact Davis had only commanded a volunteer regiment in the Mexican War], General Johnston, who, having been wounded in the first day's battle, was replaced by General Lee. The latter does not appear to have impressed his countrymen with the same enthusiasm as his predecessor; if any judgement may be formed from the opinions expressed by the *Richmond Examiner* of the 5th inst., which states that the battles of Saturday and Sunday 'were both victories; but with great difference between the promise of the first and the performance of the second. The whole affair seemed to have lost its purpose and plan when the animating mind was withdrawn; and that spirit that went up in the fiery shouts of Saturday, sunk into indifference on Sunday. Nevertheless,' adds the writer, 'the enemy was well whipped; and lost not less than 10,000 men [in fact about 5,000 casualties compared to 6,000 for the Confederates].' This is known to be an exaggeration; but few people, even without the excitement and bewilderment of war and passion, deal fairly with figures, and General M'Clellan's estimate, which is fearful enough, may be accepted as near the truth as it is possible to make it.

Lee intended to continue to attack McClellan and on 12 June sent his cavalry commander, Brigadier-General J.E.B. Stuart, on a dramatic reconnaissance which took 1,200 Confederate horsemen right round the Union army. Another occasional correspondent, clearly different from the individual who had reported from Washington in April and probably one of the British officers observing McClellan's operations, wrote from 'Hill's Plantation on the Pamunkey' on 15 June of the appearance of some of Stuart's men behind Union lines in a report published on 10 July:

Between the unfinished railway bridge at White House landing and New Castle, up the Pamunkey River, a distance of about 10 miles, I reckon, are two ferries, the nearest being Garrick's landing, some four or five miles from White House landing. There three or four schooners were lying on Friday afternoon. They were attacked by some 50 or 60 men – Confederate cavalry – who fired at the crew with carbines and revolvers, killing several people. The captain of one of the boats made his escape in a boat with some of his men, the bullets whistling over their heads. He had the presence of mind to save his papers. This schooner and another were fired and burnt. Another lying outside was cut loose, and saved by the captain of another vessel. Almost at the same time another troop of Confederate cavalry, probably belonging to the same body of troops, about 150 men strong, attacked a train at the railway station about two miles from Garrick's landing, and about two and a-half from that at White House. Some people were killed and taken prisoners, together with a number of waggons, which were burnt.

One colonel, who was taken prisoner, escaped. It was said that a strong body of cavalry was roaming in the rear of the army, intending to attack the great depot at White House, and burning the shipping there. As to the number of these troops no certain information was to be had, for some estimated them as high as 4,000, and others at so many hundreds. They were said to belong to Steuart's [*sic*] Confederate cavalry; but where they came from was doubtful. Some were of opinion that they belonged to a corps standing against M'Dowell, had been cut off, and tried to reach the army around Richmond, doing as much harm as possible on their way. Others, however, would have that these troops went round the right wing of the Federal army, having been informed by farmers living there that there were no Federals to oppose them. They also said – and their statement was so strengthened by that of some eye-witnesses of the surprise – that some overseers of plantations were with the Confederates serving them as guides. Some planters and other persons remaining on their farms hereabout have been arrested under suspicion of having given information to the Confederates.

Now sure of McClellan's exact dispositions and reinforced by Jackson, who had slipped away from the Shenandoah after a stunning success against numerically superior Union forces, Lee launched a series of attacks in what became known as the Seven Days' battles beginning with a limited offensive by McClellan at Oak Grove on 25 June and followed by the actions at Mechanicsville/Beaver Dam Creek, Gaines

The Confederate Water Battery at Gloucester Point, June 1862

Mill/First Cold Harbor, Savage Station, White Oak Swamp/Frayser's Farm, and Malvern Hill. In tactical terms many of these battles were far from Confederate successes and, overall, Lee lost some 20,000 casualties – often in crude frontal assaults – compared to about 16,000 for McClellan. Yet the Seven Days were to prove a significant strategic victory for the South, for McClellan retreated on 2 July and entrenched at Harrison's Landing on the James. McClellan had been relieved of the office of General-in-Chief by Lincoln on setting out for the peninsula in March and the President, who had then acted as his own General-in-Chief, now brought Halleck from the West to fill the post as Mackay reported on 25 July, the piece appearing on 8 August:

G eneral Halleck's promotion to the chief command of the armies of the United States was officially announced yesterday morning. The appointment does not appear to create any exuberant satisfaction. The office may be a popular, but it has not lately proved a successful one. Within a twelvemonth it has been held by four persons. General Scott was superseded in it because he was too old. General M'Clellan was next tried, and was superseded because he was too young [hardly true]. The third dignity was Mr Lincoln, who has just superseded himself, for the sufficient reason that he is no soldier. General Halleck, the fourth on the list, is neither old nor young [he was forty-seven], and has made the art of war his study. He has published an excellent treatise on tactics [*Elements of Military Art and Science*, 1846], in which he lays it down as a fundamental axiom, essential to success, that every General worthy of the name should, in his dispatches, represent his defeats to be victories. He has also shown administrative ability, but has never

Henry Halleck

had the opportunity to fight a great battle. He is neither popular nor unpopular, but seems to have inspired a certain amount of confidence by the respectability of his private and the energy of his public character.

Halleck and Lincoln concluded that there was nothing further to be gained by the campaign on the peninsula and on 3 August a withdrawal was ordered, although McClellan again procrastinated and also delayed uniting with a new Army of Virginia put together from the McDowell's command and the various Union forces that had faced Jackson in the Shenandoah. This was placed under the command of the now Major-General John Pope, who had enjoyed a measure of success on the Mississippi. Unfortunately he was something of a braggart and was cordially disliked by McClellan. Perhaps inevitably, Mackay picked up Pope's bombastic proclamation to his new command, confidently predicting his undoubted triumph where McClellan and the Army of the Potomac had singularly failed. Mackay's dispatch dated 29 July was printed on 11 August:

At present General Pope is the provocative to most of the melancholy mirth of the day. The schoolboy magniloquence of his address to his soldiers in assuming the command of the army of the Shenandoah was a little too much for plain men and for ordinary gravity. Drunkards, when sober, do not relish the spectacle of another man's intoxication, and a blustering public, somewhat sobered and toned down by adversity, does not look with complacency upon a blustering General. The people expected to find vigour of action in Pope, but as yet they have only found vigour of tongue and vain boasting. Unlike Falstaff, he may be brave. Unlike Bobadil, he may understand the art of war; and unlike Munchausen, he may keep within the boundaries of the possible when he has a story to tell the world; but he has so much in common with these three remarkable personages as to administer largely to the people's amusement. He was known to his friends to be highly imaginative in matters of fact while he was yet a captain; and his boast of the capture of 10,000 of Beauregard's army, when he had not really captured a tenth of the number, was so entirely what was expected of him as a General that nobody was much surprised at General Beauregard's little statement which put the matter right. Pope's last achievement has been of a different kind. Three days ago he publicly notified the desertion of an officer from his army, who it appears had not deserted, and offered a reward of 5c for the capture of the offender. 'It is an ill bird,' says the proverb, 'that fouls its own nest,' and the question is asked, if a captain in Pope's army be only worth 5c., what is the General worth? The laugh is at Pope's expense, and not at that of the captain, who perhaps may find or make the opportunity for a new appraisement on both sides. Surely it is not with Generals of this calibre that the great battles of the Republic are to be fought and the South subjugated?

In this view, at least, Mackay was all too correct. With McClellan still en route to the Potomac, Lee hastened to strike at Pope before any junction of the Union forces. Jackson attacked Pope's advance guard at Cedar Mountain on 9 August and Lee then took what was to become a frequent calculated risk in his generalship of dividing his

John Pope

55,000 man army by sending Jackson with 24,000 men on a flanking march around Pope's right to fall across Pope's line of communications at Manassas on 26 August. Running into Jackson on ground covering much of the former battlefield of Manassas/Bull Run on 29 August, Pope failed to realize that the remainder of Lee's army was near and was taken in the flank by Lee's other corps commander, Lieutenant-General James Longstreet, on the following day. Two of McClellan's corps were sufficiently close to support Pope, notably that of Porter, but did nothing to assist him. Suffering some 16,000 casualties to the 10,000 suffered by Lee at this second battle of Manassas/Bull Run, Pope was forced to retreat towards Washington. Approaching the capital, Pope's army was met by none other than McClellan whom, with some misgivings, Lincoln had placed in command of its defence, merging Pope's command with that of McClellan and sending Pope off to Minnesota, a rumour Mackay had already picked up on 29 August. Not yet knowing of the fighting at Manassas, he commented on the Union's apparent lack of competent leadership, in the context of Pope losing his baggage in a cavalry raid by Stuart and then suffering the descent on his supply depot at Manassas. The dispatch was published on 13 September:

Already the cry has gone up from New York to supersede him altogether, or send him to Minnesota to make that head against the wild Indians which he appears unable to make against the Southern warriors; and to appoint some better man in his place. But here arises another difficulty. Every one asks who is the better man? Is it Buell? He is in imminent danger himself [from a new Confederate advance into Tennessee], and conspicuous for doing nothing. Is it M'Clellan? He has been tried and found wanting. Is it Halleck? He has been foiled by

Beauregard, and may be foiled again by an abler General. Is it [Major-General Ambrose] Burnside [commanding the IX Corps, with which he had enjoyed success in amphibious operations in North Carolina]? He is too young and inexperienced. Is it [Major-General Ormsby M.] Mitchell [actually Mitchel, commanding 3rd Division in the Army of the Ohio under Buell], the astronomer? He is under a cloud of disgrace for the events at Athens [in Alabama, where a brigade of his division ran wild after apparently being fired on by civilians], and is not trusted by the Government. Is it Fremont? That would be madness, sufficient to justify that tritest of all trite proverbs which accuses Heaven of afflicting with dementia those whom it desires to ruin. Is it Butler? Heaven forfend! If it were he, the very women of the South would turn out with daggers – or scissors in default of better weapons – to combat the detested yankees. Is it Hunter? He has done nothing but preach a negro equality, which the whole North repudiate socially, and which nine-tenths of it deny politically. Is it [Brigadier-General John W.] Phelps? He has been dismissed for insubordination [actually resigned on 21 August when the administration repudiated his recruitment of negro soldiers at New Orleans]. Is it [Brigadier-General John B.] Turchin [who had commanded the 8th Brigade of Mitchel's division at Athens]? Not while Mitchell suffers for Turchin's misdeeds. In short, there is no General in the North in whom the people have the slightest confidence, unless it be Halleck; and he, if he be man equal to the occasion, will place himself at once in the field, and try the issue with the Confederates in one great battle for the possession of Washington. The opportunity is a noble one. If he profit by it, and win, he is master of the North, and can do and be what he pleases. If he lose, he will be but one more pebble on the great shore of necessity. The wave will wash over him, and a new name will occupy his place, to meet with worse, or better, or the same fortune. Or peace will come; and no General, good or bad, will be needed.

Back in July 1862 Lincoln had called for a further 300,000 men to come forward to join the Union armies in return for bounties normally made only upon a man's discharge from military service, but also simultaneously enacting a law making state militias liable to federal service. In early August an additional demand for 300,000 militia was also made with provision for making up shortfalls in the earlier total of 300,000 volunteers by compulsory militia enlistments. Mackay reported on 5 September, in a report appearing on 19 September, of the recruitment effort in New York:

E ver since it became evident that the 300,000 volunteers demanded by the first call would not be raised by any amount of bounty money unless the process were expedited by the threat of a compulsory levy, this city has been to all outward appearance in a fever of military excitement. The draught [sic] is so unpopular, and so likely to be a failure if rigorously enforced, that every wellwisher of the Government, as well as the many rich men who are not its wellwishers, acted together with the greatest unanimity of purpose, though not of motive, to prevent the draught. The first object to be accomplished was to fill up the quota of the volunteer army by offers of money. This done, the same process was to be adopted with regard to the quota due under the forced levy. Every nerve has been strained to accomplish both of these results. The bounties have been gradually increased from $100 to $300 and upwards. For the last month Broadway and the City-hall Park have swarmed with recruiting agents. The noble thoroughfare seemed as if dressed out for a permanent holiday. Banners in gay profusion, the numbers of stars on the 'star-spangled banner' being precisely 34 – without the omission even of one for rebellious South Carolina – have been stretched from window to window and from housetop to housetop. Troops have marched and counter-marched amid the throng of omnibuses from morning to night. The pavements have been encumbered with picturesque groups of Irish Zouaves in their brilliant uniforms, lounging on door-steps, smoking their cigars, parading up and down among the by-passers, ogling the women on the side-walks, and looking, every inch of them, as if they had a deal of money and a deal of impudence, and did not know what to do with either. The tap of the drum has been continually heard above all the noises of the traffic; and there has been such a show of warlike activity that the stranger arriving in New York might well believe that war was the chief business or favourite pastime of the people; and that Mr Lincoln would not have to appeal in vain to such a community for the men he needed. But all is not gold that glitters. The sound of the trumpet may be warlike, but it is not war. The gay appearance of New York has been deceptive. Immense efforts have been made, but cold and irrefutable figures show that as yet the efforts have been attended with slight success. Under Mr Lincoln's two calls, the county and city of New York had to provide a quota of 25,100 men. Of these no more than 16,468 had offered themselves and been accepted at the commencement of the previous week, leaving 8,632 still due. The Government with the hope of coaxing some of these into the ranks by an extension of time has allowed the Governor of New York to postpone the operation of the draught, and the Governor on his part has added another bounty of $50 per man to all who voluntarily enrol themselves within 20 days. Of the 60 counties of the State of New York only four – those of Cayuga, Franklin, Monroe, and Wayne have raised their full quotas, and of the whole levy of the State, amounting to 118,808, no less than 42,044 men, an army in themselves, are in arrear. And yet the press of New York, in face of such facts as these, supported by official documents, boils over with rage at the Englishman who asserts that volunteering is a failure – and that it would have been a failure still more disastrous if it had not been for the threat of conscription. The American who dares to say as much in public is fortunate if he do not find himself in Fort Lafayette within 24 hours. What may be the condition of the enlistment in other States of the Union I do not know, as I have no official documents on which to base an estimate; but it is difficult to avoid the suspicion, if such be the case in populous and wealthy New York, that New England and the Western and Middle States would not at this moment show a much more favourable record if the truth were promulgated.

Mackay's comment on his lack of access to official documents, of course, reflected the fact that *The Times* and its correspondents had long forfeited the goodwill of the administration. Moreover, it must be said that it would appear that some 421,000 volunteers and 88,000 militiamen had been obtained by the end of 1862, which was not an inconsiderable number, although the degree of evasion did prompt Lincoln to suspend habeas corpus later in September with a subsequent official drive to detain evaders and those judged to be inciting such evasion. As previously related, the Confederacy with a much smaller manpower reserve had already introduced conscription in April 1862 for those aged between eighteen and thirty-five years with a term of service of three years, at the same time retaining the one year volunteers of 1861 for an additional two years' compulsory service although, as with most conscript systems, there were a variety of exemptions and, in this case, substitution as well. Naturally enough, what necessitated conscription or its threat was the scale of wastage from death, wounds, disease or desertion and, indeed, it was a description of Union casualties that was one of the first articles of a new correspondent in September 1862, Francis Lawley (1825–1901). A son of Lord Wenlock and educated at Rugby and Balliol, Lawley had been Liberal MP for Beverley and parliamentary private secretary to Gladstone. He had also been offered the governorship of South Australia, but debts run up on horse racing and doubtful dealings on the Stock Exchange had ended his political career and he had gone to America in 1854, where he wrote for a number of New York magazines. Written from Baltimore on 5 September, Lawley's piece appeared on 20 September:

One of the most heartrending thoughts, in connexion with all these recent battles, is that, comparatively, a very small number of wounded has hitherto been brought into Washington. That the number of wounded in these battles is enormous seems generally believed. Humanity shudders and recoils at the thought of thousands of frail, suffering, anguished bodies, many of them famished when they received their wound, lying for 48 or 72 hours without food or water or kindly care – many a poor weary soul escaping from its racked and fevered casket from sheer want of human tenderness and sympathy. But, though there are thousands of sufferers left behind, Washington has this week seen a sight which might well draw tears from a stone, but which seems scarcely to have ruffled the serene indifference of the stolid American nature. On Monday a long train of maimed and bleeding and mangled wretches, most of them wounded the Friday before, approached over the Long-bridge. No one was there to look after them, and there for hours lay this mass of tortured and writhing humanity, while pools of blood trickled from the carriages and left a ghastly trail behind. Many a poor fellow not deprived of the use of his legs, untended in the churlish and bewildered city, wandered to the railroad station, with heart fondly turning to some far-off home, possibly among the hills of what was once happy and peaceful New England. He who could witness that sight and not from his heart abhor the grasping vaulting nature of those politicians who, rather than accept what has long been inevitable, would month after month subject poor human nature to such unutterable anguish, must have been cold indeed. But no sign of emotion did Washington deign to give or betray. The same idle poco-curante crowd at Willard's Hotel, the same knot of sharks and contractors fattening on a nation's woes, the same frail and miserable women profaning with repulsive levity streets and buildings which the Angel of Death had marked for his own, – well may the bewildered stranger ask himself with sickening horror, Is this a Christian nation which conceives the best tenants for its churches to be the maimed and agonized and dying, and can look at such sights undaunted and unmoved? Can it bear the thought that thousands of its sons should lie for days starving and with wounds festering on the field of battle, finding no relief till mortification, more merciful than Christian man, preludes a final and painless repose?

Medicine, of course, was still somewhat primitive and crude amputation was often the only remedy for serious arm or leg wounds. Neither side had been prepared for the scale of losses and it took considerable time to reorganize medical departments. Many women North and South entered military nursing such as Dorothea Dix and Clara Barton in the former and, indeed, women were prominent in Lincoln's establishment of the United States Sanitary Commission in June 1861. Nevertheless, despite such efforts on both sides, one out of every six men wounded was likely to die of his wounds while twice as many men were to die of disease as were to die from the result of battle.

In the immediate future, however, there would be the prospect of yet more hospital trains reaching Washington for, having defeated Pope, Lee launched a major incursion into Maryland, crossing the Potomac on 4 September 1862. If a victory could be won on Northern soil then, perhaps, Britain and France would be moved to recognize the South. As inhabitants of a divided border state, many Marylanders might be induced to throw in their lot with the Confederacy and, at the very least, a Confederate army subsisting on northern soil spared that of Virginia. Dispatches by both Mackay and Lawley on the repercussions of the Confederate advance appeared together on 30 September, that from Lawley being penned at Baltimore on 12 September:

It is known that not less than 150,000 Confederates are now in Maryland [actually only about forty thousand]. It is by some asserted that their numbers are 200,000. At Frederick upon Tuesday last were assembled no less than seven Southern Generals of Divisions, with General Robert E. Lee as Commander-in-Chief, and [Lieutenant-] General 'Stonewall' Jackson among the number. A proclamation [calling for Marylanders to join the Confederacy] has been put forth by General Lee, of which the moderation and calmness will commend themselves to all. A proclamation has also been put forth by Colonel Bradley Johnson [commanding a brigade in Jackson's division of Jackson's corps], who is a native of Frederick, and reported to be Provost Marshal of that city. Everywhere private property has been scrupulously respected, cattle and provisions and stores rigorously paid for, individual opinion unmolested. Union men by dozens have gone among the rebel troops, have conversed freely with them, have been allowed to go where they like without joining the Confederacy or suppressing their Union sentiments. There is only one opinion with regard to the discipline of the Southern troops, and that is that it is perfect. The men march calmly and steadily forward, looking neither right nor left, with the solemnity and immobility of marble statues. There is among them none of the thoughtlessness and levity of the Northern troops, none of that craving for newspapers which has always been so conspicuous in the Federals. Men who have gone through such a campaign as has lately been experienced in Virginia, who have been constituent units of that force which, from its rapidity of movement, is called 'Jackson's foot cavalry' [technically Jackson's whole corps], who are fighting for a cause which embodies to them ideas vastly more sacred than is 'the Union' to the mercenaries of the North, have as little dross about them as they have flesh. There is about them the calmness and self-assured confidence which spring from enthusiastic belief in their generals, and from successful experience of their own prowess. Nothing can be more ragged and deplorable than their dress and hats and shoes. But everywhere the cry is, 'Send us no clothing or luxuries. We have no waggons to carry them. Give us shoes and salt and show us a yankee.' But, ragged, tattered, and shoeless as they are, the concurrent testimony is that they are well armed and scrupulously careful of the cleanliness of their rifles, most of which, it is not necessary to say, have been taken from the Federals. Moreover, there is but one opinion as to the superior horsemanship of their cavalry soldiers and the excellence of their horses.

Lawley's admiration for the Army of Northern Virginia and his support for the Confederate cause is clear from the above and, indeed, as a constant supporter of British intervention on behalf of the South, he was to enjoy close links with the Confederate military and political leadership in the coming months when he moved south to Richmond. Lawley was still at Baltimore, however, as the Confederate campaign continued in Maryland.

Lee had been compelled to detach part of his army to take Harper's Ferry, which lay across his line of communications through the Shenandoah valley. When, therefore, on 13 September a copy of Lee's operational orders was found by Union soldiers occupying a former Confederate camp site as McClellan followed Lee, the division of the Confederate Army became apparent. For once McClellan moved uncharacteristically

Confederate dead in 'Bloody Lane' after the battle at Antietam

swiftly although still not sufficiently so to catch Lee, who was made aware of the 'lost order' through the warning of a Marylander conveyed through Stuart. Lee was thus able to block the passes across the South Mountain and summon Jackson from Harper's Ferry once the Union garrison there had surrendered, which it did on 15 September. Concentrating those troops available with their backs to the Potomac near Sharpsburg but fronted by Antietam Creek, Lee awaited McClellan's attack. However, despite having some 60,000 men available against no more than 30,000 Confederates, McClellan again delayed and did not attempt to bring on the battle until 17 September. A series of badly coordinated Union attacks failed to dislodge the Confederates and, at the moment towards late afternoon when Lee's front was in danger of collapsing Major-General Ambrose P. Hill's 'Light Division' arrived from Harper's Ferry to thwart the Union advance. Antietam had been the bloodiest day in American history with some 25,000 casualties on both sides. Lee did not immediately retreat, however, but stood his ground until nightfall on 18 February when he slipped away, McClellan failing to renew the battle or to pursue sufficiently vigorously to prevent the Confederates returning to Virginia.

Nevertheless, the Confederate invasion of Maryland had been thrown back and immediately eased the likelihood that Britain and France might intervene. Moreover, Lincoln took the opportunity provided by what was undoubtedly a strategic victory for the North to bring forward his Emancipation Proclamation on 22 September upon which he had been resolved since July – if a sufficiently favourable moment occurred. With effect from 1 January 1863 those slaves residing within states still in rebellion would be deemed free. It did not apply to slaves in those states not deemed to be in rebellion and, of course, it could only be applied in those areas under or coming under Union control. By claiming what might be termed the moral high ground, though, it had the immediate effect of yet further undermining the South's claim for European recognition. Mackay, writing from New York on 24 September in a dispatch published on 7 October, recognized some of the implications of the proclamation:

General M'Clellan having failed to crush the rebellion on the banks of the Potomac, President Lincoln has come to the rescue with a proclamation which he hopes will crush it in the cotton fields. Sixty days ago he declared that he would confiscate the property, slaves included, of all persons who at the expiry of that term should be in arms against the Government. That proclamation having remained a dead letter – having had no effect whatsoever in coercing or persuading the Southern people to re-enter the union which they abhor, [it] has been followed by a second, extending the day of grace until the 1st of January 1863. On that day, as far as President Lincoln's action can penetrate, all persons held as slaves within any State, or designated part of a State of which the people shall then be in rebellion against the Federal Government, shall be considered thenceforward and for ever free, and the naval and military power of the United States shall recognize and maintain their freedom. But the President does not take it upon himself to abolish slavery, for he proposes to purchase the manumission of all slaves within such States as may be loyal at the time specified, and which may desire to rid themselves of the institution, and to leave slavery alone in all such loyal States as may not feel disposed to try the experiment of emancipation. The document is what it is the fashion to call 'a step in advance'; but it has the fatal demerit of being insufficient to please the ultra-abolitionists, and of being more than enough to offend the Southern slave-owners, the Northern Pro-slavery party, the advocates of State rights, and all that large class of persons, American as well as Irish, who have a social, a political, and an economic objection to the negro, and who, though refusing to enslave him, would absolutely expel and banish him from their territories, as in Illinois and Wisconsin, and who would deny him all social status, as in New York and Pennsylvania. It is true that the President fore-sees this difficulty and endeavours to obviate it by his favourite, but foolish and futile project of expatriation. It is enough to say on this point that the negroes of the South are not likely to hear of it for many months, if ever; that the free negroes of the North object to leave the land of their birth to try their fortunes in Central America, in Africa, or anywhere else; that Chiriqui [in Panama, which was then a province of Colombia], the place selected for the first experiment of the new colony, does not belong to the United States; that if the scheme could be carried out it would reduce the South to a wilderness for want of labour that white men could not undertake; that it would cost more money to expatriate the 4,000,000 of men, women, and children of the South, to say nothing of those of the North, than Mr Chase could print off in three years in any form of note or bill that would pass current; and, last of all, that it is absurd, impracticable, and impossible.

Apart from the abolitionists, Lincoln's proclamation was also far from welcome to the Democratic Party and its leading adherents within the Army of the Potomac such as McClellan and Porter, and in fact the Democrats were to make some gains in the mid-term congressional, state and gubernatorial elections of November 1862. McClellan remained undoubtedly popular among his troops but Lincoln was increasingly exasper-ated by McClellan's delay in following up Lee's retreat. Consequently the President visited his general in the field from 1 to 4 October to urge action. Initially, as Mackay reported on 7 October in a dispatch printed on 20 October, all seemed resolved:

Mr Lincoln, who has a high sense of his own responsibility for the doings of his Generals, if not for those of his Ministers, has made an unusually long visit to General M'Clellan, to satisfy himself that all is right on the Upper Potomac. The telegraph has informed him daily, for the last fortnight, that all is quiet on that stream; but as the army might be too quiet for efficiency, he appears to have resolved to see with his own eyes whether it were in working order, and whether M'Clellan were as much to be trusted as he himself believed, contrary to the opinion of some, if not most, of his Ministers, and of other prominent persons who take him by the button-hole. At his return, at 10 o'clock on Saturday night, from a visit of two days and two nights to the camp [actually four days, as indicat-ed above], he immediately summoned his War Secretary [Stanton]; and on Sunday morning he convened a Council of Ministers that remained in close deliberation for five hours. It seems to be the impression that he has again been 'putting his foot down' upon M'Clellan and keeping it down, as if he were very much in earnest, and not at all kneadable by the extraneous agencies that desire to mould him to purposes not his own. He is reported to be entirely satisfied with what he

McClellan and Lincoln confer after Antietam, 4 October 1862

saw and heard, though he was by no means satisfied with the reported state of matters when he left Washington. Certainly the cordial good feeling that subsists between the General and the army – so different from the bickerings, animosities, and personal jealousies with which he himself has to do battle every day, must have come upon his jaded senses as pleasantly as a breath of fresh air in the face of a convalescent. It is no secret that General M'Clellan has more enemies and possibly more friends than any man in America, and that the most vigorous and open, as well as the most insidious and secret means are daily employed to deprive him of command.

At the same time that McClellan was coming under increasing pressure, dissatisfaction was also growing with Buell in the West, who – after Halleck's promotion to General-in-Chief – shared the command in the West with Grant, but who had been given responsibility for an advance eastwards from Corinth to Chattanooga in Tennessee with the Army of the Ohio while Grant's Army of the Tennessee was dispersed in various static duties. As cautious as McClellan and harried by Confederate cavalry raids striking his extending lines of communication, Buell had moved slowly and had then been forced to swing northwards short of his objective to counter an advance into Kentucky by General Braxton Bragg, who had succeeded Beauregard in command of the Confederate Army of Tennessee in June 1862. Following a confused engagement between the two armies at Perryville on 8 October, Bragg retreated to Chattanooga but, like McClellan, Buell was slow to follow and, as Mackay reported on 24 October in a piece printed on 8 November, it imperilled his command:

Unpopular as General M'Clellan is with the Republicans and Abolitionists, [Major-] General Buell, the next most important Federal officer in command of an army in the field, is equally, if not more so. He is accused of having stated at the commencement of his military career that he did not know who was right or wrong in the struggle – the North or the South, and to have acted throughout the war on the lazy principle of poco-curantism. He is declared to be always behind time, to have lost the battle of Pittsburg Landing [Shiloh] by his indifferentism, and to have wilfully, if not treasonably, allowed General Bragg to retire from Perrysville [*sic*], and out of Kentucky into Tennessee, without serious loss, though his army, in overwhelming force [60,000 men as opposed to 40,000 Confederates], stood idly by, within a few miles, and might have captured the Confederate army. Some weeks ago the President, moved by the urgent complaints of the Abolitionists, superseded General Buell in his command; but only to reinstate him by telegraphic dispatch a few days afterwards. He is also a West Pointer, and the innuendo is daily made that the West Pointers on both sides love each other too well to fight very desperately, and that some fine morning before anyone suspects the manoeuvre they will unite their armies, and make an end of the Republic.

Lincoln removed Buell on 30 October and replaced him in command of what was now to be the Army of the Cumberland with Major-General William S. Rosecrans, who had driven Confederate forces away from Corinth on 3 October. Meanwhile in the east McClellan had been further embarrassed by Stuart's cavalry again riding right around his army and, with no advance in prospect, Lincoln removed McClellan from his command on 7 November. His replacement was Burnside, who had commanded his corps at Antietam with less than conspicuous success and believed himself unfitted for the command of the army.

As these events unfolded, Mackay also reported on the varying attitudes of clergy on both sides to the war in a dispatch of 28 October. Perhaps not surprisingly, Mackay somewhat underestimated the passion of Southern clergy for the cause of the Confederacy – indeed, one of Bragg's corps commanders at Perryville was Major-General Leonidas Polk, Episcopal Bishop of Louisiana. His report was published on 11 November:

The part taken by the clergy in the war has been marked and decided both in the North and South. In the North, while the Episcopalians have been neutral, the Presbyterian, the Puritanic, and even the Unitarian pastors have been aggressive, violent, unreasonable, and vindictive. If the solution of the difficulty could have been left to their hands, and they had the means to convert their bloodthirsty theories into facts, the extermination of the Southern people would long ago have been attempted. They have evinced the true spirit of persecutors, and some of them in this city have manifested as little reluctance to the use of the stake and the gibbet against the friends of the South as inquisitors in Spain would have exhibited against heretics. In the South the clergy have been less violent and more charitable, with the single exception of the renegade Parson [William G.] Brownlow [a former Methodist minister turned newspaper editor in Knoxville, Tennessee, known for his virulent anti-Southern views, who had been arrested by Confederate troops in November 1861 but then deported to Union territory in March 1862]. The Episcopalians have prayed for the President of the Confederate instead of the United States, and in New Orleans and Nashville and other places temporarily occupied by Federal armies, where they have not been permitted to offer up prayers for Mr Jefferson Davis, they have refrained from substituting the name of any other magistrate. This course of proceeding has in many instances led to the closing of their churches, and in Nashville to the imprisonment of several of the most zealous clergymen, by order of Governor [Andrew] Johnson. In New Orleans, with such a man as Butler to deal with, the preachers have been unusually cautious; but hitherto that redoubtable General, foiled, or, at all events, damaged in reputation by his attack upon the ladies, has been chary of meddling with the church or the chapel.

One better placed than Mackay to assess the influence of the Southern clergy was Lawley, who was now reporting from Richmond, his dispatches much delayed by the Union blockade. Most were apparently sent through the agency of the French consul in the Confederate capital via the Paris office of *The Times*. Lawley's first report from Richmond, largely recapitulating the story of Antietam but also ironically disparaging the effect of the blockade, had been written on 8 October but did not appear in print until 4 November. McClellan was yet to be dismissed when Lawley reported next on 5 November, revealing his dislike for the argumentative Bragg, whom he would have liked to see replaced by Joseph Johnston. He also commented in passing on the attitude of the Southern clergy and what became a frequent theme, namely the loyalty of the slave population to their masters. As with his earlier dispatch, it took nearly a month to reach London, being printed on 1 December:

It is interesting to observe how much more reticent and guarded the Southern press, wholly unrestrained by censorship or supervision, is than the muzzled and stifled journals of the North. General Lee has been in this town for three days, and everybody in the streets has known it; not a word to that effect has appeared in print. Possibly it might be useful to General McClellan to be aware of this fact, and the instinct of a people whose affections are in their cause is a truer guide to discerning where silence is desirable than the surveillance of Mr Stanton and his myrmidons. In the annals of civilized warfare such harmony in support of a war has never been approached. The women are a never-failing source of wonder and admiration to the stranger, and next to the women in earnestness are the clergy, and especially those of the Romish faith. It is absurd to talk of such a word as earnestness being applicable to the coloured race, but to the fullest extent of their powers detestation of the Yankee is expressed by the negroes. I trust, hereafter, to

have full opportunities of collecting details of negro fidelity under trying circumstances during this war; for the present it will be enough to state that not one of those
prophecies which we have all believed and been deluded by in England with regard
to the weak spot of slavery festering at the heart of the South has found one tittle of
realization. Women and children without one adult white male have constantly lived
in the voiceless solitudes of the South surrounded by negroes; in no instance known
to me has anything but the greatest loyalty and affection been evinced.

Burnside had not sought the command of the Army of the Potomac and was placed
in a difficult position in trying to replace as popular a commander with the troops as
McClellan. Nevertheless he resolved that rather than make another direct advance
through the Manassas area, he would move his army eastwards to attempt a crossing of
the Rappahannock around Fredericksburg. Two of his corps had reached Falmouth
opposite Fredericksburg by 17 November, although a misunderstanding between
Burnside and Halleck meant that there was no pontooning equipment available to effect
a quick crossing of the river. As Union troops initially broke contact with the Army of
Northern Virginia to begin the move to the east, Lawley was at the Confederate head-
quarters situated at Culpepper Court-House midway between the Rapidan and
Rappahannock rivers. On 14 November he reported on the Union withdrawal and on
the effect of artillery, his report appearing on 27 December:

A long scouting ride yesterday, in company with [Major-] General J.E.B.
Stuart, in the direction of the little village of Jeffersontown, lying about 15
miles north of Culpepper Court-House, revealed to us the rear of the Yankee army

Ambrose Burnside

rapidly falling back and fighting loosely as it retreated. The woods just beyond Jeffersontown were for some time filled with the enemy's sharpshooters, and it was difficult to force them from their cover. Seldom has so much powder been burnt with so little effect. On the Confederate side not a man was wounded; the only animal I saw touched was one horse, who got a buckshot above his nostril. It may be presumed that the Federals escaped with as little damage. It is scarcely necessary to add that the normal artillery duel in this instance, protracted for less than a quarter of an hour, was as barren of results as usual. One of the lessons of this war, in which field artillery has been employed to an unprecedented degree, is that while the moral effect of artillery, especially upon undisciplined troops and among trees, is very great, the actual results attained thereby may be stated as nil. Of course I am not speaking of artillery employed when the fighting is at close quarters, and grape and canister and shrapnel are used against masses of men. But these artillery duels, which point many a correspondent's letter and fill many a reader with awe, seem usually to be as bloodless as though they were conducted with blank cartridges. It is doubtful whether by every thousand discharges from cannon so high an average as the death of one human being is attained. Some ingenious arithmetician may amuse himself by computing, taking the price of each shot and shell from a six-pounder up to a 32-pounder and determining the relative number employed, what this life has cost. As evening fell, only a small Federal force remained to the south of the Rappahannock, and night saw them all encamped on its northward bank. This morning we passed some 20-pounder Parrott guns and one long Whitworth gun going to the front, with a view to shelling a Federal camp some two miles north of the river. The Whitworth gun is spoken of as a great success, and commanding a far longer range than any other gun upon either side.

Lawley was indeed correct in seeing that artillery was most effective used in mass at medium and close range but, although the new rifled artillery did make accuracy at long range theoretically possible, it was rarely attempted successfully. The overall effect of artillery, therefore, might be small, as in the Union campaign in the Wilderness during the spring of 1864 in which only 6 per cent of their casualties resulted from Confederate artillery, which was even less than the 7 per cent put down to accidents or self-inflicted wounds. Yet in certain battles the positioning of artillery was sufficiently effective to ensure far larger casualties, as would shortly be demonstrated in Burnside's advance across the Rappahannock, for the delay in providing him with bridging equipment enabled Lee to shift his own army to Fredericksburg and to occupy Marye's Heights and other commanding ground opposite the river.

As the two sides awaited developments, Lawley sent back one of his most memorable dispatches describing Lee and his corps commanders, Jackson and Longstreet, who was to become a particularly close contact of Lawley. Dated 21 November, it finally appeared on 30 December:

General Lee is, I believe, between 50 and 60 years of age [he would turn 56 in January 1863], but wears his years well, and strikes you as the incarnation of health and endurance, as he rears his erect soldierlike form from his seat by the

Robert E. Lee

fireside to greet courteously the stranger. His manner is calm and stately, his presence impressive and imposing, his dark brown eyes remarkably direct and honest as they meet you fully and firmly, and inspire plenary confidence. The shape and type of the head a little resemble Garibaldi's, but the features are those of a much handsomer man. On the rare occasions when he smiles, and on still rarer occasions when he laughs heartily, disclosing a fine unbroken row of white, firm, set teeth, the confidence and sympathy which he inspires are irresistible. A child thrown among a knot of strangers would be inevitably drawn to General Lee in the company, and would run to claim his protection. The voice is fine and deep, but slightly monotonous in its tone. Altogether, the most winning attribute of the General is his unaffected childlike guilelessness. It is very rare that a man of his age, conversant with important events, and thrown to the surface of mighty convulsions, retains the impress of a simple, ingenuous nature to so eminent a degree. It is impossible to converse with him for ten minutes without perceiving how deeply he has meditated upon all the possible eventualities of the campaign in Virginia, and how sound and well-considered are the positions which he advances. It is obvious that the most entire and trusting confidence is placed in General Lee by his subordinate officers, whose respect and affection he seems thoroughly to have won. The General is still crippled in his hands from the effects of a fall which he sustained so long ago as the 30th of August. At dawn that day he rode across the historical stream of Bull Run, and, observing a patch of herbage, he dismounted and allowed his horse to graze, recollecting that the animal had carried him the whole preceding day almost without food. The General himself sat down on a stump. There were only a few cavalry pickets of Confederates between General Lee and the enemy. Suddenly a charge of a large body of Yankee cavalry drove in the Confederate pickets, and came close up to the spot where General Lee was. The General ran forward to catch his horse, and, grasping at the rein as his horse sidled off, he fell heavily forward entangled in his cloak, upon both hands, and jarred the nerves of the arms right up to the shoulders. His horse was caught by one of his staff, and the Yankee cavalry, not knowing what a valuable prize was close at hand, fell back without approaching more nearly. The General rode throughout the whole of that eventful day, the 30th of August [the concluding day of the 2nd Battle of Manassas/Bull Run], but for many days and nights he suffered agonizing pain; and even now, on the 21st of November, he is far from having wholly recovered the full use of his hands; though not for one day or hour has he permitted himself to be absent from duty.

A similar abnegation of self is visible in every thought and act of General Lee. 'If only I am permitted to finish the work I have on hand, I would be content to live on bread and beef for the rest of my life.' 'Occasionally we have only beef, occasionally only bread; but if we have both together, and salt is added to them, we think ourselves Sybarites.' 'Upon this occasion it was necessary to stop and procure food for some of the younger men.' These are some of the characteristic utterances which struck me as they came from General Lee's lips. In reference to the last, it would seem as though the ordinary demands of human appetite were in him subordinated and subjected in presence of the imperious exactions required from his brain. In all the varied attributes which go to make up the commander-in-chief of a great army, it is certain that General Lee has no superior in the Confederacy, and it may fairly be doubted whether he has any equal.

General Lee has three sons in the army – the one a General, under [Major-] General J.E.B. Stuart [Brigadier-General W.H.F. 'Rooney' Lee]; the second a Colonel [G.W. Custis Lee, ADC to Jefferson Davis]; the third, a lad of 18 [Robert E. Lee, Jnr], who is a private attached to one of the batteries [Rockbridge Artillery] of [Lieutenant-] General Jackson's corps. In reference to the last, General Lee told me a story which seemed to me, for the first and only time during many conversations, to have elicited from the narrator faint traces of emotion. Most certainly it was difficult to listen to the story without one's self experiencing such emotion. It appears that at the most critical moment of the Battle of Sharpsburg [Antietam], when General Lee was ordering up every gun to meet the heavy masses of Federal artillery pressing on the centre, he observed a single gun harnessed and ready for action, the sole survivor of a battery which had been engaged earlier in the day, and had been roughly handled by the Federals. General Lee immediately ordered the gun to the front. As it passed to the front, coming close to the spot where General Lee was standing, he recognized in the postilion mounted on the leading horses his young son. The boy turned and smiled brightly on his father, exclaiming, 'So I see that you are sending us in again.' It is a pleasure to add that, although slightly wounded, the boy lived to come safely out of the terrible engagement.

At a distance of seven miles from General Lee's headquarters, near the little village of Bunkerhill, were the headquarters of the hero of heroes of this struggle, [Lieutenant-] General 'Stonewall' Jackson. We had been taught to expect a morose, reserved, distant reception; we found the most genial, courteous, and forthcoming of companions. A bright, piercing, blue eye, a slightly aquiline nose, a thin, tall, sinewy frame, 'made all over of pinwire', a great disregard of dress and appearance – these are the characteristics of General Jackson's exterior. There is also about him a very direct and honest look. The disappointing circumstance is, that his voice, which is rapid in its utterance, is weak and unimpressive. Passionately attached to the [Shenandoah] Valley of Virginia, which has for so long been the principal scene of his achievements, idolized by the inhabitants of Winchester and of the Valley, General Jackson has acquired such a fame in that entire neighbourhood that it is sad to think what would happen if the one life round which such prestige clings should yield to a stray bullet or to the chance of disease. Sinewy and wiry as the General seems, it is impossible not to fancy that he is wearing himself terribly by his restless, sleepless activity, by his midnight marches, and by the asceticism of his life. The respect and consciousness of his presence, and what that presence means, exhibited by his staff, impressed me very strongly, and seemed to exceed the respect exhibited towards General Lee. He spoke a few hearty words of admiration of General Lee, saying that he never should wish to serve under an abler commander. But his heartiest and most enthusiastic utterances were in admiration of the Cathedral edifices of England, and notably of York Minster. He dwelt with great animation upon the vibration of the air produced by the deep notes of the organ in York Minster, and which he had never heard equalled elsewhere. It is rare to find in a Presbyterian such appreciation and admiration of Cathedral magnificence.

There are such endless stories about General Jackson that to repeat them would fill a volume. Stories of his being wrapt in prayer in the midst of a fierce engagement, – stories of the unaffected earnestness and piety of his life in his tent, and of his black servant saying that when his master, who invariably prays morning and evening, rises also in the middle of the night to pray, he knows that great and critical events are imminent. A most undemonstrative, reticent man, doubtless, in all that regards his vocation of a soldier. There is every reason to think that, when the war is over, General Jackson will be the very first man to bury himself in the deepest obscurity of private life. Throughout this war it has been the practice of General Jackson to throw himself, disregarding his own inferiority of numbers, upon large bodies of his enemy, and the day is ordinarily half-won by the suddenness and desperation of the attack. His usual policy then is to retire, upon which the correspondents of the Northern journals, who upon the day of General Jackson's onslaught have been half-frightened out of their lives, announce with their usual fanfares a great Federal victory, and joy and exultation are universal. In a few days, however, when the Federals have reached some spot where it suits General Jackson to attack them, he pounces upon them again, and frequently the very fame of his second approach drives his opponents to a precipitate retreat without fighting, if the ground admits of such a possibility. The upshot of nearly a year and a half of General Jackson's conduct of the war, frequently at the head of no more than a handful of men, is that no permanent foothold has been gained by the Federals in the Valley, and that, at will, General Jackson has run his opponents, sometimes including at once two or three Federal Generals of rank, out of the Valley. As there are many conflicting reports about the origin of the name

'Stonewall', it may be interesting to repeat the true circumstances under which it was given. In the first battle of Manassas, on July 21, 1861, [Brigadier-] General [Barnard] Bee, of South Carolina (himself subsequently killed in the same action), observing his men flinching and wavering, called out to them to stand firm, exclaiming, 'Look at Jackson's men; they stand like a stone wall!' In his official report of the battle, General Beauregard employed the same expression in connexion with General Jackson's command, and the name has clung to General Jackson ever since.

It remains for me to say a few words respecting one other of the most valuable officers of the Confederacy – an eminently combative man – [Lieutenant-] General Longstreet. His frame is stout and heavy, his countenance florid and cheery, and eminently English in appearance. In every position he has occupied – first, as commanding a brigade; secondly, as commanding a division; thirdly, a *corps d'armée* – he has grown in the affections of his men and in the confidence of his commanding officers. As brave and imperturbable under fire as in his tent, remarkable for his promptitude in thinking correctly when in the greatest danger, his value to the Confederacy can hardly be overestimated. A review of some 10,000 of his men took place when we were at Winchester. Among this body there were no shoeless or barefooted sufferers; a finer or more spirited body of men has never been assembled together on the North American continent. In conclusion I can safely say that, although I saw much suffering, great want of shoes, frequently very inadequate clothing, among the men of General Lee's army, I was astonished to observe how confident was the spirit pervading the entire body. No such army has ever yet been assembled to fight for the Confederacy. Any battle into which these men enter is half won when the first shot is fired. Again and again they have

James Longstreet

joined issue under most unfavourable circumstances with their opponents, and have gained victories. It is not likely that the tide will be turned now that the Federals are every day fighting with less and less appetite, and now that the experi- ence of 18 months of war has given such confidence to the Confederates in them- selves and in their commanding officers that the day of battle is surely and triumphantly looked on as necessarily the day of victory.

Lawley's eulogy did much to establish the cult of Lee in Britain where, as in North America, the man would become a near legendary figure beyond reproach – the 'marble man' as he has been described. Lawley also found time while at Fredericksburg to send back accounts of two more Confederate personalities, the first on Major-General J.E.B. Stuart being written on 26 November and appearing on 1 January 1863:

E ach General has his warm admirers, gained by such opportunities of inter-
course as have brought individuals within the said General's orbit; but it is safe to say that in the race for popularity the foremost places are held by General 'Stonewall' Jackson and General J.E.B. Stuart. Each has attached to him the pres- tige of entire absence of failure. *Il n'y a rien qui réussit autant que le succès.* But while in the Shenandaoh Valley the achievements of General Jackson have aroused towards him a generous feeling of gratitude for danger averted and pros- perity preserved, it is doubtful whether east of the Blue Ridge the 29 years of General Stuart, added to that indefatigable energy which teaches him, after he has ridden 50 miles during the day, to regard it as his highest happiness to ride a dozen more miles at night, 'to tread but one measure' in a Virginian country-house, do not incline the scale, especially if the balance be adjusted by fair hands, in favour

J.E.B. Stuart

of the younger General. There have been many English officers, particularly in the East Indian service, whose endurance in the saddle has been regarded as unequalled, but I doubt whether any Englishman ever exhibited such superiority to bodily fatigue as is almost nightly evinced by the gay cavalier who knows every hospitable roof within a dozen miles of his head-quarters (and what roof is not hospitable?), and, accompanied by his banjo player, visits them by turns night after night, returning usually to his hard-earned rest long after midnight hour has flown. With the earliest dawn of morning, the first voice, calling gaily for break-fast, is that of the midnight merrymaker, who rises the picture of health, good-humour, and strength. It may be noticed *en passant* that to the circumstances that he has never touched tobacco in any form, or any wine or other liquor, General Stuart attributes much of his health and vigour. Certainly so jovial and merry a company as is assembled at General Stuart's head-quarters it has never been my fortune to see paralleled in either the Federal or the Confederate camps.

Reporting again on camp life in Stuart's headquarters on 8 December in a report published on 13 January 1863, Lawley also referred to another young general officer, the thirty-one-year-old Brigadier-General John B. Hood:

The apparent imminence of a battle has had its usual effect in heightening the spirits of the soldiers, and disposing the camp to such gaiety as life in a pine wood and a total absence of women may be supposed to admit of. The usual frol-ics at General J.E.B. Stuart's head-quarters are of nightly recurrence, except on the occasions when the General is absent upon one of his long scouting rides, which keep him out all night, and afford a respite to 'General Stuart's head-quarters' band', which consists of one excellent banjo-player and one 'bones', and is thus temporarily released from serenades and the discourse of other music. But all other entertainments of the camp have for the moment been thrown into the shade by the performances enacted two nights ago by General Hood's Texans, and which by particular desire will be repeated to-night. General Hood, a tall, sinewy, eager-looking soldier, is universally admitted to have led his Texan brigade into some of the hottest places which could be found throughout this war, and if the palm of valour could by acclamation be voted to any one brigade there is little doubt that Virginians, Louisianians, and every other State would combine in acknowledging the superior and paramount claims of Hood's fighting Texans. General Hood, who is much beloved by his men, knows that listlessness and want of interest and occupation in camp are fatal obstacles, when the day for action comes, to efficiency in the field. He has been at pains, therefore, to encourage the organization, among his men, of a band of Aethiopian [*sic*] minstrels, ten or twelve in number, who, on Saturday night discoursed very eloquent music and elicited rapturous applause, especially one soldier successfully dressed up as a *danseuse*, and conspicuous for a remarkably neat foot and ankle. The long prepa-ration which such performances exact, the interest of the discussions which they subsequently awaken, are great incidents in the monotony of camp life, and very healthy stimulants to men so disposed to listless apathy as the Southern soldier. It cannot be questioned that the banjo, the national musical instrument of the

Francis Lawley

Southern Confederacy, is a great addition to the amusements of soldiers on a campaign, and would be beneficial in spiriting away some of the proverbial spleen and
dullness of the British soldier in camp. Add to this the natural appetite for music
which makes every negro a musician and ready for dance and song, and there are
elements of entertainment which cannot be found in connexion with any European
army in the field, and are no slight circumstances in influencing and elevating the
spirits of the dejected, tatterdemalian, lack-lustre, half-starved scarecrows who are
nobly conducting this brilliant struggle for independence, which it is obvious to
the least far-sighted observer they are on the eve of bringing to a successful issue.

If Lawley's predictions were to be somewhat over-optimistic in the long term, he had
the measure of the confidence of Lee's army in its positions overlooking the
Rappahannock. On 11 December Burnside finally began to construct bridges over the river
at Fredericksburg and entered the town, which was severely damaged, after a brisk
engagement with its defenders. Two days later, however, while the left wing of Burnside's
army had limited success against Jackson's corps before being driven off, an unimagina-
tive and sustained frontal assault from the town on Longstreet's prepared positions on
Marye's Heights, including a stone wall flanking a sunken road at the foot of the hill,
resulted in utter carnage. Having suffered 15,000 casualties compared with but 5,300
Confederate losses, Burnside withdrew across the river on 15 December. Lawley
described the aftermath for his readers on 20 December, his dispatch being published on
23 January 1863:

Gone, indeed, they were; but in what fashion? A glance at the long slope between the town of Fredericksburg and the foot of Marye's Heights gave the best idea of the magnitude of the toll which had been exacted for their passage of the Rappahannock. A ride along the whole length of the lines told also a sad tale of slaughter; but when the eye had once rested upon the fatal slope above mentioned the memory became fixed upon the spot; nor for 50 years to come will that scene ever fade from the memory of those who saw it. There, in every attitude of death, lying so close to each other that you might step from body to body, lay acres of the Federal dead. It seemed that most of the faces which lay nearest to Colonel [James B.] Walton's artillery [Washington Artillery Battalion] were of the well-known Milesian type. In one small garden, not more than half an acre in size, there were counted 151 corpses. I doubt whether in any battle-field of modern times the dead have ever lain so thick and close. By universal consent of those who have seen all the great battles of this war, nothing like it has ever been seen before. It is said that the morning after a victory always breaks upon naked corpses. It was not so in this case, but the sole reason was that the pickets of both armies swept the slope with their fire, and that any living thing which showed upon it was the target for a hundred bullets. But three or four mornings after the battle it was seen that the furtive hand which invariably glides into the pocket of victory had been busily at work, and naked corpses and others from which everything but their under clothing had been rifled were visible in abundance. So tremendous was the fire, chiefly emanating from [Brigadier-General Thomas R.R.] Cobb's Brigade [but named for his elder brother, Howell Cobb, now commanding the District of Middle Florida], posted in the lane at the foot of Marye's Heights, that even chickens in the gardens in front fell pierced by it. It was remarked by a Confederate General [almost certainly Colonel Edward P. Alexander, commanding Lee's Battalion, Reserve Artillery] intimately acquainted with the Federal [Major-] General [Edwin V.] Sumner, who commanded the Federal right, 'Was there ever any other General but Sumner who would have got his men into a place in which not even chickens could live?' But the fire across the slope was fatal not only to men and chickens, but also to every other living thing. Horses by dozens were strewn along the hillside; and occasionally a dead cow or a dead hog lay close to the silent and too often fearfully torn and mutilated human bodies which everywhere met the view. Such a sight has rarely been seen by man. It is doubtful whether any living pen could do justice to its horrors; but it is certain that it would be easy to write more than any ordinary reader would care to read. It is known that during the nights of the 13th and 14th very many bodies were carried off and buried by the Federals; but when the party of Federals detailed to bury their comrades had completed their task it was found that under Marye's Heights they had buried 1,493 corpses, and 800 more on the Federal left. Computing that 3,000 Federals fell dead on the field, and adding six or seven times that number of wounded, you may gain an approximate estimate of the Federal loss on the 13th of December. To this must be added upwards of a thousand prisoners taken by the Confederates, and all the stragglers and deserters who strayed away from the Federal army. It is incontestable that the 13th of

The Confederate position behind the stone wall at the foot of Marye's Heights, Fredericksburg after its later capture by Union forces, 3 March 1863

December will be graven as deep in the annals of the great republic as is the anniversary of Jena [Napoleon's victory in 1806] upon the hearts of the Prussian people.

Lawley exaggerated the Union losses but not that greatly and there could be no doubt that, at the end of a year of fluctuating fortunes for both sides, a peaceful resolution was not at hand.

1863

Following the gains made by the Democratic Party at the midterm elections in November 1862, there had been speculation that Lincoln would not go ahead with the implementation of his Emancipation Proclamation. However, as Mackay reported from New York on 2 January in a report published on 15 January, New Year's Day ended such speculation:

The President has kept his word. He issued his Proclamation of Emancipation yesterday, but it was not published until to-day in any of the journals, though publicly read last night at Boston, at an Abolitionist meeting, to the promoters of which an early copy was forwarded. Mr Lincoln abolishes slavery as far as his words and signature can abolish it in ten of the States of the Southern Confederacy, leaving it intact in such portions of those ten States as are occupied by the Federal forces, and in the Border States of Maryland, Delaware, Kentucky, Tennessee, and Missouri. He admits, by these exceptions, that he has no power under the Constitution to touch the question of slavery in any place where the owners of slaves are loyal to the Government of which he is the head, but declares at the same time that he sincerely believes the emancipation of such negroes as have the good fortune to be slaves of the rebels 'to be an act of justice'. He does not say whether it is justice to the slaves, or justice to their masters, that inspires his policy. If it be justice to the slaves, why does he not emancipate those who belong to loyal owners? And if it be justice upon the owners – justice inflicted in the shape of fine or deprivation of property, does he not admit the negro to be a chattel, which he has as much right to confiscate as lands and houses, and so place himself in antagonism with his Abolitionist friends, who maintain that the negro is not, and never can be, a chattel? And when he invokes 'the considerate judgement of mankind and the gracious favour of Almighty God' on his act, does he think the one will approve or the other bless a course of proceeding which ought to make the slaves of loyal men curse the loyalty of their masters as the greatest affliction that could befall them, and which, in the case of the rebel owner, uses the slave as an instrument of vengeance just as Mr Lincoln would use a sword, a rifle, a cannon, or any other offensive weapon? The proclamation is as cruel and illogical as the war of which it is the climax. It only declares slaves to be free in States where the President has no more power either to make them free or white than the Imaum of Muscat has, while it retains them in bondage in every place in which his armies could give effect to his words, and convert his theories into facts. The whole document rests upon a false foundation, and has no other justification, even in

'Contraband' slaves at Follies Farm, Cumberland Landing on the Pamunkey River, May 1862

the mind of its weak and irresolute author, than the old, stale, and wicked plea of necessity, that plea which evil doers, oppressors, tyrants, and weak rulers have always employed since the creation of the world, and will continue to employ until its end in support of the foregone conclusions of their own passion, prejudice, and madness. It is, moreover, a direct and palpable incentive to a servile war – of which no imagination, however truculent and prurient, can exaggerate the horrors. Though it enjoins upon the negroes the policy and duty of abstaining from violence, it expressly permits and advocates violence if it seem to them to be necessary for self-defence or the procurement of their liberty. In other words, Mr Lincoln deliberately counsels the negroes to defend by force the liberty which his proclamation but not his arms has bestowed upon them in case their masters should resist, as they assuredly will, their escape from bondage. It is impossible to put any other construction upon the words, and should a war of races and a repetition of the atrocities of St Domingo [the slave revolt during the French Revolutionary and Napoleonic Wars on Haiti] be the result every drop of blood that may be shed in the struggle – whether it be the blood of white men, women, and children or the blood of the unhappy negroes themselves – will lie upon Mr Lincoln's head and on the heads of those who counselled him to do evil that good might follow.

Mackay had recognized that the proclamation now issued had been redrafted in order to qualify the original impression that the administration was inciting slave revolt although, from Mackay's point of view, the qualification made little difference. It was also the case that the new draft expressly encouraged the recruitment of negro units, to which the Confederacy reacted by threatening to execute white officers leading such units. In all, possibly between 180,000 and 200,000 negroes eventually served in the Union Army. Ironically, one of the last acts of the Confederate Congress was to authorize the raising of negro troops in March 1865 but no more than a few companies were organized before the South collapsed a month later.

If the ultimate emancipation of slaves rested on the successes of Union armies then there was seemingly little immediate prospect of it. In the East, of course, Burnside had been thrown back at Fredericksburg. In the West, having succeeded Buell, Rosecrans had also attempted an advance, clashing with Bragg's Confederate Army of Tennessee at Murfreesboro/Stones River in another typically confusing battle of changing fortunes over the three days from 31 December 1862 to 2 January 1863. The unpopular Bragg was compelled to retreat on Chattanooga but, with some 12,000 casualties on each side, Rosecrans was in no position to follow up his opponent for all that the battle was portrayed as a Northern victory – as Mackay reported on 6 January in a dispatch printed on 20 January:

The long tide of ill-fortune that has been running against the North seems to have turned. For the last three days the public mind has been filled with disquieting presentiments of evil in the South-West. On Sunday it was reported that [Major-] General Rosecrans had been defeated at Murfreesborough [*sic*], and that he had surrendered with his whole army to General Bragg. Yesterday it was asserted on better authority that the battle had raged for five days [actually three] with awful slaughter on both sides, but with no definite result. This morning there

William Rosecrans

is news from General Rosecrans himself, admitting the terrific obstinacy of the contest, but claiming a victory, purchased with the loss of from 7,000 to 10,000 men. Nashville, the prize on which the Confederates had set their hearts [and from which Rosecrans had set out], has been saved; and if the great Confederate army of the South-West has not been destroyed or rendered incapable of further offence, it appears to have received so heavy a blow as to incapacitate it from any immediate resumption of hostilities. The telegraphic dispatches represent it as in full retreat to Tullahoma, about 30 miles distant, on the line of the Nashville and Chattanooga Railway. One dispatch adds the words, 'in disorder'; but a careful perusal of the two bulletins of General Rosecrans leads to the belief that General Bragg saved his army as secretly and unexpectedly to the enemy, and in as good order, as [Major-] General Burnside saved his at Fredericksburg. When the struggle ended on Saturday night General Rosecrans evidently calculated on its renewal, and only awakened to find, at 7 o'clock in the morning, that the foe had escaped without exciting his suspicions. [Brigadier-] General Robert Mitchell [commanding the 4th Division of XIV Corps in Rosecrans's Army of the Cumberland], dating from Nashville yesterday, says 'The Lord is on our side. The rebels are whipped.' But the profane supposition in the first sentence, and the confident assertion in the second, may be put to the test at Chattanooga, should General Rosecrans pursue the enemy to that strong position and again offer battle.

Rosecrans had been sufficiently successful to retain Lincoln's confidence but this was not the case with Burnside and, when an attempt to again cross the Rappahannock bogged down in mud, he was replaced on 26 January with one of his leading critics within the army, Major-General Joseph 'Fighting Joe' Hooker. Mackay reported the change of command a day later, his dispatch appearing on 16 February although he confused Burnside's two earlier offers to resign with his demand in meeting Lincoln after the 'Mud March' that either several of his subordinates, including Hooker, be removed or he would resign:

A fter floundering in the peculiarly tenacious mud of Virginia for a few hours [in fact the 'Mud March' lasted from 20–22 January], General Burnside resolved to lead his dispirited and insubordinate army to the attack, unaccompanied by the artillery, which he found it impossible to move, arguing that the storms which had done him so much damage had done as much to the enemy, and that if they could fight without cannon so could he. At the council of war called to consider the matter General Burnside found none to agree with him. Hesitating under such circumstances – as well he might – to assume the responsibility of continuing a movement so inauspiciously begun, so certain to be inefficiently supported by his reluctant subordinates, and so likely to lead to the capture or annihilation of the whole force, he resigned himself to his fate, countermanded the movement, left his horses, his waggons, and his guns in the mud, marched his troops back to their old cantonments, and proceeded to Washington, determined to resign his command. The President did not wish to accept the resignation, but General Burnside was peremptory and would listen to no advice or persuasion. The result was that on Saturday morning he ceased to be commander of the Army

Joseph 'Fighting Joe' Hooker

of the Potomac; and that [Major-] General Hooker, the 'fighting Joe' [*sic*] of the soldiers, was appointed to his place. For some reasons not yet explained – perhaps from the appointment of a junior over their heads, perhaps from disapprobation of the unconstitutional acts of the Government, perhaps from dissatisfaction with the continued interference of the President with military matters, which he does not understand, and perhaps from despair of achieving any good with the Army of the Potomac, [Major-] Generals [Edwin V.] Sumner and [William B.] Franklin – old, experienced, and trusted soldiers – have also resigned. The distrust and demoralization are widely spread.

In fact Franklin had come under heavy criticism after Fredericksburg and was also one of those critics whose removal Burnside had demanded, while the sixty-six-year-old Sumner was to die just two months later. Nevertheless, there was clearly a significant morale problem within the Army of the Potomac and Hooker, who was as popular with his troops as McClellan had been previously, undertook a major reorganization.

On the southern side of the front in Virginia there was equally little action, and Lawley had travelled south to Charleston and then on into Georgia. On 26 January he reported from Augusta, one of those centres becoming vital in the attempt by the Confederacy to match the industrial might of the North. In Atlanta and also at Selma in neighbouring Alabama a wide range of manufacturing was now under way, but Augusta's significance lay in its powder mills which were eventually to produce 2,750,000 lbs of gunpowder. With Lawley's dispatches increasingly delayed in reaching England, his report from Augusta did not appear until 18 March 1863:

Unquestionably, if the spectacle which I have seen to-day could by anticipation have been foreseen by President Lincoln and Mr Seward two years ago they would never have hardened their hearts and refused to let the South go. When upon the 13th of April, 1861, Fort Sumter surrendered to General Beauregard and the Confederates, not one single pound of gunpowder was anywhere manufactured in the Confederacy. A rigorous blockade of the seaports of the South was immediately commenced, through which the principal ingredient of gunpowder (saltpetre) had to be largely sucked in. At this juncture it seemed advisable to President Davis to intrust to Colonel [George W.] Raines [actually Rains], formerly an officer of the United States' army, the responsibility of planning and building a large Government mill for the manufacture of gunpowder. For this post Colonel Raines possessed eminent qualifications. He had been Professor of Chymistry [sic] at West Point, and, for some years, since leaving the army [in 1856], he had been at the head of some large ironworks at Newburg [actually Newburgh], on the Hudson [in New York State]. Augusta in Georgia, was selected as the site of the intended mill, and never, both as regards the person and the situation pitched upon, was happier sagacity evinced by the President. Following, so far as he was acquainted with it, the plan upon which the gunpowder-mill at Waltham Abbey [Essex], belonging to the English Government, is built, Colonel Raines proceeded to construct the works necessary for his purpose; and the success which has attended his efforts has been such as could never have been believed before the pressure of war and privation had awakened Southern ingenuity and enterprise. The result is that, at the cost of about $20,000, one of the most perfect gunpowder-mills in the world has been produced, which turns out 5,000 lb. of powder a day, and could produce double that quantity, if worked day and night, and much more if worked under the exigency of a pressing demand. The cost of this powder, in spite of the costliness of the saltpetre which has been introduced through the blockade, is about 4c. a pound, which is believed to be about the same as its cost in England. The mill has now been constantly at work for many months, and, consequently, more powder than the Confederacy is likely to require for years to come has already been produced. There is another Government powder-mill, at Columbia, in South Carolina, working, I believe, to supply the wants (not very large as yet) of the Confederate navy. But all the gunpowder issued for the service of the Confederate armies of Virginia and the West, and also for the defence of Charleston and Vicksburg, has come out of the mill at Augusta, and it was stated to me by an Ordnance officer in Charleston that the powder which he had recently received there and tested was very nearly, if not entirely, up to the standard of the finest English manufacture.

From Georgia, Lawley moved to Vicksburg on the Mississippi, regarded by Jefferson Davis and others as of vital importance to the Confederacy, although it could be argued that complete Union control of the Mississippi would not and ultimately did not confer particular advantages on the North, at least in terms of those resources available to the Confederacy west of the river. Indeed, the loss of the Confederate Army of the Mississippi commanded by Lieutenant-General John C. Pemberton when Vicksburg eventually fell was of far greater significance than the loss of the city itself. In fact Davis had reinforced Pemberton at the expense of Bragg's Army of Tennessee in December 1862, the same month in which Grant's first advance on Vicksburg was thrown back by a damaging Confederate cavalry raid on his depot at Holly Springs, Mississippi led by Major-General Earl Van Dorn. In turn, this left Major-General William T. Sherman's Union XV Corps – advancing more directly on Vicksburg down the Mississippi – isolated and on 29 December Sherman's forces were easily repulsed at Chickasaw Bluffs. Grant was left to examine various ways of approaching Vicksburg and it would not be until April 1863 that he would set out to outflank the city by moving down the west bank of the Mississippi. When Lawley reported on 6 February in a dispatch published on 31 March, however, Vicksburg still appeared impregnable:

What are the chances, under existing circumstances, of Vicksburg being taken? It requires some patient tranquillity to discuss them. There are three methods of attack, of which two have been tried already. The first is the bombardment of the town and batteries by gunboats and mortar-boats on the river, in the hope of silencing the Confederate guns. This was tried elaborately at an enormous cost last summer, and the result is known to the world. The second is landing troops on the Yazoo River [emptying into the Mississippi from the east about twenty miles to the north of Vicksburg], and marching them through swamp and bayou to attack the line of bluffs which run back from the Mississippi to the Yazoo river, and strike the latter at Snyder's-mill, about 13 miles from Vicksburg. This was attempted on the 27th of December last [by Sherman], and an attempt was also simultaneously made to force the obstructions stretched across the Yazoo at Snyder's-mill. Both of these efforts met with signal failure. The *Benton*, which was regarded as the best of the Mississippi ironclads, was very roughly handled by the batteries. The 45,000 men whom [Major-] General Grant led up from Chickasaw Bayou [in fact 32,000 men under Sherman] (a small stream which empties into the Yazoo) found the natural obstacles and difficulties of the country almost more than they could surmount, and when some 6,000 of these men got sufficiently near to the bluffs to encounter opposition they were met by an advanced guard of 1,500 Confederates and routed with inglorious facility [in fact about 21,000 Union troops were opposed by 14,000 defenders]. The third, and, apparently, the only possible method of attack which remains is to land men in transports right under the guns of Vicksburg, and to carry the batteries by storm. It is hardly necessary to say that this plan of attack would exact much more desperate valour than either of the others. It is inevitable that several transports must be sunk as they approach the batteries, while the men who land from the surviving transports would be exposed to a tremendous fire of grape and canister and musketry. It is not probable that an army so demoralized as that which [Major-] General [John A.] M'Clernand commands [in fact the Union XIII Corps under Grant, but McClernand had aspired to an independent command in the West] could be induced to undertake so desperate and hopeless a venture; but, if they do, the result is 'beyond a peradventure'. There is some talk of pontoons being thrown across the stream and troops being thus conveyed across, either below or opposite the town. The idea of building a pontoon-bridge in the face of the Confederate batteries is manifestly absurd. The difficulties of building it anywhere upon the

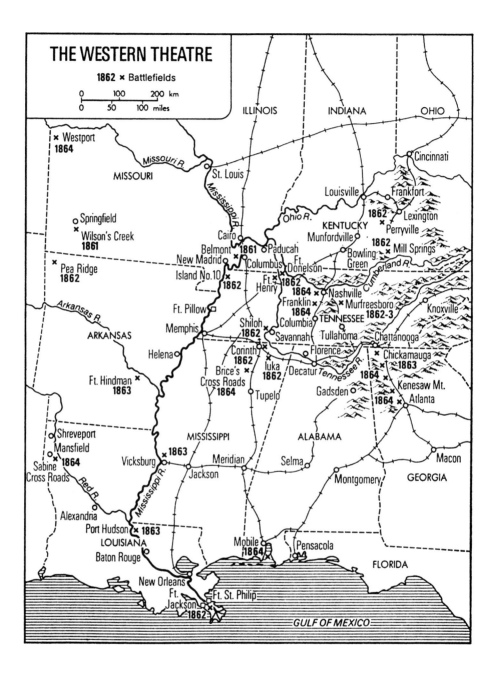

THE WESTERN THEATRE

1862 × Battlefields

0   100   200 km
0   50   100 miles

Mississippi are so stupendous that it is hardly worth while to further discuss such a possibility. It is impossible to witness the vagueness and aimlessness of the Federal efforts at Vicksburg, at Baton Rouge [from which a Union force under Major-General Nathaniel P. Banks was preparing to advance on Port Hudson on the lower Mississippi], at Murfreesborough, no less than in the neighbourhood of Fredericksburg, without coming to the conclusion that the whole head is sick and the whole heart faint – that there is no man in the North bold enough to face resolutely the desperate, but inevitable necessity, and at all hazards to stop a war which has already cost at least 500,000 lives, and of which the result is unalterable, although 500,000 more were added to swell the total.

With equally few developments on which to report in the North, Mackay gave his readers a guide to the terminology of Northern politics, his article of 17 February being published on 6 March:

The English student of Transatlantic public life is apt to become bewildered by the copious vocabulary of American party nomenclature. While in England Whig, Tory, and Radical, Free-trader and Protectionist, Liberal and Conservative, Obstructive and Destructive have been for five-and-twenty years almost the only party epithets that have obtained general currency and acceptation, America has employed a whole dictionary of phrases, invented by the exuberant humour, no less than by the equally exuberant hatred of contending factions. 'Locofocos', 'Hard Shells', 'Soft Shells', 'Dough-faces', 'Know-nothings', 'Nigger worshippers', 'Black Republicans', etc., have done duty, with such words as 'Whigs', 'Old-line Whigs', 'Federalists', 'Nullifiers', 'Straight-out Democrats', and numerous other phrases, to designate the various divisions and subdivisions of parties. These were, however, the shibboleths and watchwords of a period of peace, and nearly all of them have disappeared. At the present time the political and Parliamentary belligerents of the North are separable into only two great bodies – the Democrats and the Republicans. But these lines do not, in reference to the war for the Union and the social and political status of the negro, make a clear demarcation. There are Democrats who love the Union more than they love liberty and happiness, or who imagine they do, and who even approve negro emancipation, provided the emancipated slaves are not allowed to leave the South. On the other hand, there are Republicans who differ from the majority of their party on the question of slavery – who think that the President has done wrong in meddling with it, and who do not value the Union so highly as to look with complacency upon the ruin of the Northern people in the difficult, and it may be futile, attempt to restore it. Hence there are the divisions of 'White Republicans' and 'Black Republicans'. The one is composed of Democrats and Republicans, who would not grant the negro any social position or political right whatever, and who maintain that [George] Washington and [Thomas] Jefferson intended the Republic to be a Government of white men, and of white men only. The other is composed of philanthropists, preachers, lecturers, and zealots, who proclaim that they would ruin and slay every white man, woman, and child in the South, rather than acknowledge that the negro was not a brother, and not as fully entitled as themselves to political equality; and who would obey – or say they would obey – a black President as implicitly as they would obey a white one, if, by the lawful agencies of that wondrous machine the ballot-box, Mr Frederick Douglass [a former slave, who had founded the abolitionist newspaper *North Star* and become a prominent political activist in the North], or any other whole or half-caste negro [Douglass's mother had been a white slave owner and his father a slave] were nominated to the perilous position. The terms 'Secessionists' and 'Unionists' explain themselves, as do those of 'Disunionists', 'Peace Democrats', 'War Democrats', and 'Exterminators'. Lately, however, three new words have obtained currency and fashion, – 'Butternuts', 'Copperheads', and 'Woolly Heads'. A 'Butternut' is one who sympathizes with the South – one, in fact, who wears the uniform or livery of the Southern army, which is a brownish-gray colour, commonly the colour of butternut, a species of walnut peculiar to America [in fact a term long used to denote southerners who had moved to the north-western states]. The term 'Copperhead' is employed by the Republicans to designate all persons, whether Republicans or Democrats, who are in favour of an armistice with the South, to be followed by a convention of the people to debate the terms of peace. The name is derived from that of a little venomous serpent very common in America – in the North as well as in the West and South, – which has a bright shining head of the colour of a new farthing. It haunts rocky places and stone walls, and its sting is supposed to be even more deadly [than] that of the rattlesnake. It is asserted that the word has a peculiar aptness not imagined by those who first applied it [apparently Republicans in Ohio describing Peace Democrats]. The 'rattlesnake' was the emblem of the State of South Carolina before it adopted the Palmetto. At certain seasons of the year, in the greatest heats of the summer, the rattlesnake becomes blind, and at such times, says popular tradition, it is always accompanied by the 'copperhead', which acts towards it the part of a faithful friend in its calamity. Hence, say the Republicans and Exterminators, no term can be more appropriate for a venomous Northern man, who aids, comforts, and abets such a rattlesnake as South Carolina, than that of a Copperhead.

'Woolly Heads' is the new name given to the Negrophilists and Abolitionists by the Democrats. The chiefs of the party are Mr Horace Greeley, Mr Charles Sumner and Mr Wendell Phillips.

The chief of the 'Copperheads' is Mr [Clement L.] Vallandigham, of Ohio. Awaiting the appearance of some more uncompromising logician than himself, who will more boldly look all the facts in the face and accept the issues whatever they may be, the 'Copperheads' accept him *ad interim* as the exponent of their sentiments. Mr Vallandigham has on many previous occasions, both in and out of Congress [he had lost his seat in Congress in November 1862], spoken with greater courage than any other public man in America in denunciation of the war and the despotism of the Administration.

Mackay was to become increasingly critical of what he saw as the suppression of citizen rights in the North, as represented by Vallandigham's arrest and deportation to the South in May 1863, without perhaps making sufficient allowances for the fact that there was a war being fought. However, he was certainly correct in seeing some of the paradoxes of Northern attitudes, not least towards emancipation. Moreover, for all his open Southern sympathies he could still be informative on some of the darker corners of a society at war, as in a dispatch from Washington on 28 February, which appeared on 17 March:

Raw lads of 18 and 20 form the bulk of the army that defends Washington against the imminent aggression of General Lee. These youths revel and riot in their premature manhood, and exhibit their exuberant strength and insolence in drunken and other orgies that seem to have no limits but their purses. To inveigle the 'greenbacks' out of their pockets and those of their officers a whole army of brazen courtesans and 'painted Jezebels' has invaded the city, who ply their trade by advertisement in the newspapers and by public exhibition in the streets after a fashion so gross that it would shame even the Haymarket. The places where they have congregated have received the name new to American slang, and peculiar to Washington, of 'Ranches', a word that in Texas signifies an enclosure for cattle. The 'Ranches' of Madame This or That are as openly conducted as the hotels or boarding-houses, and the Provost Marshal and his officials make little or no effort to interfere with them. At every street corner, and place of public resort are to be seen printed notices, warning simple-minded strangers against the multitudinous thieves who have congregated here from all parts of the world. In those 'howling caravanserais' the leading hotels, where the utmost possible discomfort is paid for at the highest possible price, and where the bad cookery and the bad wine are only equalled by the bad accommodation and the bad attendance, are posted up at every angle of the vestibules, corridors, and reception rooms conspicuous warnings against the hotel thieves who have come hither from England and France, as well as from New York, to break into ladies' bedrooms at the dinner hour and decamp with their jewelry. Three days ago one of them succeeded in making off with the money and private papers of Mr Ex-Secretary [Simon] Cameron [Lincoln's first Secretary at War, who had resigned in January 1862 and had also resigned from his subsequent post as minister to Russia in November 1862], while that unsuspecting diplomat was quietly dining at Willard's. Another class of thieves, not so designated in polite society, but worthy of the name – the people who sell the Government rotten and unseaworthy steamboats for the conveyance of troops and stores; shoes for the army, that wear out in one day's march; and shoddy garments, nether and upper, that rot like blotting paper in a shower of rain; the 'respectable' people who plunder under form of law and with the decent observance of trade, feed daily at Willard's and other public places, and make themselves conspicuous by the magnums of claret and champagne which they consume, and by the general loudness of their talk and behaviour. Then there are the 'wire-pullers' and 'log-rollers'; that is to say, men who have schemes before Congress, and who 'engineer' their bills through both Houses by the vulgarest agencies of dinner and drink, as well as by other means not so visible to spectators, though perhaps more satisfactory to such members of the Legislature as are neither too honest nor too proud to be purchased. But the roguery and rascality of Washington are equalled by its misery. There are estimated to be no less than 40,000 sick, wounded, and mutilated soldiers within the District of Columbia, receiving such poor relief and consolation as circumstances will allow, not one twentieth part of whom will ever again be in a condition to fight the battles of the North. In addition to these are the negroes, or 'contrabands', as they are called in the slang which [Major-] General Butler originated and made popular, who have escaped from Maryland and Virginia into the Federal lines, and are maintained by the Government at a heavy cost. Many of these poor creatures are able-bodied men, for whom no work is to be found even as teamsters – an occupation for which they are well fitted; but a large proportion are aged and infirm persons and young children. All of them are huddled together in wretched shanties at a remote corner of the town. Smallpox is making fearful havoc among them, and thence extending its ravages among the white population. Washington, though an immense city upon the map, is not sufficiently built up to accommodate the 250,000 people who have been drawn within its focus by the necessities of the war and the Government. Its drainage is so miserably defective that the wonder ought to be that it has not long ago been the theatre of pestilence as well as of war, and thus suffered the second as well as the first scourge of humanity.

On the same day that Mackay reported from Washington, Lawley was back in Georgia after his trip to Vicksburg and, though at Atlanta, devoted some attention to some of the less obvious aspects of the Northern coastal blockade of the South. The article eventually appeared on 15 April:

It is unquestionably competent to the Federals to increase the pressure of want by their possession of some of the finest grain-growing districts of the Confederacy. All the Northern moiety of Virginia, the fruitful valley of the Shenandoah, the Eastern sections of North Carolina, produce in ordinary times most of the grain which supplies bread to the South, or is exported through New York to Brazil and South America. Upon each of these districts the iron heel of the invader is planted. Furthermore, in that portion of Tennessee which is in the Federal grasp General Rosecrans has forbidden every kind of agriculture, and aged men and women and children (the sole denizens left in that region) who reject the oath of allegiance are driven down South at the point of the bayonet, to increase the number of mouths which the Confederacy has to feed. Another great source of supply is cut off by the suppression of the North Carolina fisheries, which ordinarily yield millions of herrings and shad, salted on the spot by large groups of male and female negroes. In this respect the North Carolina herring far surpasses the Nova Scotian, which is caught out at sea, thrown into the hold of a ship, and not salted for many days after it is secured. The salt herring of North Carolina is here asserted to be the finest in the world. A gentleman who owns one of these fisheries told me that he had caught at one draught enough herrings to fill 180 barrels. The offal of the fish is valuable as manure, and the yield of Indian corn from fields sprinkled with the heads and entrails of the shad is said to be something fabulous. It has been customary to feed the negroes upon salt fish, which, as well as salt pork, they infinitely prefer to fresh meat. But this great staple of Southern food has been cut off by the Federal possession of Albemarle and Pamlico Sounds. Nevertheless, such is the wealth of the interior waters and bayous and lagoons which still remain to the Confederacy that it is doubtful whether,

if only transport could be commanded, the whole population might not be supported on fish alone. For instance, the bay of Mobile seems literally paved with oys-
ters, not less delicious than the bivalves of the James River with which Richmond
is bountifully supplied. The 'shell roads' at Mobile and New Orleans, constructed
of oyster shells, testify to the abundance of the yield in the neighbourhood of those
cities. Again, the extraordinary affluence of game and deer and wild ducks
through the Southern States assists their commissariat, and supports hundred of
families in remote country districts. For some time the scarcity of shot militated
against the destruction of small game, but recently a wooden shot tower has been
successfully established at Petersburg, in Virginia, and shot is becoming cheap
and abundant. It is extravagant to fancy that enormous districts, teeming with the
richest gifts of nature, and blessed with a climate incompatible with the consump-
tion of an Englishman's allowance of animal food, are inadequate to the support
of a sparse population, even though agriculture be partially suspended. The sole
difficulty is to bring the food and the mouths together. This is the enigma with the
solution of which until the wheat harvest of July scatters plenty over the land the
Confederate States will have to grapple. It would materially assist them if twine
for making seines and fishing nets could be brought in through the blockade.

It is probable that five out of every six blockade runners, operating from ports in the
Caribbean such as Nassau in the Bahamas, got through to those ports remaining open
such as Wilmington in North Carolina or Charleston but, since they were built for
speed, blockade runners did not carry much freight. Consequently, while a considerable
amount of cotton was exported and perhaps 600,000 small arms and other supplies
imported by the South, the quantities still fell far short of actual requirements and
shortages fuelled the inflation from which the Confederacy increasingly suffered. As it
happened, another of the 'Occasional Correspondents' reported on 4 March – it
appeared on 11 May – on his experiences in earlier reaching Charleston through the
Union blockade:

On the 14th of January we sailed from Nassau for Charleston, and on the following day were caught in one of those terrific gales which burst with such
fury over that part of the Atlantic which lies immediately to the north of the
Bahamas. The tempest subsided on the 17th as we got nearer the land, but we had
left the tepid waters of the Gulf Stream, and the air became bitterly cold. A biting
north-east wind swept over the deck, and the sleet and rain fell incessantly. It
seemed impossible for us ever to get warm, and our teeth chattered as if we had a
shivering fit. But in the morning we saw in the hazy distance the shore of South
Carolina, and then shortly afterwards the low, dark hull of one of the blockading
ships. This was a fresh source of anxiety, and great was our relief when we found
we had not been observed. We passed the vessel, and got in safely half a mile
ahead up the channel. We had scarcely done so when the look-outs whispered
'Two more forward.' We thought we had eluded them also, but we were mistaken.
A bright flash, the rush of a ball over head, and then the loud report of a gun let us
know that the fleet was aware of our presence. Then rockets were discharged on
all sides, and more guns were fired. We were within no great distance of the bar

that guards the entrance of Charleston, some four miles or so from Fort Sumter, inside of which the hostile fleet never venture. In another 10 minutes we should have been perfectly safe; but as we approached two more ships were seen lying right in the narrow channel over the bar, through which it was necessary to pass. The captain hesitated about proceeding further, and so nervous did he become that he turned the ship's head round and ran her out to sea again. She was followed by a howling pack of cruisers, but speed, good luck, and the darkness favoured us, and by daybreak we were some 30 miles from shore, tossing about again in the Gulf Stream. The same programme was gone through the next night, and then we had to return to Nassau for coals. Under another captain we returned on the 29th of January to try our fortune again, and this time there was no hesitation. 'Charleston, or beach her', said our new commander, and in one hour we ran through the north channel, and arrived safe and sound under the guns of Fort Beauregard.

Naturally enough the North wished to close those ports remaining open to the South, and on 7 April 1863 Rear-Admiral Samuel F. Du Pont attempted to take Charleston with a fleet of nine ironclads. Lawley reported on the attempt on 18 April in a dispatch printed on 1 July:

It will have been known to your readers, long before the arrival of this letter, that the attack on Charleston, which commenced on the 7th inst., and was upon that day kept up with vigour for nearly three hours by nine Federal iron-plated vessels, was abandoned, finally as some think, upon the afternoon of the 12th. Of these vessels, the 'new Ironsides', a *soi-disant* seaworthy frigate, nominally the rival of the *Warrior* and *La Gloire* [respectively Britain's and France's first sea-going ironclads], and mounting 16 heavy guns, two of them rifled 100-pounders, was reputed by far the most formidable. Built somewhat like the iron-clad gunboats of the Mississippi, though with less shelving sides, looming up the harbour large and low, like an immense house with a roof flat at the ridge, and then sloping steeply both ways – the house itself submerged in water up to the rain pipes under the eaves – the Ironsides slowly and majestically advanced in the van of the attacking squadron, carrying the flag of [Rear-] Admiral Dupont, and impressing all spectators with the conviction that, if the success of this day's attack upon Charleston were commensurate with the anticipations of some of the assailants, the advance of Admiral Dupont's frigates into action was likely to be celebrated in song and story when [British Vice-Admiral Cuthbert] Collingwood's bold onslaught at Trafalgar had been forgotten. Behind the Ironsides advanced in two lines her lesser sisters of the deep – seven of the Ericsson Monitors, each with one revolving turret and two guns, built upon a design and in a fashion with which your readers have long been familiar, and one new aspirant to the honours of invulnerability in the shape of the double turreted *Keokuk*, called also the Whitney battery. The turrets of the *Keokuk* do not revolve, but in each a heavy gun is fixed, one of them throwing, I believe, an 11-inch, the other a 15-inch shot or shell. The solemnity of the scene, as these mailed pioneers of a new system of nautical warfare wore slowly in towards Fort Sumter, their ports closed, their exterior presenting no sign of life or action, their propelling power unseen, their tremendous guns withdrawn from view, forced the blood through the heart of the spectators in long and quickening pulsations. Suddenly 'the long roll' beat to arms in Fort Sumter, the crescent and palmetto tree of the sovereign State of South Carolina rose side by side with the stars and bars of the infant Confederacy, and as the twin flags flung themselves out upon the breeze the well-known national air of Dixie rang out in defiance, and the painful silence was broken by a salute of 13 guns from the fort. Everywhere along the wharves of Charleston, upon the sea-wall of the battery, on the tops of every house commanding the harbour, spectators of both sexes stood eagerly observant; while the student of history, had he possessed calmness enough at such a moment, might have recalled Thucydides' thrilling description of the Piraeus when the ill-omened Sicilian expedition went forth [in 415 BC during the Peloponnesian War between Athens and Sparta] freighted with the prayers and aspirations of the entire population of Athens, impotent though they were to avert its inexorable doom.

Du Pont's squadron was unable to penetrate the harbour boom and took over 400 hits before withdrawing, although there was only one Union casualty. Du Pont was promptly dismissed and replaced by Rear-Admiral John A. Dahlgren who, in conjunction with Union land forces, now concentrated on a prolonged bombardment and blockade of Battery Wagner on Morris Island. With additional Union threats to the coast of both Virginia and North Carolina, Longstreet was detached from Lee's army with two divisions to Suffolk, Virginia, leaving the Army of Northern Virginia with only some 60,000 men at the moment when Hooker, who had now amassed over 130,000 men, was ready once more to attempt the break through on the Rappahannock. Hooker's plan was certainly bold, his cavalry sweeping far to the west in a diverting raid and some 40,000 men under Major-General John Sedgwick demonstrating before Lee's positions at Fredericksburg. At the same time Hooker took 70,000 men in an outflanking move across the Rappahannock and the Rapidan to converge on Chancellorsville to Lee's seven miles from Fredericksburg and effectively in Lee's rear.

Starting his movement on 27 April, Hooker was at Chancellorsville three days later but then hesitated. By the time he renewed the advance on 1 May Lee had taken the gamble of leaving only 10,000 men under Major-General Jubal A. Early at Fredericksburg opposite Sedgwick and taking the remainder of his outnumbered army west. Apparently losing his nerve, Hooker drew back into defensive positions around Chancellorsville and surrendered all initiative to Lee. That evening Lee and Jackson conceived another extraordinary gamble by which the Confederate army would again be divided, with Jackson taking 26,000 men on a wide flanking march to the west while Lee held the Union forces with only 17,000 men in the expectation that Hooker would do nothing. While Jackson's flank march did not go undetected, it was not correctly interpreted and Jackson's troops burst with complete surprise into the right flank of Hooker's army in the early evening of 2 May. Intending to continue an attack which had petered out in the darkness, Jackson went forward to reconnoitre in the gloom only to be shot by nervous Confederate picquets as he returned to his own lines. On the following day Sedgwick forced his way across the Rappahannock at Fredericksburg but Hooker, who had been badly concussed by a shell hitting a pillar of a house against which he was leaning, abandoned the commanding ground at Hazel Grove – a relatively open space amid the forested area of the Wilderness which surrounded Chancellorsville – enabling Lee to reunite with Jackson's command (now under the control of J.E.B. Stuart) and to detach troops to meet the new threat from the east. Sedgwick withdrew back over the river and, against the wishes of his subordinates, Hooker also retreated whence he had come on the night of 5/6 May. Lee had won his greatest victory, although his 13,000 casualties were proportionally much greater than the 17,000 suffered by Hooker. But, as Lawley reported from Chancellorsville on 6 May in a dispatch printed on 16 June, the greatest blow suffered by the Confederacy was the wounding of Jackson:

W hat might have been the result but for one casualty which alone almost countervailed the victories of a week who shall say? Formation or order the Federals had none; reserves, tactics, organization, disposition, plan, all went down before the whirlwind suddenness of the surprise. The loss of the Confederates was ludicrously small; their advance like that of a white squall in the Bay of Naples. Night had fallen. About 8 o'clock [Lieutenant-] General Jackson rode forward with two or three of his Staff along the plank road, and advanced 150 yards in front of his foremost skirmishers, peering with those keen eyes which you might fancy could be seen through the deepest gloom forward into the night. He turned to ride back – a heavy fire from one of his own regiments, hailing from South Carolina, but whose number I will in mercy withhold [the 18th North Carolina], saluted him. One bullet struck his left arm four inches below the shoulder, shattering the bone down to the elbow. The wound was intensely painful; he half fell,

Thomas 'Stonewall' Jackson

half was lifted from his horse. An aide galloped back to [Major-General] A.[mbrose] P. Hill to report that Stonewall Jackson was wounded and lying in the road. General Hill galloped hastily up, flung himself from the saddle, began, choked with emotion, to cut the cloth of Jackson's sleeve, when suddenly four of the Federal vedettes appeared on horseback, and were fired on by the Staff officers. The vedettes fell back upon a strong and swiftly advancing line of Federal skirmishers. General Hill and all the officers and couriers of both Staffs had no alternative but to mount and ride for their lives, leaving Jackson where he lay. Right over the ground where was stretched the wounded lion the Federals advanced. Within their grasp lay the mightiest prize, the most precious jewel in the Confederate crown; but it was not destined that Stonewall Jackson should be struck by Federal bullet, or yield himself prisoner to a Federal soldier.

As General Hill and his companions galloped back they also became the target of the same luckless North Carolinians [sic]. General Hill's boot was cut by a bullet, but his leg uninjured; Colonel [Stapleton] Crutchfield, chief of artillery to Jackson, was seriously, if not mortally, wounded [Crutchfield lost his leg but did return to active service, only to be killed in April 1865 just three days before the final surrender of Lee's army]; [Captain James K.] Boswell of Jackson's Staff, killed; [Captain Conway R.] Howard, engineer to A.P. Hill, knocked from his horse, but whether killed, or wounded, or a prisoner, is not known [he was captured when inadvertently riding into Union lines in the darkness, apparently some time before Jackson was hit]; two or three couriers killed. Without losing a moment, General Hill threw his own skirmishers forward, backed by heavy supports, and the ground on which lay General Jackson was again occupied by the Confederates. But in the meantime two more bullets, both from his own men, had struck him as he lay on the ground, one passing through the wrist of his shattered arm, the other entering the palm of his right hand and coming out through its back. He was at once carried to the rear, and his arm instantly amputated under chloroform. Grave fears were entertained that he would lose his right hand also, but I am happy to add that they have since abated. Again may it be hoped that, if he is wanted, Stonewall Jackson will carry into action a guilelessness, simplicity, and unselfishness which are all his own, and combine with them Cromwell's fiery zeal, saintly earnestness, and dauntlessness of purpose.

Lawley's account is not entirely accurate. Jackson's three wounds were all suffered in the initial volley from the Confederate lines, which also cut down most of those staff officers accompanying Hill and himself – fourteen dead horses were later counted at the spot although there appears no tally of the precise number of staff killed or wounded. While two Union picquets did indeed approach Jackson while he lay wounded, they were both quickly secured and Jackson was never fought over in the way Lawley implies. However, the whole area was being constantly swept by Union artillery fire and it was this that subsequently wounded Hill, who was hit in the calf by a shell splinter and was compelled to turn over command to Stuart. Nevertheless the degree of loss involved in Jackson's wounding was certainly not exaggerated by Lawley. Jackson was taken to a plantation building at Guinea Station, which Lawley visited on 7 May, his report appearing on 17 June:

A few hundred yards from Guiney's lies a comfortable Virginian farmhouse belonging to a Mr Chandler. In it 'Stonewall' Jackson is understood to be lying wounded. With a beating heart I rode up to ask after him, for rumour had stated that his condition was not favourable. Dr [Hunter H.] Maguire [actually McGuire], his staff surgeon, met me outside the house. He stated that until 2 this morning nothing could be more favourable than his patient's progress towards recovery, that he had ceased to entertain any fears about the wounded right hand, and that it had been his intention to convey the General to Richmond to-day. But at 2 this morning the General woke with an acute pain in his side, and, although Dr Maguire hoped that it might proceed from neuralgia, he had the greatest apprehensions in regard to pneumonia. The General was asleep while I was talking with the doctor. Shortly after he awoke, and upon examination it was pronounced that the symptoms were decidedly those of pneumonia. The Doctor proceeded to cup and leech him; from that moment I gave up all hope of his recovery. General Jackson's physique was far from being robust. It is an unerring indication of the fiery earnestness with which he entered into this war that from the time the first musket was fired he forgot his feebleness, and exposed himself to hardships, privations, destitution of food, exposure by night and day, such as I verily believe have never been submitted to by any General, whether modern or ancient, since first war desolated the earth.

Jackson died of pneumonia on 10 May and was the further subject of a long article by Lawley seven days later which, ironically, appeared in *The Times* on 11 June, six days before his description of Jackson's illness and death, indicating the difficulties of sending dispatches out of the Confederacy. In a postscript to the article on Jackson dated 19 May, Lawley also reported on the progress of Grant's army in its march down the west side of the Mississippi and the success of Porter's gunboats and other vessels running past the Vicksburg batteries on the night of 16/17 April, which had enabled Grant to cross the river south of the city on 30 April and advance on the Confederate forces posted at Port Gibson:

The great and absorbing interest of the recent operations near Fredericksburg fixed the eyes of both sections mainly upon that neighbourhood, and it was not until the smoke which overhung the valley of the Rappahannock had cleared away that the attention of the Confederate public was attracted to the fact that, contrary to my own and the general anticipation, another formidable attack, conducted along the approach which has long been felt to offer most promise to the assailants, was threatening the little hill city of Vicksburg. For a considerable time past it has been found that it was almost impossible to check the passage of Federal transports and barges under cover of night down the Mississippi, and accordingly a large number of vessels have successfully run the gauntlet of the Vicksburg batteries, subject only to the loss of a heavy percentage of their numbers. As there has throughout this war been a reckless disregard of property on the Federal side – a disregard which at the present moment may very possibly be nothing but wise economy – [Rear-] Admiral Farragut did not scruple to sacrifice many of his vessels in order to get a larger number than he sacrificed below the obstruction offered at Vicksburg. His troops [they were Grant's troops of course] were marched over the tongue of land across which the attempted canal has been carried, and were embarked upon the surviving transports beyond the range of the Vicksburg batteries. It appears that the defences thrown up by the Confederates at Grand Gulf, which is situated at the mouth of the Big Black River, some 30 miles below Vicksburg, were only seriously taken in hand after a large number of Federal vessels had succeeded in getting past the batteries at Port Hudson and Vicksburg. These defences were designed to obstruct the passage of vessels up the Big Black, which is navigable, though not without great damage to large vessels, for a considerable distance from its mouth. A heavy bombardment of the few and light guns planted by the Confederates at Grand Gulf necessitated the abandonment of that post, and a subsequent battle at Port Gibson [1 May], which was again abandoned by the Confederates, let their enemy in, and opened a door along the Big Black to the rear of Vicksburg. The evacuation of Port Gibson was followed by that of Bayou Pierre, and [Brigadier-] General [John S.] Bower [actually Bowen] fell back with his small Confederate force towards Vicksburg, but not until his gallant little band had done some excellent fighting.

Lawley indicated that he had suppressed the vulnerability of Vicksburg from the south in his previous dispatches but he still anticipated that Grant would be caught between Pemberton's forces in Vicksburg and those being gathered by General Joseph Johnston who, fully recovered from his wound during the Seven Days Battles, had been appointed to command the Department of the West in November 1862.

An integral part of Grant's operational plan had been to divert Confederate attention through a long-range raid by 1,700 cavalry under Colonel Benjamin H. Grierson, who left La Grange, Tennessee on 17 April and emerged sixteen days and 600 miles later at Baton Rouge, Louisiana. A trail of destruction was left in its wake, Southern railway lines and rolling stock being a target. Mackay commented on the role of cavalry in the light of this raid in a piece written on 19 May, which appeared on 3 June:

At the commencement of the war, and until within the last six months, when the brilliant achievements of the Southern cavalry attracted attention to the subject, the Northern Government and people rather despised than encouraged the cavalry arm of the service. But now cavalry raids are all the fashion, and have superseded even the iron-clads in popular estimation, as the means by which the horrors of war can be most effectually brought home to the experience of the Southern people. The North has not yet produced a cavalier equal to the Confederate [Major-] General J.E.B. Stuart, but has several candidates in the field for similar fame, among the foremost of whom are [Major-] Generals [George] Stoneman and [William W.] Averill [actually Averell] and Colonel Grierson. General Stoneman's raid in the rear of Fredericksburg to within five miles of Richmond, though not attended with the results anticipated, shows how much damage may be done with comparative impunity by a daring cavalry officer with a few hundreds of well-picked men and fleet horses. Colonel Grierson's raid was still more dashing and effective. With about 2,000 men, well mounted, he rode between six and eight hundred miles in fifteen days, in and through the State of

Mississippi, from La Grange, near Memphis, to Baton Rouge, in Louisiana, committing an immense amount of damage on his way, burning factories and stores, tearing up railways, destroying bridges, and carrying off a huge quantity of plunder. But *cui bono*? The Federals are not in want of supplies; and have no such justification for their raids as General Stuart had when he entered Maryland and Pennsylvania, to provide the Confederate armies with shoes, clothes, and provisions. If all be fair in foreign war, which is doubtful, all is not fair in civil war. Raids like these, which are attended with wanton mischief, and the destruction of the property of people who may at heart be loyal to the Union cause, have no other effect than to embitter the passions of the people and prolong the miseries of the war. Brilliant and dashing as they may be, and forming ample materials for future romance, they are not the kind of warfare that should be adopted towards a people with whom it is the duty as well as the interest of the North to be at peace some time or other, if not as political partners, which the North still foolishly and passionately hopes, at least as commercial friends and political allies, which will be their natural relationship when the war is ended.

Mackay's distaste for the emergence of a more 'total' warfare is understandable and he did correctly identify the way in which Stuart's initial activities in Virginia had set the pattern for cavalry being used for raiding rather than in the massed battlefield formations familiar to Europeans. Ultimately Union cavalry would be trained for a more effective role as mounted infantry, but in the meantime many raids were of little real strategic value, although Confederate cavalry in the West operating under talented tacticians such as Major-Generals Joseph Wheeler and Nathan Bedford Forrest had a decided impact upon Union operations. Stoneman's raid in conjunction with Hooker's advance to Chancellorsville had merely deprived the Army of the Potomac of the ability to gather battlefield intelligence through mounted reconnaissance. As it happened, Stuart's taste for raiding was to have precisely the same effect on the Army of Northern Virginia as Lee prepared to follow up his victory by once more invading the North.

Longstreet, who had rejoined Lee's army from his detachment to the Virginia coast, would have preferred to reinforce the Army of Tennessee and, indeed, this was also the suggestion of Beauregard, now commanding at Charleston. Johnston, too, believed Tennessee more important than Vicksburg since the loss of the former would do far more to open the deep South to Northern penetration. If Rosecrans could be thrown back and Tennessee and even Kentucky freed of Union forces, it was reasoned that it must compel Grant to abandon operations before Vicksburg. Lee, however, was convinced that by again seizing the initiative, and carrying the war to Northern soil, pressure would be taken off Virginia's resources. Subsequently, even more expectations were invested in the invasion of the North, a significant victory being likely not only to strengthen the hands of the Peace Democrats in the North but also perhaps revive the possibility of European recognition of the Confederacy. Having won the strategic argument at a crucial meeting in Richmond on 15 May, Lee reorganized his 75,000-strong army into three corps under Longstreet and the newly promoted Lieutenant-Generals A.P. Hill and Richard S. Ewell. Moving westwards and then north through the Shenandoah, Ewell led the advance across the Potomac on 15 June, compelling Hooker to withdraw from Virginia and follow suit ten days later. By 28 June Ewell was closing

Richard Ewell

on the Pennsylvanian capital of Harrisburg but the Confederate army was strung out all the way back towards the Potomac. What made the situation worse was that, smarting at a relatively minor reverse at the hands of Union cavalry at Brandy Station in Virginia back on 9 June, Stuart had used the discretion allowed him to take off virtually all Lee's cavalry far to the east on another attempt to ride round the Union army, as a means of restoring his pride. Thus, like Hooker at Chancellorsville, Lee was operating blindly and had little idea of the Union army's location. Travelling with Lee's Headquarters, all still appeared well when Lawley reported from Chambersburg in Pennsylvania on 29 June, his dispatch being printed exactly a month later:

A ny time during these last 10 days a traveller might sit by the wayside in the [Shenandoah] Valley of Virginia, or on the edge of the Potomac – that Rubicon which the Confederates have at length crossed to teach their pertinacious enemy some of the anguish which Virginia, Tennessee, Louisiana, North Carolina, and Mississippi have in different degrees so long endured – and at Hagerstown in Maryland, or at Greencastle in Pennsylvania, and wonder at the endless files of footmen and horsemen, accompanied by troops of negro camp-followers which passed before him; the men still ragged and unkempt, but hardly one with-out good substantial shoes; the mules and horses for the most part sleek and fat, the army altogether in infinitely better case than I ever saw it before. It is not like-ly that any such traveller would occupy his post long without being subjected to any amount of 'chaff', all the more so if his dress or appearance offered any salient points of attack. With jest and song and banter for each and all that they met, with saucy cheers as they tramped through Pennsylvanian hamlets to the tune of 'Dixie' villainously interpreted by a Confederate field band, heedless of the half-cowed, half-menacing looks of the groups of Yankee men and women, the ragged rebels press insolently forward, as though defeat and discomfiture were possibilities not dreamt of in their philosophy. Within the county of Franklin, of which Chambersburg is the county town, hardly a horse, or mule, or head of cattle has escaped the Confederates; and it is hard to see, even if the Confederate army was withdrawn to-morrow, how the harvest, which lies thick and promising in many a fair field, could be saved or garnered. The farmers gather ruefully in the streets, emboldened by the impunity which they have learnt from the experience of the last fortnight is everywhere extended to them by the Confederates, and moodily discuss the future and anathematize President Lincoln and Governor [Andrew] Curtin [of Pennsylvania] and General Hooker. But it is a strange commentary upon this war, especially in the eyes of one who has during these last four months visited hundreds of Southern towns, and encountered hardly a soul but old men and young boys and women, to see thousands of young and middle-aged stalwart men standing idle in the market-place, glaring as fiercely as they dare at their ragged invaders, but declaring that 'it is none of their business to fight'. Surely, if the men of Chambersburg are not goaded into rising by the presence of their foe, by the seizure of all their horses and cattle, and by grievous exactions in the shape of any number of rations, paid for, it is true, in Confederate scrip, but demanded at their hands by the Southern army, it is hard to say what amounts of pressure will constrain the men of Pennsylvania to acquit themselves like men. Hitherto, though I have conversed with many of them, and have heard the measure of their irritation against the Confederates expressed in various keys, there seems, so far as I can discern, no sense of individual responsibility among the men, no consciousness that the tread of an invader on their soil is the worst of pollutions. There has been, it is true, some little 'bushwacking' as the Confederates advanced, but it has been checked by the capture of the offenders, some 15 or 20 in number, and their dismissal as prisoners to Richmond.

Lawley was unaware that Hooker was no longer in command of the Army of the Potomac, having resigned on 27 June after a minor dispute concerning deployments around Harper's Ferry and had been replaced on the following day by Major-General George G. Meade of the Union V Corps. Mackay reported on the new appointment on 1 July in a dispatch published on 13 July:

The action of the Federal Administration has not been of a nature to show that it had any foresight a month ago, or that it has any now. General Hooker, knowing that his army was demoralized by its want of confidence in him – a fact on which he ought to have acted long before General Lee had foiled and outwitted him – desired in the very face of the foe to be relieved of his command. The President granted the request – unaware, apparently, of the immensity of the peril involved in such a change at such a moment – and appointed as his successor [Major-] General G. B. [*sic*] Meade, of whom few had ever heard, who has gained no laurels in the battlefield, but who is known to the Army of the Potomac as an excellent topographical engineer, and a painstaking, hardworking General of Division [he had commanded a corps since November 1862]. It is in favour of General Meade that he is not, like his predecessor, a 'rowdy', a profane swearer,

George Meade

and what is called in America a 'blower' or boaster; but a quiet unassuming man, with the language, manners, and reputation of a gentleman. This is a great though unappreciated advantage. The democratic soldiers of America may consider themselves the political, or even social equals of their officers, but they like to see a gentleman in command – if rowdies themselves they detest rowdyism in their officers. And this was one of the secrets of M'Clellan. He was just to his men, careful of their health and comfort, never indulged in the language of the bar-room and the 'groggery', never lost his temper or his good manners, or forgot what was due to his own dignity or that of the humblest person with whom he was brought into contact. In these respects General Meade is said to be his equal. A few days will show what other qualities he has to fit him for his perilous station. If he be not as good a soldier as General Lee – which few venture to hope – it will fare ill with the luckless Army of the Potomac, which now serves under its seventh commander [actually fourth, the others being McClellan, Burnside and Hooker. Mackay may be counting McClellan twice and McDowell and Pope but the army was not so designated when McDowell commanded it, Pope commanded a differently designated army and McClellan did not effectively cease to be army commander either when dismissed as General-in-Chief or when both he and Pope were in the field simultaneously before his being given the responsibility of defending Washington], and never put any confidence in [but] one of them. Had Mr Lincoln seen fit to re-appoint that one [McClellan] – the unfounded rumour of whose recall sent gold down one-and-a-half per cent yesterday, and stocks up in a still greater proportion; had he sent to him the instant that General Hooker desired to be relieved, he would have inspired it with new life and hope, and deprived the

coming battle of much of its inequality. He has not done so, and the consequence
is that the great majority of people look upon General Meade's defeat as all but
certain, and resign themselves to it with a kind of bewildered curiosity, like that of
children at a play, asking with their eyes rather than with their tongues, 'What
next?'

It was only on 28 June that Lee realized that the 90,000-strong Union Army was
north of the Potomac, and ordered a hasty concentration on Cashtown, which was relatively central for Ewell to the north and east at Carlisle and York, Hill already in the
vicinity and Longstreet around Chambersburg. Contrary to Lawley's report of the
well-soled infantry of the Confederate army, the marching had taken heavy toll on
footwear and one of Hill's divisions approached the small town of Gettysburg on 30
June in order to secure supplies from a shoe factory there. They ran into Union
cavalry, bringing on a classic 'encounter battle' in which, both sides having been
caught by surprise, each attempted to concentrate widely scattered forces as quickly
as possible. The battle began in earnest on 1 July as Hill's corps and then Ewell's
arrived and drove two Union corps back through the town in disorder but, with his
troops exhausted, Ewell chose not to press the attack that evening as the Union forces
rallied on Culp's Hill and Cemetery Hill to the east of the Gettysburg. As with Stuart,
Lee's discretionary orders assisted Ewell's decision, the prevailing opinion thereafter
assuming that had Jackson been alive the attack would have been pressed and the battle won that first day.

While he had not intended to bring on a general engagement with his army dispersed, Lee now resolved to fight where he stood and renew the attack, declining to
accept Longstreet's advice to move southwards between the Union army and
Washington and to find a strong defensive position which would compel Meade to
attack. Thus on 2 July the battle continued, but with an attack by Ewell in the north
around Culp's Hill and Cemetery Hill badly coordinated with Longstreet's attack in the
south towards the prominent feature of the Big and Little Round Tops and the southern
section of Cemetery Ridge. Longstreet's divisions were certainly slow to reach their
start lines and Longstreet was to be greatly criticized in later years, but there were
undoubted difficulties in marching tired formations a considerable additional distance
in order to avoid observation from the high ground occupied by Meade's rapidly growing army. Even so, Longstreet came close to seizing the Little Round Top after one
Union corps commanded by Major-General Daniel E. Sickles had been caught by taking up positions much further forward from the line of Cemetery Ridge than had been
intended. Lee, whose judgement may have been affected by diarrhoea, again chose to
persist in attacking on 3 July, this time committing two of Hill's divisions and the fresh
division of Major-General George E. Pickett of Longstreet's corps – in all, no more
than 15,000 men – in an optimistic frontal assault in the very centre of Meade's position on Cemetery Ridge. Lawley, who had himself been ill while accompanying the
Confederate army and in receipt of treatment from the medical staff of Lee's headquarters, noted that Longstreet seemed 'reluctant' and Lee uncharacteristically 'anxious and
ruffled' during the battle. Somewhat recovered, Lawley witnessed the climatic
'Pickett's Charge', his report on the battle as a whole, which he completed on 4 July,
being published on 18 August 1863:

George Pickett

The division of [Major-] General Pickett, shorn of two of its brigades, lately left in the vicinity of Suffolk [Virginia], but likely, I believe, shortly to join Lee's army, did not in number much exceed 4,000 men. The strong division of [Brigadier-General James J.] Pettigrew, which in its engagement of the lst [under its original commander, Major-General Henry Heth, who was wounded], against [Union Major-General John F.] Reynolds, sustained inconsiderable loss, numbered, with the addition of [Brigadier-General Cadmus M.] Willcox's [actually Wilcox] Brigade, temporarily attached to it, about 10,000 men. It was naturally desirable before their attack was delivered that a heavy cannonade from the Confederate batteries should, as far as possible, exhaust and perhaps silence some of the Federal guns. Accordingly, under the instructions of Colonel [James B.] Walton, Chief of Artillery to [Lieutenant-] General Longstreet, and Colonel [Reuben L.] Walker, Chief of Artillery to [Lieutenant-] General A.P. Hill, battalions of artillery, numbering in all 140 guns, were got into position, while similar arrangements were made by [Lieutenant-] General Ewell on the left, so that in all upon the Confederate side alone there must have been a concert of about 200 guns. It can hardly be doubted that their thunder was echoed back from a similar number of pieces on the Federal side, and to the reader's imagination must it be left to conceive the diapason of 400 guns. The thundering roar of all the accumulated battles ever fought upon earth rolled into one volume could hardly have rent the skies with fiercer or more unearthly resonance and din. Far back into the mountains the reverberations rolling from hillside to hillside startled strange and unmusical echoes. Vast cumuli of cloud, such as would have shrouded 10,000 Homeric goddesses, had they cared in these days of villainous saltpetre to mingle in the melee, floated over the strife; horses, the suffering and tortured ministers of man's fury and wrath, lay thickly dead or horribly mutilated upon the ground; constantly from out of the white pall of vapour issued wounded and mangled men, and rumours that this or that General was killed, that this or that regiment was reduced to a corporal's guard, traceable to no authentic source, neither believed nor disbelieved by the listeners, rose as it were out of the ground, until the spectator, a prey to that whimsical caprice which at moments of fierce and absorbing excitement seizes on men's minds, found himself wandering in thought to strange and far-off scenes, to happy valleys which had never seen war, and vaguely speculating how their echoes would awake and respond to such a thunderous din.

Precisely at 1 o'clock, responsive to the warning summons of two signal guns, the 110 pieces in the Confederate centre and right opened fire; nor were their voices hushed until 40 minutes after 2. Then came [Major-] General Pickett's turn, and nobly did he spring to the head of his undaunted men, and marshal them to the attack. With long floating locks, with a seeming recklessness, which is, perhaps, partly assumed, but which stamps him of the [Napoleonic Marshal and cavalry commander, Joachim] Murat type, General Pickett, of more demonstrative courage than other Generals, but not less unflinching than his own sword, seemed as he advanced to lead his men into the very jaws of death. Slowly emerging into the open ground, with shells (singularly ineffective, as it seemed to me, considering the apparently murderous precision with which they all burst) cracking and snapping over them at every stride, General Pickett's men seemed to take hours to surmount the mile of interval which divided them from the Federal batteries. At length their destination is reached; with a wild yell they spring into the Yankee earthworks; astride of each Federal gun rides a Confederate soldier; the group around General Longstreet congratulates him that the advance is a complete success, and for a few moments breath is drawn more freely. But the quick eye of General Longstreet discerns that Pettigrew's division, upon whose almost simultaneous advance depends the retention by Pickett of the captured guns, is in confusion. Upon their left Pettigrew's men, when they close up to the Yankee batteries, perceive a large column of Federals descending the hill to flank them. Retaining that fatal habit of thinking for themselves which is so pernicious to a soldier, the Confederates first halted, then got into confusion, then broke and fell back. The frightful damage from grape and canister which, shrinking at this perilous moment, they could not but sustain, was compared by an eyewitness of both scenes to the punishment inflicted on the Federals from the heights of Fredericksburg in December last. In vain did General Longstreet send Major [Osmun] Latrobe to General Pettigrew, shortly before the latter's troops broke, urging him in military language 'to refuse his left' – that is, to meet the flanking column by a line thrown obliquely out to meet it. Major Latrobe's horse was shot as he sped on his message, and on foot he could not get up to General Pettigrew in sufficient time to instruct and guide him. When Pettigrew and his men fell back, the flanking column of Yankees, meeting with no resistance, swept round until they approached and overlapped Pickett. Then and not till then he commenced to give way. 'Hide, blushing glory, hide' the cost of that retreat. Out of a division of 4,300 men he brought out, in the first instance, about 1,500, though I believe that another 1,000 straggled in next day. His three Brigadier-Generals lay dead or desperately wounded upon the field [Richard B. Garnett, dead; Lewis A. Armistead, mortally wounded; and James L. Kemper, wounded and a prisoner]; out of all his field-officers only one major came out unwounded; 11 out of the 13 colours which he carried into action were lost. Since the commencement of this war I know of no division on either side which has ever made so resolute an advance, or been so rudely and murderously handled. Long will the 3rd of July be remembered in anguished Virginia, from which State almost all Pickett's division was drawn. General Pickett and his staff, all of whom miraculously escaped, were torn by grief at the loss of friends known for a lifetime, but doubly and trebly endeared by the common perils and sufferings of these last two years.

But if at an earlier stage of this letter I fancied that less than his usual calmness was visible in General Lee's face, all trace of cloud and anxiety passed away in this hour of our deepest gloom. Riding from knot to knot of the stragglers, with kind, firm, calm words encouraging the disheartened, rallying every man who could carry a musket or was only slightly wounded, he infused confidence and spirit into his men at the moment which of all others is most trying to volunteers. General Willcox, riding up to him with tears in his eyes, exclaimed, 'General, I have tried to rally my men, but as yet they will not stand.' General Lee responded, 'Never mind, General; the fault is all mine. All that you have to do is to help me to remedy it so far as you can.' If any testimony to the affection and confidence inspired by General Lee were wanting, it might be found in the cheers issuing from the interior of ambulances as they passed him, bearing their ghastly load of wounded to the rear. This scene was witnessed by [Lieutenant-] Colonel [Arthur J.] Fremantle, of the Coldstream Guards, who has returned to England, leaving behind him many a friend in the Confederate army, which he has accompanied for the last three weeks.

In fact, Lawley exaggerated the degree of success enjoyed by Pickett's leading brigade under Armistead, who penetrated only a short way into the Union positions with a few hundred men. In all, while Union casualties over the three days amounted to perhaps 23,000 or approximately a quarter of those engaged, Lee's 28,000 casualties were a full third of his army. Meade did not choose to counter-attack in this moment of Confederate weakness and, after standing in position much as he had done after Antietam, Lee was able to withdraw successfully. Nothing, however, could disguise the magnitude of the defeat, the responsibility for which ultimately did lie with Lee.

It was also on 4 July, as Lee's army retreated, that Vicksburg surrendered. Advancing from the south, Grant had forced Pemberton back within his defences after an action at Champion's Hill on 16 May although he then failed in two frontal assaults on the city on 19 and 22 May respectively. However, with Sherman fending off Joseph Johnston's not altogether whole-hearted attempts at relief – Johnston felt Pemberton should abandon the city and break out – the forty-two day siege that ensued could have only one outcome. Accordingly both city and some 31,000 men were lost in the capitulation, which was followed swiftly by the surrender of the last Confederate position on the Mississippi at Port Hudson on 8 July. Vicksburg and Gettysburg together could certainly be said to have ensured that the Confederacy could no longer win the war but they did not necessarily mean that the North had yet won and those like Mackay attuned to real or imagined Union weakness found some comfort in the reaction to the introduction of fully fledged conscription, those men obtained under the militia draft of July and August 1862 being due to reach the end of their term of service by mid-1863. With the new legislation passed by Congress on 3 March 1863 the first ballot of those aged between twenty and thirty-five became due in July. In New York the first ballots were held on 11 July but, on the following day and the next three after that, possibly as many as 50,000 people rioted, looted, destroyed and, in some instances, murdered. At least eleven negroes were victims of the mob although the overwhelming majority of the estimated 105 dead were rioters themselves, since troops recently engaged at Gettysburg had to be rushed to the city to restore order by force.

The riots embraced a complex kaleidoscope of fears and prejudices well beyond mere opposition to the draft, as Mackay recognized in a memorable dispatch from New York of 14 July, which appeared on 28 July:

Early in the day [12 July] gangs of workmen went from workshop to workshop to call upon their fellows to leave their labour and proceed to the building in the Third-avenue where the formalities of the draught were to be resumed. By eleven o'clock some thousands of persons had collected. They commenced by throwing stones at the windows. They next rushed into the office, seized the wheel by which the lots were drawn and broke it into fragments, got hold of the enrolment lists and tore them into shreds, – thus rendering the prosecution of the draught impossible until a new enrolment had been completed – assaulted and severely ill-treated the functionaries employed, and were debating what was next to be done, when a man suddenly appeared on the platform with a pail of turpentine, which he deliberately poured upon the floor. A lucifer match was immediately applied. The turpentine blazed up furiously, and in less than half an hour afterwards the whole edifice was in a blaze from the basement to the roof. The firemen arrived to extinguish the conflagration. They were received by the mob with loud cheers; but were not permitted to throw water on the flames. The fire spread rapidly until eight contiguous houses were enveloped in one common destruction. The crowd assisted the terrified inmates to escape; but otherwise manifested a stern resolution to suffer no interference with their vengeance. Their next business was to tear up the iron of the street railways [presumably tram lines], to prevent the passage of cars with troops or police to the rescue, and to provide themselves with weapons. This done, they cut the telegraphic wires in all directions, and broke up into several mobs, each bent on its own purpose, or going wherever chance conducted it. Of course, such a riot became the holyday of all the rowdies, blackguards, and thieves of this city, who, scenting plunder as the crow scents carrion, turned out in large numbers to swell the volume and disgrace the character of the crowd. Hitherto no blood had been shed. A detachment of the Provost Guard that had been hastily sent from the Park Barracks, to prevent further destruction, if they could not restore order, arrived at Forty-first-street, in the very heart and focus of the riot, and found their further progress impeded by a dense mass of people, supposed to amount to 5,000 or 6,000, who received them with shouts and yells of execration, and pelted them with stones and brickbats. Thus hemmed in and surrounded, and in danger of being torn to pieces, they fired a deadly volley into the crowd, and about 20 people fell mortally wounded. No one knows whether or not they received orders to fire, or whether the fatal discharge was the unpremeditated and unauthorized act of their own fear; but the consequence, as might have been expected, was only to add to the fury of the multitude. The Provost Guard no sooner fired than it retreated, pursued by the crowd. The men threw away their firearms to facilitate their escape, and these being picked up by their pursuers seemed to suggest to the mob that in a future conflict with the troops it would be necessary that they should have muskets and rifles. Several soldiers and policemen – it is not yet known how many – were killed [eight soldiers and two policeman died during the rioting], and the crowd, growing larger and more furious as it rolled, invaded an armoury on the Second-avenue, belonging to Mr Opdyke, the Mayor of New York, where a large store of arms and ammunition for which this gentleman and his brother had contracted to supply the Government was known to exist. It was defended for a short time by the servants and workpeople of Mr Opdyke. But all resistance was in vain. The people overflowed into the building like an advancing sea, and in a few minutes the musketry and ammunition were seized and distributed among the insurgents. Whatever was not of a nature to be made available as a weapon was destroyed. This done the torch was applied to every corner of the edifice, which in a short time was in such a blaze as would have defied all the efforts of all the firemen of New York to extinguish. While this scene was being enacted another body of rioters, who had chased an obnoxious soldier or policeman into a large stone house at the corner of Lexington-avenue, surrounded the building, and demanded that he should be given up. The cry was raised that the house belonged to a 'shoddy contractor', who had made a fortune out of the war. The allegation, true or false, was fatal to the house.

The mob burst into it, tore down the pictures from the walls, cut them to pieces with their knives, or dug holes in them with railroad iron, demolished a large and costly pianoforte, threw the fragments out of the windows, took the books from the library and set fire to them in the street, broke open pantry and larder, wine cellar and plate chest, closet and wardrobe, and carried off every portable article of value and the wearing apparel of the male and female members of the household as trophies of their achievement. Finally they set fire to the building; and, watching the progress of the flames until they were quite assured that the work of destruction would be complete, marched off to commit new outrages. The next place that received a visit was the splendid house of Mr Opdyke, the Mayor, in the Fifth-avenue, a gentleman particularly noted for the fervour of his war sentiments, the richness of his contracts, and the vehemence of his Black Republicanism, or philanthropic love for the negroes. Cries were raised to gut and fire the house, and in one minute more the thing would have been done, had it not been for the opportune presence and judicious speech of one of the city judges, Mr Barnard, who endeavoured to calm the fury of the mob. Having obtained a hearing, from a doorstep, he bade them remember that Mr Opdyke was the legally elected chief magistrate of the city, and, as such, entitled to their respect and obedience. He entreated them not to sully their just cause by acts of violence. He declared that, in his opinion, as a lawyer and judge, the Conscription Act was illegal and unconstitutional; and added that, if any citizen, taken from his home in pursuance of that Act, applied by his counsel for a writ of habeas corpus before him, he would grant the writ, and bring the question to a test in the State and city of New York. This restored the crowd to good humour, and with three cheers for the judge they proceeded on their way, leaving Mr Opdyke's mansion unmolested.

But, although opposition to the draught was the main motive that impelled the people to these lawless deeds, another passion took possession of them as the day wore on. In their hatred of the war and the draught which had grown out of it, they remembered that Mr Lincoln by his Proclamation of Emancipation had so embittered the South as to render a restoration of the Union impossible. Hatred of the war and hatred of the negro, whom they supposed to be the cause of it, were equally strong in their minds. No negro could venture into the crowd without insult or danger. One unfortunate man of colour, being hooted and pelted with brickbats and brought to bay by a furious gang of assailants, drew a revolver from his breast and shot the foremost man dead. He was immediately pursued by a mob of hundreds of excited ruffians, seized, thrown to the ground, beaten on the head with clubs and pieces of iron, stamped and spat upon, and next, after every shred of clothing had been stripped from his back, hung, stark naked from a lamp-post, and pelted with stones and mud by an assemblage of juvenile ruffians, from the age of 12 upwards. After dangling for a few minutes all the available combustible rubbish of the neighbourhood was piled under his feet and set fire to, the maniac crowd dancing around in a frenzy of blood and horror. In another part of the city a second negro met a similar fate; and toward 6 in the evening a body of several thousand persons, breathing vengeance against that unhappy race – most of whom this day in New York would have been glad to exchange the peril of liberty in the North for the security of Southern slavery and protection – marched up to a large building, called the 'Coloured Orphan Home', an institution, as its name implies, devoted to the maintenance and education of orphan negro children. Giving the inmates an hour to escape, they declared their intention to set fire to the building, which intention they ruthlessly carried into execution at the appointed time. One life only appears to have been lost, – that of a poor negro child, who was accidentally trampled to death in the rush of the inmates to escape destruction. Amid scenes like these, the local authorities being almost, if not entirely, powerless to resist the progress of the insurgents, the night darkened down upon a city that would have been doomed to destruction if the mob had had as much leadership as it had ferocity.

Substitution, commutation and exemption were all actually provided for in the operation of the draft and it has been calculated that of the 776,000 men drawn in the draft of 1863 and the three that followed in 1864, only just over 46,000 ever served personally in the ranks. However, the contemporary perception was that the draft discriminated against the poor, and especially immigrants unable either to commute or to hire a substitute – commutation was abandoned in July 1864 – and the Irish community figured prominently in the New York riots.

Mackay shortly proceeded on leave but other aspects of the strain of war in the Northern and especially the Western States were to be illuminated by a new correspondent for *The Times*, the Italian-born Antonio Carlo Napoleone Gallenga (1810–95). A former professor of modern languages in Nova Scotia and of Italian language and literature at University College, London, Gallenga had returned to Italy in 1859 to sit in the Piedmontese parliament despite having become a naturalized British subject in 1846. He had then reported from Italy for both the *Daily News* and *The Times* and would later be a leader writer on the latter. Arriving in July 1863, Gallenga made his way to the West. Saddened at the number of men required to garrison both Boston and New York against riots, he went on in a report from Chicago on 30 August to describe the particularly bloody internecine warfare being fought out in Kansas and Missouri. The article appeared in print on 15 September:

Unless my inexperience of men and things on a first arrival greatly deceive me, we shall soon require no less vast a display of force in the West. As many as are willing are free to desert from the Federal army; and the breaking up of the Confederate force on the Mississippi has scattered many thousand desperate characters loose into the thinly settled districts of this western world. The affair of Vandalia [in Illinois, where an armed mob overpowered the local militia trying to arrest deserters] is perhaps only a first specimen of what parties here may attempt with utter impunity. Any strong measure adopted either to catch deserters or to enforce the draught can scarcely fail to multiply similar scenes. But far more startling tragedies are being played further south, on the Missouri and Kansas borders, countries long used to the raids of Bushwackers, Jayhawkers, Redlegs, and malefactors of every description, by whatever strange names they may be known. A leader of one of these marauding parties, one [William C.] Quantrell [usually rendered as Quantrill], nothing but a robber, but pretending to have a commission from the Confederate Government [he had received a commission as Captain in August 1862], fell suddenly upon the town of Lawrence, in Kansas, beyond Leavensworth [21 August 1863], and slew nearly the whole male population in cold blood, plundering their habitations, and setting fire to them. I shall enter into no particulars about that awful butchery, as it was already an old story by the time I arrived in this part of the country, and more than one account of it will have reached you from other quarters. What is important to note is merely that there was, naturally enough, a raising of bucklers throughout Kansas; that a large body of the 'boys' of the country instantly set out on the traces of the Missouri robbers and murderers, and that they have been slaughtering more than 80 persons, three or four of whom were known as Quantrell's followers, the others being only supposed to be sympathizers with his cause. The Kansas boys declare they will have no rest till they have laid the four border counties of Missouri, from which the marauding party took its start, into a howling and smoking wilderness. The reprisals may be just, and vengeance may be a sacred duty, but it is awful to think that this country, in which three years ago 500 muskets could not have been mustered, should now betake itself to the practice of private war; that it should set up the maxim of 'an eye for an eye, a tooth for a tooth', and that Government should look on while the avenger visits on four counties the sin of a few hundred ruffians.

A meeting of Kansas boys was held on Friday evening last, the 28th, in which it was resolved that 'loyal men' should meet at Paola on the 8th of September, all armed and fully equipped and organized, under the command of General [James H.] Lane [a US Senator and leader of Jayhawkers, who was a self-styled 'General'], who trusts he shall by that time have assembled 5,000 men ready for an onslaught into Missouri. At the same meeting the commander of the department, [Major-] General [John M.] Scholefield [actually Schofield, commanding the Department of Missouri], was denounced as imbecile and inefficient, and his removal demanded. [Brigadier-] General [Thomas] Ewing, who also commanded in the name of the Government [Department of the Border], telegraphed Lane, saying 'that he will defend Lawrence and Kansas, and requesting Lane to use his influence to prevent unauthorized raids into Missouri'. Lane answers that 'he will, on the 8th inst., assemble 5,000 men at Paola, and tender his services to him (Ewing), and, if rejected, he will appeal to a higher power'. General Ewing has placed two companies at Platte city to protect the borders against avengers from Kansas. The 'loyal men' cause hardly less trouble and anxiety than the 'Bushwackers'.

From all these crude items of information it appears clearly that the worst passions of that fierce border population are strongly excited, that Government has lost all influence or control over them, and is in as great fear of its friends as of its adversaries. Nothing seems more likely than we shall have a long internecine struggle between the lawless marauders on either side. Guerrillas are also very active throughout the regions of Kentucky and Tennessee.

In many respects the bitter fighting in Kansas and Missouri merely continued that which had occurred there before the war, but it had been exacerbated by the support obtainable from both Union and Confederacy. Neither 'side' had a monopoly of virtue in a conflict that had a dynamic all its own, bearing little relation to the wider war. Quantrill's raid on Lawrence left 182 dead and resulted in Ewing deporting some ten thousand people from the four border counties of Missouri, but it would only be the defeat of an attempted invasion of the state by Confederate forces commanded by Major-General Sterling Price and reinforced by many pro-Southern guerrilla groups in September and October 1864 that would finally disperse the latter. One notorious guerrilla leader, 'Bloody Bill' Anderson, was killed during the repulse of the invasion in October while Quantrill died a Union prisoner in June 1865 as a result of wounds received in an earlier skirmish in Kentucky. Some who had ridden with him, however, such as Frank and Jesse James and the Younger brothers, were to gain further notoriety after the war.

Gallenga's arrival in the West was fortuitous since attention was now principally drawn to the renewed advance of the Union Army of the Cumberland under Rosecrans, which had commenced in June after six months of inactivity. The intention was to seize Chattanooga, a key rail junction on the Tennessee river which also barred passage into Georgia through the Cumberland mountains. Despite the formidable natural obstacles in his way, Rosecrans skilfully manoeuvred Bragg out of Chattanooga in early September. Consequently Longstreet was hurried west with two divisions to reinforce Bragg, whose poor relationship with his own corps commanders resulted in a failure to capitalize upon the way in which the three Union corps became separated from each other as they advanced over the mountains. By the time Longstreet arrived, Rosecrans had been able to reconcentrate his army at Chickamauga. Nevertheless, on 19 and 20 September 1863 in

Braxton Bragg

yet another characteristically confused engagement, Longstreet was able to find a gap in the Union line on the second day and split Rosecrans's army, only a stubborn defence by Major-General George H. Thomas – the 'Rock of Chickamauga' – saving a total collapse. Rosecrans, who suffered 16,000 casualties, fell back on Chattanooga but Bragg was so shaken by his own 20,000 casualties that he declined to attempt the rapid pursuit urged by his subordinates. Gallenga reported on the battle from Louisville, Kentucky on 23 September in a dispatch printed on 15 October:

I had devised to go down the Mississippi River from St Louis, and visit the various posts of Cairo, Memphis, Vicksburg, Port Hudson, Natchez, and New Orleans, when, in an evil moment, the warlike exploits of [Major-] General Rosecrans diverted me from my purpose, and here am I, now, on my way to Chattanooga, with very little hope ever to be able to reach my destination. The news of the sanguinary affairs in East Tennessee of Saturday and Sunday last only reached St Louis on Monday, and threw that city into a perfect fever of frantic expectation. The movements of General Rosecrans across the Tennessee River had caused my friends the officers of the Union party to look grave, and they professed, rather loudly than earnestly, their full confidence in that General's prudence and coolness, asserting that 'he knew what he was about, and if he deemed it safe to move forward there could be no reason why he should keep back'. That great uneasiness beset my friends the Union officers' minds there could, however, be no doubt, and when the intelligence came, like a clap of thunder, that Rosecrans had unexpectedly found himself in presence of superior forces, that he had been attacked by the combined corps of Bragg, Johnston, and Longstreet, summing up altogether a force of no less than 140,000 combatants [actually less than 100,000 and without the presence of Johnston], people began to feel sure that he had now been caught in a trap and decoyed into a position from which he could not extricate himself without grievous losses. The first news reached St Louis by private telegrams, generally forwarded by the correspondents of the local press; these first bulletins – hasty, perhaps, but genuine – talked of a 'positive defeat' of Rosecrans's army, of its centre being broken through, of two divisions in complete 'deroute' and confusion, and the Commander-in-Chief being forced back to Rossville, eight or ten miles from Chattanooga. Since that first instalment of news the telegraph has been closed against all private intercourse, correspondence is at an end, and all the information that reaches us in the West comes in a roundabout way from Washington, where the United States' authorities monopolize the wires, and prescribe what we shall read, hear, and believe.

There was, however, no disguising that Rosecrans had been defeated and Mackay, now back on duty in New York reflected, on 29 September in a dispatch printed on 13 October, on the likely fate of the hapless commander of the Army of the Cumberland:

Ten days ago [Major-] General Rosecrans was the only genuine Napoleon of the war. All others, including General M'Clellan, were fictitious, or, in American parlance, 'bogus'. Rosecrans was the man of the hour; the non-political General who was to win battles, pierce the heart of the Confederacy, and bring the Southern leaders to their knees howling for mercy. But General Bragg has wrought a change, and Rosecrans has been thrown from his pedestal, and will, unless he gain a victory even now – which no one expects, – be consigned to the lumber-room where rest, more or less broken and dilapidated, the once heroic statues labelled with the names of M'Dowell, M'Clellan, Fitzjohn Porter [who had been dismissed from his corps command in November 1862 following Pope charging him with disobedience and disloyalty for his conduct during the Second Bull Run campaign], Pope, [Brigadier-General Charles P.] Stone [who had been arrested and imprisoned for 189 days without charge in February 1862 for alleged sympathy for the South after a subordinate's disastrous attack at Ball's Bluff, Virginia], Butler, and others, who have served their turn, and are now considered neither useful nor ornamental. Disheartened by one reverse, the supporters of the Administration are calling for the dismissal of Rosecrans, and the appointment in his place of [Major-] General Thomas, whose division in the great battle of Chickamauga on Sunday, the 20th inst., saved the army of the Cumberland from total rout and annihilation. But the Administration, knowing that it ordered Rosecrans to advance against his better judgement, hesitates to adopt this course. Knowing at the same time that a scapegoat of some kind is necessary to appease the people, and help to divert attention from its own mismanagement, it has found the victim in the person of [Major-] General Burnside, who, whether as military satrap of Ohio [he had commanded the Department of the Ohio since March 1863] or a leader in the field, has been without exception the most unfortunate person the Federal Government has ever had in its employ. The General has had a keener appreciation of his own demerits than the Government. He has never willingly assumed high command; he protested against his own nomination to succeed [Major-] General M'Clellan; he went reluctantly to Cincinnati to play the part of a dictator, but having once tasted the sweets of arbitrary power, he appears to have become unfitted for a secondary position, and to have yielded but a grudging obedience to General Rosecrans, his junior in the service. A fortnight ago he resigned his command, but was persuaded by the Government to reconsider his determination. He did so, and was ordered to march from Knoxville to the support of Rosecrans. This for some reason he failed to do [in fact primarily for lack of adequate supplies]. The battle of Chickamauga was fought in his absence, and Rosecrans was defeated. Though the same fate might have befallen the army of the Cumberland had Burnside been present with his 25,000 men, the Government assumes the reverse, and has marked its displeasure at his ill luck, or his inability, by relieving him of his command, and appointing [Major-] General Joseph Hooker, the defeated of Chancellorsville, in his place.

Hooker's arrival at Chattanooga with 20,000 men detached from the Army of the Potomac – he did not replace Burnside, who remained in command of the Department of Ohio – was one of the largest instances of rapid rail transportation in the entire war, the men, horses and equipment covering the 1,200 miles from Virginia in just twelve days. Sherman was also sent, with 17,000 men from the Army of the Tennessee, and on 17 October Lincoln appointed Grant to command a new Department of the Mississippi embracing all forces in the West. Grant hastened to take personal charge of the situation at Chattanooga, replacing Rosecrans with Thomas while still en route.

Ironically there was equal pressure for command changes among the Confederate

George Thomas

forces, who now occupied the seemingly dominating positions of Lookout Mountain and Missionary Ridge to the south and east of Chattanooga. The abrasive Bragg had never been popular with his subordinates and, when he attempted to shift blame to them for the failure to achieve a more complete victory at Chickamauga, they broke into open revolt. Jefferson Davis himself was compelled to come to the West and in an extraordinary meeting on 6 October listened to the demands of all four corps commanders in the presence of Bragg that he be replaced. Longstreet apparently declined the command and recommended Johnston, but the president would accept neither Johnston nor Beauregard and left Bragg in command. A number of men were transferred to other duties, however, and Longstreet detached in an effort to recapture Knoxville. Lawley, ever a partisan of Longstreet and no friend to Bragg, had also come out to the West in September and, while he had missed Chickamauga, he was now on hand to record the divisions within the Army of Tennessee. Lawley's first impressions of Bragg's army in a retrospective account of Chickamauga were written on 8 October and appeared in *The Times* on 24 November:

S hortly after 9 [on 20 September] the battle began raging furiously along the whole Confederate right, where fought [Lieutenant-] Generals Polk, and D.H. [Daniel Harvey] Hill, and [Major-Generals John C.] Breckinridge, and [Patrick R.] Cleburne, and many more, as gallant men as ever set squadron in the field. But here, coming, as I have, to the army of General Bragg, a stranger to its Generals and familiar only with the Army of [Northern] Virginia, where I have spent so many pleasant hours, I must profess my surprise at observing the want of harmony and the utter absence of enthusiasm which prevail in this Western camp. It is not that the men are one whit less brave, or the Division Generals less able than those under General Lee; but, if I read matters aright, there is not at the head of this army that firm, mild, sagacious, temperate wisdom, before which petty differences are hushed, which daunts political intrigue and self-seeking, and which presents to every man, from the highest to the lowest, a living example of purity, unselfishness, and patriotism, before whose lustre all historical characters of modern times, except, perhaps, Wellington and Washington, pale their ineffectual fires. To the merits of General Bragg, by no means inconsiderable, I am far from being blind. But it is no injustice to him to say that he never can inspire enthusiasm such as is wanted in a mighty and unequal struggle of this kind in either his officers or his men. That this Western Confederate army if subjected to the command of a General whose character is electric, as was Stonewall Jackson's, might become the rival of the army of General Lee I have no manner of doubt; but in its present condition its choicest achievements will be, when engaged, level battles like Murfreesborough, or unimproved and unreaped victories like Chickamauga; and, when at rest, dissatisfaction, heartburning, recrimination, such as never have been absent from the Federal armies, will continue to sweep like pestilence through its ranks, and disqualify it daily more and more for bringing its work to perfection.

Lawley wrote a further dispatch in similar vein on 19 October – it appeared on 30 November – concluding that the 'best interests of the Confederacy and of General Bragg himself demand that he should seek some position which will emancipate him from the prejudices, animosities, and heart-burnings which now surround him on every side'. He then journeyed south to Georgia and again visited the powder-mill at Augusta before returning to Richmond in November where, on the 14th, he wrote a dispatch eventually printed on 15 December describing the effects of inflation on the South:

Would that I could see promise of future and final Southern triumph in any corresponding quality of the Southern mind! In many fashions Southern unfaith crops up and recoils upon the Confederate Government, making, for instance, Mr [Christopher] Memminger's [Confederate Secretary of the Treasury] task, though he takes his stand upon raw material worth 60 or 70 millions of pounds sterling, Herculean as compared with Mr [Salmon P.] Chase's [Lincoln's Secretary of the Treasury], who issues vastly larger promises to pay on a security of breadstuff exports worth only 60 or 70 millions of dollars. There are, of course, other reasons to account for the fact that three dollars in 'greenbacks' will buy two dollars in gold, while it requires 30 paper dollars of the Confederacy to buy a like sum; but the fundamental explanation of the discrepancy in value of the irredeemable paper issues of the two sections lies in the vastly superior faith in themselves of the Northern people. For many months we have heard throughout the Confederacy the cuckoo cry, 'Do something to arrest the depreciation of the currency, or we perish;' but hitherto nothing has been done, and, as is now seen by everybody, we are on the brink of a precipice. It is universally admitted that the country is richer in everything that constitutes wealth than it was 12 months ago; that there is a sufficiency of meat and far greater abundance of cereals than last year; that fruit and vegetables have been granted us in unusual abundance; that Richmond has supplies of coal and wood vastly in excess of those laid in against last winter – in proof of which I may mention that the streets are now as well lighted as those of London, whereas last year their Cimmerian darkness was a favourite theme of the *New York Herald*; but in spite of these facts unfaith in Confederate currency grows apace, the farmers refuse to part with their crops on any terms, flour fetches $100 per barrel, and is rising, bacon is close upon $3 a lb, everything is proportionately dear, and nothing plentiful, save Confederate currency, until at last a woman going to market has been heard to exclaim, 'I carry a basket to market to hold my money, and I carry a pocketbook to fetch home the slice of beef which it buys.'

   In this emergency all eyes turn to the Confederate Congress, which meets upon the 7th of December; and never was graver question submitted to a deliberative assembly than that which awaits its immediate discussion. Some 800 or 900 millions of dollars are afloat in a community which could with difficulty sustain a circulation of 200 millions, and, worse than all, Mr Memminger's paper mill is harder at work than ever, until the dollar, which now represents a value of fourpence English, promises shortly to be worth only four farthings. The redundant currency has somehow to be funded, fresh issues to be suspended, a limited amount of circulating medium to be put forth, and a solemn pledge given that this amount shall not hereafter be exceeded. I am bound to record that the people are in a temper to stand extravagant taxation. For many weeks past the Confederate Cabinet has been eagerly engaged in discussing and excogitating a scheme of relief, and a financial convention of the presidents of Southern banks is to assemble at Augusta on the 16th inst. I have reason to think that some such plan as the following has found favour in the eyes of influential men. Authority will be given to the Secretary of the Treasury to issue 1,000 millions of 6 per cent coupon bonds, and simultaneously to impose an annual tax of 5 per cent on real and personal estate capitalized, of which tax one-half is to be paid in currency and the other half in specie or coupons of the 1,000 million loan. There will be inducements offered (such as a bonus of 5 per cent) at once to buy up or convert currency into this loan, and it is hoped that so much of the existing circulation will be quickly retired as will immediately reduce prices, and admit of a limit being put to the outstanding currency. Other details of this scheme there are in abundance, but, concisely stated, its outline is not far from what I have sketched. My own apprehension is that it will not be prompt and drastic enough in its operation to sweep away at once the vast redundancy of the currency, to inspire confidence in a distrustful people, and to bring supplies promptly into market. If it fails there is no alternative left for the Government but to seize and impress whatever it wants with a high hand, and to this step it will be impelled, rather than yield to the hated Yankee, by the almost unanimous voice of the Confederate people. It was long ago remarked by Machiavelli that no people once embarked in war is ever forced into peace by reason of pecuniary inanition, and never were there nations less amenable to considerations of cash than the two sections of a sundered republic, which three years ago exhibited an average of individual wealth among its citizens such as could be found nowhere else upon earth. The embarrassments of the Confederates in adjusting their currency, in getting the supplies which abound in distant Florida and elsewhere up to the mouths which need them, and in introducing through an increasingly stringent blockade all that is vital for their continued struggle, may be, and probably will be, grievous and perplexing; that they will be such as to extinguish or paralyse future resistance will not be lightly credited by one who knows what difficulties have already been surmounted, what shortcomings supplemented, what energy and ingenuity displayed.

Lawley was undoubtedly correct in seeing the issue of confidence as crucial to the value of the Confederacy's currency. Unfortunately, since Memminger was constrained by public and congressional opinion from either raising taxes or tariffs, recourse was had to loans and printing ever more paper money. As Lawley anticipated, bonds failed to take paper money out of circulation and forced Memminger into an even more grandiose bond issue in February 1864, but this also failed and he was to resign in June 1864. By early 1864 prices of commodities were twenty-eight times higher than in early 1861 and were to approach a level ninety-two times higher than early 1861 by April 1865.

A certain wavering in Lawley's usual confidence in the Confederate cause was clearly evident in his dispatches by the end of 1863. His confidence was hardly restored when, in the absence of Longstreet operating unsuccessfully against Knoxville, Grant's forces attacked Bragg's positions at Chattanooga in a three-day offensive from 23 to 25 November. Ironically, it was the discredited Army of the Cumberland under Thomas unexpectedly carrying entrenched Confederate positions on Missionary Ridge that

Chattanooga seen from Missionary Ridge

forced the result rather than the main assaults by Sherman on Tunnel Hill to the north and Hooker on Lookout Mountain to the south as Grant had anticipated. At a cost of fewer than 6,000 casualties the Union forces pushed Bragg into headlong retreat: his resignation was accepted by Jefferson Davis on 1 December although he was then subsequently appointed military adviser to the Confederate president. In a dispatch written over the period from 19 November to 1 December, which was to be published on 1 January 1864, Lawley could see only one culprit:

In conclusion, reviewing the situation at this moment of the Confederate States, I cannot but be of opinion that President Davis, by his well-intentioned, though ill-judging, obstinacy in adhering to his friend General Bragg has done more to shake the stability of his hold upon the affections and confidence of the Confederate people than by any other act which has signalized his two and a half years of troubled and agitated power. It would seem that Mr Davis has failed to discern that the competency of a General, like the virtue of a woman, cannot afford to be discussed in public. The very fact of the discussion by his soldiers of their General's competency adds most alarmingly to his incompetency, and no one can have watched General Bragg's army for the last two months without noticing the fearful deterioration to which its want of faith in its head has visibly subjected it. War in a republican country, with a daily press which is its interpreter, and which is read by every soldier that conducts it, is very different from the wars of Marlborough or Napoleon, and so Mr Davis has long ago discovered. It is greatly to his honour and credit that he has not emulated Mr Lincoln's example and imposed upon the journals which surround him a decorum of criticism and comment which is, indeed, strange and exotic upon American soil. But a defiance of an almost unanimous public opinion, for which, in reference to General Bragg, Mr Davis is responsible, even assuming that public opinion were wrong and Mr Davis right, is, to say the least, an error. May it not be converted by persistence in it from an error into an irreparable calamity, and may there be truth in the rumour which circulates through the feverish streets to-day to the effect that [Lieutenant-] General [William J.] Hardee is about to assume the command from which General Bragg by transgression fell!

A well-known military theorist in the pre-war regular army, Hardee had been one of Bragg's more prominent critics in the Army of Tennessee until transferred to Mississippi in July 1863. In the event, however, it was Johnston whom Davis reluctantly appointed to replace Bragg on 27 December, a certainty of which Lawley was already aware when he wrote his last report of the year on 21 December. Appearing on 23 January 1864 it also gave some space to a brief description of a visit he had made to the main Confederate prisoner of war camp for Union officers in Richmond, Libby Prison, then holding 1,040 captives and the subject of growing controversy in the Northern press:

There was at one moment a great deficiency of the Commissary-General's stores at Richmond, occasioned by temporary causes, and of not more than four days' duration. During these four days the prisoners experienced what has again and again been endured unmurmuringly by Confederate soldiers in the field, and were obliged to live entirely upon farinaceous food. Loud as have been the outcries in Yankeedom about their starving prisoners, there has been no less uproar in the Confederate Congress against Commissary-General [Lucius B.] Northrup [actually Northrop], by reason of the deprivation of meat which, during these four days, he inflicted upon the prisoners. Mr [Henry S.] Foote, the Thersites of the Southern Congress, has made the rafters ring with his denunciations of President Davis, who is understood to be a friend of Mr Northrup, and who for divers reasons is especially obnoxious to Mr Foote. It will not, in my opinion, be possible for New York journals to awaken a fresh burst of European indignation by factitious representations of miseries which have no existence in fact. That the condition of a prisoner of war is at best triste and unenviable need hardly be stated to any sensible man or woman. If the Federal officers confined in the Libby could be admitted to a sight of the heartrending letters which I have read from Confederate officers confined on Johnson's Island [Sandusky Bay, Ohio], they would face their lot with a little more manliness, and not aggravate trials already sufficiently irksome by permitting themselves to imagine that their sufferings are exceptional and peculiar, and such as were never borne by any other prisoners of war upon earth. For the present it will be sufficient to state that I hope shortly to give such facts and statistics as will establish, at least to the satisfaction of Europe, the true condition of the unhappy starvelings whose imaginary agonies have been such a rich mine to the press, and especially to the illustrated journals, of New York.

Lawley was a little ingenuous in his report of the condition of Union prisoners and, in fact, never did go on to furnish the statistics he had promised. However, it was perfectly true that the Confederacy was hard enough stretched to feed its own armies, let alone prisoners of war, and in this sense the retaliatory action by the Federal authorities in May 1864 of reducing the rations of Confederate prisoners to those of Union prisoners in the South materially reduced the living conditions of the former. The situation was exacerbated by the subsequent refusal of the North to exchange prisoners since it was reasoned that the Confederacy could least afford the attrition of its manpower, although exchanges were restored in January 1865 when the Confederacy agreed for the first time to exchange negro as well as white prisoners, this having been the ostensible explanation for the original suspension of exchanges. The most notorious camps on either side were Elmira in New York and Andersonville in Georgia. At the latter some 13,700 Union prisoners died in thirteen months, its Swiss-born commandant, Henry Wirz, being the only individual executed for war crimes after the surrender of the Confederacy.

Lawley would shortly return to England for an extended period of leave. At the same time Gallenga had also left the United States, his last dispatch having been written from New York on 7 December. Supposedly Gallenga was suffering from ill health but it would appear that, like Russell before him, the absolute refusal of the Federal authorities to have any representative from *The Times* accompanying its armies in the field was the major factor. As the New Year opened, therefore, it would be left once more to Mackay to report on the war's progress.

1864

Grant's success at Chattanooga, following that at Vicksburg earlier in 1863, clearly enhanced his reputation but, writing from New York on 12 January in a dispatch printed on 25 January, Mackay was not disposed to regard Grant as any different from other Union generals who had been tried and failed. Mackay's remarks were framed in the context of 1864 being presidential election year:

But, although the military situation pleases the unthinking multitude, who are taught to believe that Grant's victory at Chattanooga has brought the war within three months of its close, the political situation is scarcely so satisfactory. The time has come for the wire pullers and the professional politicians to begin the work of president making, and the difficulty is where to find the material out of which to carve him. If the North had provided a thorough General – bold and successful enough to win great victories, in spite of the obstructiveness and meddlesomeness of the White House and the War-office – such a man would override all opposition and be elected to the Presidency with a unanimity never witnessed since the days of Washington. But such a General has not yet appeared. An attempt has been made to represent [Major-] General Grant as the coming man, on the strength of his achievements at Vicksburg and Chattanooga; and it cannot be denied that for the time being he stands in greater popular favour than any other General in the Federal service. But the people are too impatient to pin their upon him even for so short a period as the traditional 90 days, unless in the interval he follows up his previous by new and greater successes. If he will capture Atlanta, and thoroughly defeat the army of Joseph Johnston in the ensuing Spring, he may become President or Dictator of the Republic, whichever he will; but if he rely upon the victories he has already won, the wave of popular favour will pass over him, and he will stand no more chance than Pope, Burnside, or Hooker, and not half or a quarter the chance of M'Clellan. The initial letters of his Christian names are employed by his friends in a variety of devices to keep up an enthusiasm in his favour among the soldiers, the rowdies, and the half-educated multitude, and U.S. Grant becomes Uncle Sam's Grant, United States Grant, Unyielding Successful Grant, Uncompromising Swordbearer Grant, Unconquerable Soldier Grant, Unrelenting Slaughterer Grant, etc., as it pleases the fancy of his vulgarest friends and most jocose supporters to call him. General Grant himself has neither spoken nor written a word, nor made move nor sign in the matter. And he is wise. The moment that he thinks his bygone achievements or

Ulysses S. Grant

his present popularity a sufficient foundation on which to erect a claim to the Presidency, that instant his doom will be sealed. He will meet the fate of M'Clellan and Fremont, and be relieved of military duty, to brood as a private citizen over the instability of fortune and the ingratitude of Republics. The only other candidates whose names are received with any degree of favour are Mr Lincoln, Mr Chase and [Major-] General M'Clellan. There are, it is true, some fanatics who still speak of [Major-] General Fremont; and others who put forward the names of Mr Charles Sumner and Mr Wendell Phillips. Nor are there wanting a few beaters of the pulpit drum ecclesiastic, who would go so far as to give the world a noble example of American philanthropy, sound statesmanship, and advanced Christianity, by casting their votes for Mr Frederick Douglass, the negro orator; but the appearances indicate, should no American Cromwell or Napoleon appear within a few months, that, Mr Chase having been otherwise provided for, the only real competitors will be Mr Lincoln and General M'Clellan. Mr Lincoln's inability to carry on the war with success is much more generally admitted than it was six months ago, but he has the great advantage of possession; and if Incompetent I is not equal to his place, no one knows whether Incompetent II might not prove a more hopeless failure. For this, among many other reasons, no Republican candidate will oppose Mr Lincoln, and the struggle on which so many hopes and so many fears are concentrated will be sharply defined, with Mr Lincoln as the champion and representative of the abolition of slavery and of State rights, and of the centralization of the Government; and General M'Clellan as the representative of the Constitution of 1787, and as the champion of all the local rights and public liberties sanctified by that document.

Mackay was right, of course, in his prediction that Lincoln and McClellan would contest the election in November although he was also correct in seeing that Lincoln would not be an automatic choice of the Republicans. Grant, in fact, declined to be drawn into the fray and the military reputations of Fremont and Butler were too tarnished, leaving the principal challenger in Chase. The latter's campaign, however, was badly handled and he dropped out of contention in March. After a number of earlier threatened resignations had been declined by Lincoln, one was accepted in June 1864.

While Mackay reported extensively on the political machinations in the North, Lawley was preparing to come home. His last dispatch from Richmond was dated 16 January and, in the company of Frank Vizetelly, he made a successful passage of the Union lines to appear in New York which, together with Washington, he contrasted with Richmond in an account on 27 January printed on 15 February:

There is a strange shadowy sense of unreality attached to passing 16 months in and about Richmond, and then waking up to find oneself in Washington. To describe such a transition would demand not only unrivalled descriptive and antithetical excellence, but also some such quaintness of conceit as has exhibited Rip Van Winkle starting from his long slumber in Sleepy Hollow. In Richmond the spectator has for months and months been familiar with war about his path and about his bed, and at all his meals and under every roof. War is breathed in at every breath, wafted upon every breeze, heard in every sound, visible at every step. For grace and elegance and lettered ease there is neither time nor superfluity of resource; nor, it must be added, are they compatible with the sublime earnestness of temper exhibited by man and woman. Sentries at the head of every street substantiate the passer's identity and investigate his right to be absent from the army. As earliest dawn breaks, you are awakened by the long monotonous chorus of thousands of negroes, engaged in completing the defensive works around Richmond, and going forth cheerfully to their labour, which has long ago assumed such proportions as to defy the assault of 200,000 men. This is no idle statement of my own, but taken from the lips of the oldest, ablest, and least boastful of Confederate officers, whose name will suggest itself to every reader [presumably Lee]. Cannon are constantly seen in the streets – either new 12-pounder Napoleons going up to the army from the Tredegar Works, or guns which have undergone repair, or field-pieces which are going North or South; the well-known lean, lank, ragged, 'gray-back' troops, with the same lordly defiant air of individuality and self-assertion as ever, constantly troop through the city, with their old wild, discordant yells, making day or night hideous. The familiar Southern tunes of 'Dixie' or 'The Mocking Bird', execrably interpreted by a few fifes, a cornet, and a drum, contrast marvellously with the rich swell of fine German bands in Washington, which render to perfection the 'Last Rose of Summer', or one of Mendelssohn's superb marches, crashing among the distant echoes of Pennsylvania Avenue. And yet there is a heart, a verve, and a sauciness about the Southern 'Dixie' and the mien of its interpreters, which are looked for in vain among the stolid German musicians of Washington and the gaudy troops bedizened with gold lace who follow them.

But other symptoms of war, with the exception of the uniforms in the streets,

Washington has none to show. The redundancy of 'greenbacks' – those evidences, according to Mr Seward, of a mighty nation's exuberant prosperity – is very perceptible in the increased crowd of the streets and the hungry look of greed which every face wears. But, perhaps, there is no sadder sign of the times which have brought sudden wealth to all, and moral thoughtfulness to none, than the ubiquity and boldness of the frail sisterhood who throng every avenue and public resort, seeking the smiles of the contractors, peculators, and nouveaux riches, and blending in a scene which could alone be photographed in language by the pen of a Juvenal. On every side money flows as though the Potomac were the Pactolus. The dome of the Capitol, which once promised to share the fate without rivalling the beauty of Cologne Cathedral, is finished, and surmounted by a Goddess of such Liberty as even Madame Roland never conceived. The hotels are thronged to bursting; Willard's, in particular, is occupied by an excited, pike-eyed, seething crowd such as vibrates in the *coulisses* of the Parisian Bourse. At night theatres, gambling-houses, 'Varieties', and worse dens of infamy, veiled under no pretence at disguise, vie with the attractions of the 'inspired Maid of Philadelphia,' Miss Anna Dickinson. Mr Seward's optimism is accepted without thought or comment; no sound of war save the occasional boom of cannon being tried at the Navy-yard (a sound soothing to Yankee vanity) ever flutters the senses; Mr Lincoln and Mr Chase openly, and Mr Seward secretly, are speculating much more as to their chances for the next Presidency than as to the strength of General Lee or the designs of President Davis.

Proceed next to New York, and the recollections of Richmond, blurred by intercourse with Washington, fade into the hazy distance, and can be recalled only by a vigorous effort of the understanding. But as he journeys northwards from Washington the passenger cannot but dreamily contrast the memory of his recent sufferings upon the overtasked railroads of 'Dixie' with the speed, the comfort, and the roominess of the Northern car. I shall not attempt to carry your readers into Broadway – a thousand times described, but as indescribable as Niagara – nor to enter upon any attempt at detail. There is such matter for all feeling in this street that the mind sinks crushed. Luxury, ostentation, heedlessness, heartlessness – the richest furs, the gaudiest silks, the brightest bonnets, the most glittering diamonds, operas, theatres, concerts, *cafés chantants*, rare shows of every hue – why should I seek to prolong the list? At Delmonico's famous Restaurant, or at the Maison Dorée, Spaniards, Frenchmen, Italians, Englishmen can discuss wines and viands to which nothing superior can be exhibited at Philippe's or at Vefour's. As for a thought of the war, of the 500,000 souls which it has hurled into eternity from the North, or the 200,000 Confederates who have died grimly *pro aris et focis* – why speak or think of such a ghastly theme?

Relatively little had happened in the eastern theatre since Lee's retreat from Gettysburg, but on 28 February Union Brigadier-General H. Judson Kilpatrick led a raid on Richmond to release those held at Libby Prison. Not only did the raid fail but it was alleged that orders found on the body of Union Colonel Ulric Dahlgren showed an intention to assassinate Jefferson Davis and to burn the Confederate capital. Mackay reflected on the raid and a raid by Sherman's forces in Mississippi on 9 March, the day after Grant had arrived in Washington to become General-in-Chief with the rank of Lieutenant-General – the first full appointment to that rank since George Washington, Winfield Scott having held it only by brevet. Grant's predecessor, Halleck, was made Chief-of-Staff. The report appeared on 23 March:

General [Brigadier-General] Kilpatrick, misled by the reports of dishonest or over-sanguine deserters and escaped prisoners from Richmond, took it into his head that he could capture that city by a cavalry coup de main and make his name illustrious for evermore. He laid a wager at heavy odds with another cavalry officer, [Major-] General [Alfred] Pleasanton, that he would do it within a fortnight, and, though opposed by every real soldier [Kilpatrick had graduated from West Point in May 1861] to whom he submitted his notion, obtained, it would appear, the sanction of the President to try what he could do, with the best wishes of that amiable but most unmilitary Commander-in-Chief [Lincoln] that he might 'go in and win'. He went in accordingly; committed a large amount of ruthless and wanton destruction in the rear of General Lee's army, broke down bridges, burnt corn mills and factories, frightened the women and children and the impotent or bedridden old men in all his line of march; reached the suburbs of Richmond, threw a few harmless shells into the city, and, fearing the capture of his whole command of 6,000 horsemen – which would have been the befitting punishment for his foolhardy experiment – rode out of the enemy's lines into those of [Major-] General Butler, with the loss of four colonels and 500 soldiers – admitted, but which time, perhaps, will show to have been treble that number. He only escaped by sheer good luck, having accomplished nothing by his raid, but the exasperation of the Southern people and the embitterment of all previously existing bad feeling. Nor has [Major-] General Sherman's more magnificent raid across Mississippi been attended with happier results. The utmost mystery is preserved with respect to him; but not all the art and efforts of the Government to conceal the unwelcome truth can prevent the diffusion of unfavourable reports, to the effect that, less fortunate than General Kilpatrick, he has been defeated in a pitched battle with tremendous loss, and that his army has been virtually annihilated.

In reality, only a cavalry force marching to meet Sherman had been defeated by Confederate cavalry under Forrest but it had forced Sherman to curtail his operations, which might have been aimed at Selma in Alabama. Nevertheless, there were to be more substantial setbacks to Grant's strategic plan for Sherman to apply constant pressure on Johnston while Meade's Army of the Potomac asserted similar pressure on Lee and other Union armies in the east assisted with diversionary operations. First, Nathaniel Banks's advance up the Red River in Louisiana was turned back in early April by Confederate forces under Major-General Richard Taylor, the son of Zachary Taylor [President of the United States, 1848–50]. Then Butler's Army of the James landing in the Bermuda Hundred at the head of the James between Richmond and Petersburg was compelled to withdraw by Beauregard in early May, while Major-General Franz Sigel's advance in the Shenandoah Valley was decisively halted by a scratch force commanded by the former Vice-President under Buchanan and presidential candidate of 1860, John Breckinridge, at New Market on 15 May.

These failures undoubtedly complicated matters for Grant who, locating his own headquarters beside those of Meade, had directed the latter to advance across the Rapidan on 4 May. Attempting to outflank Lee but anticipated by the latter, Grant's forces ran into the Confederates in an encounter battle on 5 and 6 May in the dense woodland of the Wilderness. Mackay reported on these first clashes of the main eastern summer campaign on 10 May in a dispatch appearing on 24 May:

O n Wednesday [Major-] General Meade passed the Rapidan without opposition. On Thursday [5 May] the Army of the Potomac was assailed by General Lee in great force, the object being to crush the advancing columns before they were in position, or within supporting distance of each other. The shock was so severe and the issue so doubtful that the reserves under Burnside [commanding a reconstituted IX Corps in the Army of the Potomac] had to be ordered up. They arrived in time, and saved the fortune of the day. The number of killed and wounded on the Federal side amounted, according to Federal authority, to

Grant and his staff at Bethesda Church, Massaponax, 21 May 1864

upwards of 8,000. One peculiarity of the encounter was that no artillery was brought into play. The ground, near and in advance of the former battlefield of Chancellorsville, where Hooker lost the day, and his reputation along with it, was so thickly wooded that cannon could not be used on either side, and the conflict was hand to hand, with the bayonet or the rifle. How stubborn it must have been is evident from the number of the killed and wounded, which, if at all balanced on the Confederate side, would not fall short of 16,000. The battle, like that of the subsequent day, was fought in a place called the 'Wilderness'. Both sides claim the victory, General Lee on behalf of the Confederates, and Mr Stanton on behalf of the Federals, for [Lieutenant-] General Grant himself either sent no dispatch or it has been suppressed. As hitherto General Lee has never been known either to exaggerate a victory or to claim one if he has not achieved it, and as the same cannot be said of Mr Stanton, the probability is that the advantage rested with the Confederates. The fighting was renewed on Friday at daybreak. The battle raged for 14 hours with scarcely an interval of rest, still in the thickly wooded, stubbly, and thorny region stretching from Chancellorsville to Mine Run. The carnage is described to have been more awful than in any previous battle of the war, and to have been attended with a loss of 12,000 men to the Federals and as many to the Confederates. General Lee, in an address to his army which found its way to the possession of [Major-] General Butler, and was by him forwarded to Mr Stanton, claims the victory on this, the second, encounter, and thanks a merciful God that every advance on Grant's part had been gallantly and successfully repulsed. If Mr Stanton, who has promised to publish all authentic intelligence immediately it reaches the hands of the Administration, had, instead of garbling and quoting from General Lee's proclamation, sent the whole document to the press, he would have enabled the public to judge far better than it now can of the true results of Friday's fighting. It appears from General Lee's admission that [Lieutenant-] General Longstreet – who is about as much beloved and confided in by the Southern army as [Lieutenant-] General Stonewall Jackson used to be – was severely wounded [hit in the throat by fire from Confederate troops close to where Jackson had been mortally wounded a year earlier], and [Brigadier-] General [Micah] Jenkins killed [by the same volley that wounded Longstreet]. On the Federal side [Brigadier-] General [James S.] Wadsworth, formerly the military commandant of Washington, and competitor with Mr Horatio Seymour, in the autumn of 1862, for the Governorship of the State of New York, was shot in the forehead while leading his division, and instantaneously slain, and [Brigadier-] General [Alexander S.] Webb, son of the United States' Minister in Brazil, was seriously wounded.

The Wilderness battle was certainly costly for both sides with Confederate casualties of some ten thousand and Union casualties of perhaps seventeen thousand, the impact being the greater for the close nature of the fighting and the fact that the intense musketry set the woods alight and many wounded burned to death. In the past such losses had led the Army of the Potomac to retreat, but Grant was determined to press on regardless of casualties and now tried to outflank Lee's right and open a route to Richmond by marching for the key crossroads at Spotsylvania Court-house. Again, Lee anticipated Grant's move and on the evening of 7 May ordered Longstreet's successor, the newly promoted Lieutenant-General Richard H. Anderson, to seize the crossroads first. In Lawley's absence another occasional correspondent, who may have been named R.W. Anderson, had reported from Richmond in April but it was a 'Confederate Correspondent' who supplied the Southern perspective on what now occurred in a report also dated 10 May but which, in contrast to that of Mackay, did not appear in print until 17 June:

I came on to this place (Spotsylvania Court-house) this afternoon [Sunday 8 May, though the article at this point is wrongly headed Sunday 9 May]. General Lee's order to occupy the village was given none too soon, for when Anderson's corps arrived, at 8 o'clock this morning, he found the Federal cavalry, reinforced by infantry and artillery, already in possession. His men had been marching rapidly, and for two miles had double-quicked it, and consequently were much jaded, but they were ready for the work, tired as they were. [Major-General Joseph B.] Kershaw's division led the corps, and was the first to reach the ground. Two brigades were sent against the cavalry force holding the Court-house, and two others were placed behind a thin rail fence and some frail obstructions which had been thrown across the road by which a force of Federal infantry was advancing. The latter fell into the error of supposing that the force behind the fence was dismounted cavalry, and rushed forward with the utmost confidence. The Confederates reserved their fire until their foes got within a few paces, and then, taking deliberate aim, gave them a volley which covered the ground with their slain. The combat was short and sharp; some of the Federals got to the fence, and actually used the bayonet, but in less than half an hour they were driven rapidly back, leaving 500 dead and mortally wounded, and 200 prisoners in the hands of the victorious Confederates. The Court-house was cleared with equal success by the brigades sent against it, and when I reached the ground at 3 p.m., I found the advance of General Lee's army in quiet possession. [Lieutenant-General] Ewell's corps came up this afternoon and was put in position, and [Lieutenant-General A.P.] Hill's will be here to-morrow morning.

Thus General Lee has succeeded in throwing his entire army right across the path by which Grant must march if he would get 'on to Richmond'. He not only repulsed all his assaults at the Wilderness, but held him there until he could throw his own army in front of him. It was a masterly performance, and makes it necessary for Grant to deliver battle here, or make another effort to turn General Lee's position. The Confederates are in splendid condition, and full of spirit and cheerfulness. They all realize the importance of victory, and are ready to endure any privation necessary to its achievement. Several officers belonging to the Quartermaster's and Commissary Departments in the field, though against positive orders, procured muskets, and went into the fight. They said it might possibly be the last great battle, and they desired to help to make it successful. Three of them were killed – two at the Wilderness and one at this place. Is it probable that such an army can be overborne by the mercenaries who reluctantly follow at the heels of General Grant? But the great battle of the campaign has not yet been fought; it will occur at this place or in its vicinity.

The unnamed correspondent was perfectly correct since Lee's forces entrenched at Spotsylvania and from 10 to 19 May Grant attempted a series of attacks, mostly just out-

A more formal view of Grant and his staff

right frontal assaults, which cost his own army some 17,000 casualties and Lee some 9,000. Though occasionally penetrating the Confederate defences as in the assault on the 'Angle' on 12 May, Grant failed to force Lee back. Among those killed in the fighting were the popular Union corps commander, John Sedgwick, hit by a Confederate sniper as he inspected the Confederate lines on 9 May and J.E.B. Stuart, who was mortally wounded in a cavalry clash at Yellow Tavern on 11 May. What made such encounters so bloody, of course, was the effectiveness of an entrenched defence armed with rifled muskets. Civil War soldiers rarely indulged in fire fights at the full extent of range of these relatively new weapons – perhaps up to 500 yards – and, in many respects, fought as if still in the age of Napoleon. Nevertheless, the stopping power of a weapon which, while still single shot and muzzle loading, enjoyed a higher rate of fire over previous smoothbore muskets was considerable and enabled an outnumbered army such as that of Lee to defend positions with far fewer men than in the past. Moreover, if the opponent obliged by crude frontal assaults in the manner of Grant during the spring campaign of 1864, it was inevitable that heavy casualties would result. Small wonder that Grant came under increasing criticism in the North, as Mackay revealed in a dispatch of 13 May, which was printed on 27 May:

Hitherto the march of Grant – though, if it be ultimately successful, it will be considered heroic – is the advance of a piece of mechanism. He sees no obstacles, and goes blindly and ruthlessly on. He trusts to nothing but superior numbers and hard fighting. The lives of his men are of no value. He throws them away by thousands, to gain half a mile of jungle. He has pushed on for five leagues, and paid about 9,000 lives for each. At every step he fights at a disadvantage, on ground of the enemy's choosing. But he fights on. His men are picked off by unerring sharpshooters from behind every tree, but his order is still to push forward. His Generals fall as if they were of no more account than private soldiers. Up to Tuesday evening [10 May] – the seventh day of the conflict – he had lost 13 of them in killed, wounded, and prisoners and at least 45,000 men. This loss is admitted by friends and admirers, while those who are neither incline to add 15,000 to that enormous estimate. But still he holds his way undaunted, seeing nothing, caring nothing, but Richmond, which if he ever reach upon the terms of these seven days he will reach without so much as a body guard – a solitary prisoner. The havoc committed in his ranks is sickening to reflect upon. One New York regiment, the pride of the city, which not long since marched down Broadway amid flaunting banners, waving kerchiefs, loud huzzas, and the music of drum and fife, suffered so terribly that out of its full complement but four officers and 15 men were left after half a day's fighting. Whole brigades have lost their officers and two-thirds of their rank and file, and, having none to lead them, have been incorporated with other brigades, only less cruelly decimated than themselves in having a brigadier left to reorganize their shattered remnants. And all this time the desperate struggle has only been waged on the outskirts of the Confederate works, and in such positions as General Lee would prefer to see an enemy in [,] whom he wished to annihilate. The line of the North and South Anna has yet to be reached; and if Grant march through it and pay no dearer for the privilege than he has paid for the honour of marching from the Rapidan to Spottsylvania [*sic*] Court-house, his original army, whether it numbered 150,000 or 250,000 will have dwindled to one-half, and will have more dreadful work before it than it has yet attempted. But it is all one to [Lieutenant-] General Grant. With the sublimity of genius, or of madness (the fortune of war must determine which), he has declared to Mr Stanton, who has communicated the news to the public, 'That he will go to Richmond by that line, if it takes him all the summer to do it.' Impulsive, and easily led, as the people are, and apt to be astonished at nothing, they are astonished at this audacity. They do not know how to account for it on any other supposition than that Grant is the greatest as well as the most daring General whom the world ever saw, and are content to wait a little longer for the results before they change their opinion. But the voice of wailing and lamentation is heard in too many thousands of households in this and all the cities of the North to permit unqualified approbation of a system of war so costly as this, or silence the buzz of adverse criticism.

Eventually realizing that he could not break through at Spotsylvania, Grant tried another move to the south-east, this time in the direction of the Virginia Central Railroad junction at Hanover between the North and South Anna rivers. Lee once more detected the move and on 22 May Grant found his way blocked by more Confederate entrenchments. Rather than attempt a frontal assault here, Grant shifted south-eastwards again across the Pamunkey but, as before, found Lee entrenched in front of him along Totopotomy Creek on 28 May. The same manoeuvring was repeated to find both armies confronting each other at Cold Harbor on 1 June and, two days later in one of the most disastrous episodes of the entire war, another Union frontal assault saw Grant lose some 7,000 casualties in little more than twenty minutes. Grant had certainly closed on Richmond and inflicted 40,000 casualties on Lee but a deliberate attritional strategy is essentially double-edged and he had suffered 55,000 casualties himself, equating to over half the numbers he had led into the Wilderness a month before. Lawley, who had returned to the South by blockade runner into Wilmington on 5 June, penned his thoughts on the campaign to date from Richmond two days later, his dispatch appearing on 18 July:

O nce more have the shouts of the combatants and the roar of their numerous artillery been heard in the streets of Richmond, and by the calm and imperturbable President of the Confederacy himself. Once more have the hills and valleys in front of the Southern capital been stained with blood and ploughed by cannon balls, and the night air made hideous by the wail of the wounded and the groans of the dying. For one month the armies of the North and the South have been wrestling for the mastery – have been grappling each other in a death struggle. During that brief period torrents of blood have been spilt, and thousands of hearts have ceased to beat for ever. And yet the Federal army, notwithstanding it has been handled so roughly, has marched with such rapidity, has made such numerous and desperate assaults, and has lost so heavily, is believed to be not one whit nearer to the goal of its ambition than it was when it crossed the Rapidan. True it is not so far from the Confederate capital if you measure the distance by

The pontoon bridge across the James at Harrison's Landing, 14 June 1864

miles or leagues; but if you measure it by the obstacles in the way – the steady lines and glittering bayonets of Lee's dauntless veterans – the Federal commander would seem to be as far from the accomplishment of the object of his campaign as when he stood upon the red hills of Culpepper.

Despite Lawley's belief that the campaign had failed, Grant had firmly shifted the front close to the Confederate capital and now made the bold move of withdrawing from Cold Harbor, marching rapidly to the south-east again and, by way of a hastily constructed pontoon bridge, shifting his entire army over the James river between 14 and 16 June. With Lee caught completely by surprise for the first time in the campaign, Grant's leading formations had a golden opportunity of seizing the critically important rail and supply centre of Petersburg, which lay virtually undefended. However, a procrastination perhaps understandable in the light of the heavy losses of Cold Harbor deterred the Union forces from pressing their advantage against a brilliant defence by Beauregard, which masked his utter weakness of numbers. By 18 June leading elements of Lee's army had arrived to reinforce Beauregard and Grant could only settle for a lengthy siege, although one which Lee himself recognized must ultimately result in Confederate defeat.

Part of Grant's attempt to divert Lee's attention from the move to the James had been to send Union cavalry under Major-General Philip H. Sheridan to link with the forces in the Shenandoah, which after Sigel's repulse at New Market, had advanced again under the command of Major-General David Hunter. Lawley recounted the progress of the diversion on 20 June in a report published on 23 July:

It is known to your readers that the Federal [Major-] General Hunter, after capturing Staunton and sending raiding parties to burn the military institution at Lexington [Virginia Military Institute] and insult Stonewall Jackson's grave, advanced with his main force in the direction of Lynchburg. It is singular that in all military operations which have for three years been conducted in Virginia by Federal Generals, I can recall no instances of celerity and vigour of action except those exhibited in May by [Lieutenant-] General Grant. It is easy to see that Hunter, by rapid marches, might have taken Lynchburg, and possibly marched to Danville; but such has been the snail-like torpidity of his movements that he allowed [Major-General John C.] Breckinridge to throw several thousand men into Lynchburg from Charlottesville, and [Lieutenant-General Jubal A.] Early to advance thither with one whole corps from Lee's army. It will be believed that, when, upon the evening of the 17th, Hunter made a feeble attack upon the earthworks around Lynchburg he was astonished at the vigour with which his men were repulsed. His force is estimated at 18,000 men; the joint forces of Breckinridge and Early amount to very much more. Hunter is said to be now in full retreat; but it is doubtful whether, if vigorously pursued by the Confederate cavalry, he will be able to extricate so large an army from the bowels of Virginia into which he has plunged. Be this as it may, it is certain that Grant will get very small aid and comfort, as he fumes and frets before Petersburg, out of the co-operation of Hunter.

But a worse catastrophe than has up to this time overtaken Hunter has cut short the career of another General, in whom Grant is said to repose great trust, and

John Breckinridge

from whom a diversion was confidently expected. Simultaneously with the trans-ference of his own army from the northern bank of the Chickahominy to the southern bank of the James, Grant sent forth [Major-] General Sheridan at the head of what was deemed an irresistible cavalry force, to cross between the Rappahannock and Richmond, and pass near Charlottesville, in the direction of Lynchburg. It was imagined that the Southern cavalry was so reduced in num-bers and so poor in equipments as to be likely to oppose but feeble resistance to the finely-appointed squadrons of General Sheridan; but it appears that Grant reckoned without his host. At Trevillian's depot [actually Trevilian Station] upon the Virginia Central Railroad, the combined forces of [Major-] Generals Fitzhugh Lee [a nephew of Robert E. Lee] and Wade Hampton encountered the Federal raiders, and it appears that, considering the small amount of men engaged, few more complete victories have been gained in this war than the one which is now put to the credit of the two successors to [Major-] General Stuart. Sheridan is said to be on the northern bank of the Pamunkey, greatly shattered, and unable to cross in the face of the victorious Confederates upon the southern bank. No relief or assistance can be looked for by General Grant from this quarter. What will he do next?

Sheridan, of course, did not lose Grant's confidence and, in fact, while not entirely succeeding, he had drawn away Confederate cavalry and thus made Lee less able to detect Grant's final movements towards the James. The detachment of Early's corps was less dangerous to Lee once the front had shifted to Petersburg, for the whole Army of Northern Virginia was not required to man the city's defences.

While the readers of *The Times* were contemplating the events in Virginia, the war had come very much closer to Britain with the dramatic naval battle off Cherbourg on

19 June between the Federal warship, USS *Kearsage*, and one of the most successful of
the Confederate commerce raiders, the *Alabama*, which had been built at Birkenhead
and then slipped out to sea in July 1862 before the British Government was persuaded
to detain it. Under Captain Raphael Semmes, the *Alabama* had sailed some 75,000
miles in the Atlantic and Indian oceans and taken sixty-four Federal merchant vessels.
Like the cruise of other commerce raiders such as the *Florida* and the *Shenandoah*,
however, it did not change the course of the war although relations between Britain
and the North were undoubtedly made worse by the orders for vessels placed by
Confederate agents with British yards. On 20 June a correspondent of *The Times*
reported from Southampton on the action, based on the testimony of John Lancaster, a
Lancashire gentleman, who had viewed it from his private steam yacht, the *Deerhound*:

Throughout the action the *Deerhound* kept about a mile to windward of the
combatants, and was enabled to witness the whole of it. The *Kearsage* was
burning Newcastle coals, and the *Alabama* Welsh coals, the difference in the
smoke (the north country coal yielding so much more) enabling the movements of
each ship to be distinctly traced. Mr Lancaster is clearly of opinion that it was the
Kearsage's 11-inch shells which gave her the advantage, and that, after what he
has witnessed on this occasion, wooden ships stand no chance whatever against
shells. Both vessels fired well into each other's hull, and the yards and masts were
not much damaged. The mainmast of the *Alabama* had been struck by shot, and as
the vessel was sinking broke off and fell into the sea, throwing some men who
were in the maintop into the water. Some tremendous gaps were visible in the bul-
warks of the *Kearsage*, and it was believed that some of her boats were disabled.

The action between the *Alabama* and the *Kearsage*

She appeared to be temporarily plated with iron chains, etc. As far as could be seen, everything appeared to be well planned and ready on board the *Kearsage* for the action. It was apparent that Captain Semmes intended to fight at a long range, and the fact that the *Kearsage* did not reply till the two vessels got nearer together showed that they preferred the short range, and the superior standing power of the latter enabled this to be accomplished. It is remarkable that no attempt was made by the *Kearsage* to close and board the *Alabama*, and when the *Alabama* hoisted sails and made as if for the shore the *Kearsage* moved away in another direction, as though her rudder or screw was damaged and out of control. Great pluck was shown on both sides during the action. On board the *Alabama* all the hammocks were let loose, and arrangements had been made for sinking her rather than that she should be captured.

The *Alabama* sank after about an hour-and-a-half of battle, Semmes and thirty-nine of his officers and men being picked up by Lancaster while others of the 150-strong crew were rescued by the *Kearsage* and French vessels. Subsequently, through the Treaty of Washington of 1871 between Britain and the United States, independent arbitration commissioners awarded the latter $15.5 million worth of damages in settlement of the so-called 'Alabama Claims' for the destruction wrought by thirteen British-built Confederate commerce raiders during the war.

With the retreat of Hunter in the Shenandoah, the Confederates too resolved on a diversionary effort though one necessitated by the need to ensure that the agricultural

Officers of the 1st Connecticutt Volunteer Heavy Artillery at Fort Richardson, Arlington Heights, Washington defences

produce of this 'bread basket of the Confederacy' continued to reach Richmond and Petersburg. Accordingly Early advanced northwards through the valley with some 15,000 men and crossed the Potomac into Maryland on 2 July, penetrating to the all but unmanned outer defences of Washington itself: at one point Lincoln viewed the skirmishing from one of the Federal fortifications. However, the rapid reinforcement of the city persuaded Early that he dare not risk an attack, and he had retired back into Virginia by 14 July. For a short time, though, there had been considerable panic both in the Federal capital and wider afield as Mackay described on 12 July in a report published on 26 July:

The 'raid' of the Confederates into Maryland – at which all New York laughed last week – if it ever condescended to bestow a thought upon the matter, has grown into a formidable invasion. Even yet there are a few optimists or incredulous persons who think that the South is bankrupt, beggared, dispirited, famished, and demoralized; who insist that Lee has made a mistake in sending his horsemen into the rich cornfields of Maryland; that they will infallibly be cut off with their booty; and that Grant will take advantage of their absence to capture both Petersburg and Richmond. But the bulk of the public has awakened, though somewhat tardily, to the conviction that Washington is in imminent danger; that Washington and not Baltimore is the destination of the Confederate General, and that it will require the presence of the whole Army of the Potomac to prevent its capture. The invading hosts, of which no one knows the numbers, though they are variously estimated at from 40,000 to 80,000 men, carry everything before them. The affrighted farmers leave their fields and their cattle and betake themselves to the great cities for safety. The great cities are in as much terror as the rural districts. Washington and even Philadelphia are sending their valuables to New York, and everybody who up to Saturday last could get away from Maryland and the more exposed districts and cities of Pennsylvania hurried off as fast as possible. To-day they have no longer a chance. The Confederates are within four miles of Baltimore and six of Washington. They have defeated the army [actually an understrength scratch corps] of [Major-] General [Lewis] Wallace [later the author of *Ben Hur*], who sought to withstand their advance on the Monocacy, and driven him into Baltimore [9 July]. They have burnt down the house of Mr [Augustus W.] Bradford, the 'loyal' or anti-Southern Governor of Maryland, and that of Mr [Montgomery] Blair, the chief friend and adviser of Mr Lincoln. They have captured the private dispatches of Secretary Stanton, [Lieutenant-] General Grant, and others. They have cut the telegraphic wires connecting with this city [New York]. They have broken up the railroads, destroyed the bridges, and prevented all communication with the North except by the byroads and the sea. Consequently, a few chance pedestrians or horsemen who may be willing to run the risks of capture in the attempt and passengers by the coast steamers are the only persons on whom the Northern public can at present rely for information from Maryland and the Federal capital.

Determined to prevent any recurrence of Early's raid and to sweep the Confederate presence from the Shenandoah, Grant gave command of a newly constituted Army of the Shenandoah to Sheridan. However, with the retirement of Early from the environs of Washington, attention was drawn once more to events in the West.

Having succeeded to the command of the Department of the Mississippi when Grant was promoted to General-in-Chief, Sherman now directed the Army of the Cumberland under Thomas; his own former Army of the Tennessee, now commanded by Major-General James B. McPherson; and the Army of the Ohio commanded by Schofield, who was no doubt relieved to have escaped Missouri. Tasked with the elimination of Joseph Johnston's army, which was entrenched some 25 miles south of Chattanooga at Rocky Face Ridge, Sherman had resolved in May to outflank the Confederates from the west. Johnston, however, slipped away and much the same kind of manoeuvring that had characterized the campaign in Virginia now ensued, with Johnston constantly concerned to preserve his army until a favourable moment should occur when he might entrap some of Sherman's forces. Consequently, with the exception of an engagement at New Hope Church between 25 and 27 May and an unsuccessful Union assault on a Confederate position at Kenesaw Mountain on 27 June there had been little actual fighting but Sherman had pushed Johnston back within a few miles of Atlanta. The sense of frustration in Richmond with Johnston's failure to attack Sherman had communicated itself to Lawley when he reported on 14 July, in a piece published on 23 August:

Encouraged as the inhabitants of Richmond are at this moment by the consciousness that Grant with the shattered residuum of his once mighty host is impotently held in check at Petersburg by an army which is more than a match for his own, and by a General who is markedly his superior, it must be admitted that great and increasing anxiety is here felt as telegram follows telegram announcing that General Johnston has again and again fallen back until the Chattahoochie River has been passed, and his bold antagonist, [Major-] General Sherman, is seen to be within three leagues of Atlanta. The mingled accents of defiance and dismay which ascend from New York and Philadelphia and herald the advance of [Lieutenant-] General Early and his Confederates into Maryland and Pennsylvania are counterpoised by the gloom which is here inspired at the mere mention of General Sherman and Atlanta. We need a Scipio Africanus [the celebrated Roman general of the Second Punic War against Carthage] to remind us, as in the famous speech which Livy puts into his mouth, that if Sherman has seemingly had the best hitherto of the Western campaign, Lee has foiled greater numbers and (as the world thinks, though I cannot agree with it) a more formidable chieftain than Sherman in the Eastern, and *hae secundae res illas adversas sustinuerunt*. In order to explain the position of affairs in the West it is desirable that I should say something as to what is, in my belief, the character of General Johnston. It is impossible to converse with General Johnston without perceiving that he is a more deeply read and scientific theorist on the art of war than General Lee. He is a grave, dignified, and self-contained man – one who has meditated much upon manoeuvres, and would probably study with delight those adroit moves and countermoves which have made [the late seventeenth-century French Marshal, Henri de] Turenne and [his contemporary, the Austrian Marshal, Raimondo] Montecuculi [actually Montecuccoli] famous as chessplayers of war, and were so highly com-

Joseph Johnston

mended by Napoleon. But this scientific study of the military art, and a conscious-ness of the reputation which he has thus gained as a strategist, supervening upon a cautious and sensitive temperament, seem to disqualify General Johnston, fearless though he be personally, for the command of a Confederate army in such a war as this.

Having requested Johnston to outline his intentions and receiving an intimation in reply that Atlanta might well be abandoned without a fight, Jefferson Davis dismissed him on 17 July and replaced him with one of his corps commanders, the thirty-three-year-old John B. Hood. Hood was clearly courageous – he had lost his left arm at Gettysburg and his right leg at Chickamauga – and he had been an outstandingly aggressive subordinate, but whether the newly promoted full General possessed the intellectual capacity to direct an army was a matter of considerable doubt. Certainly, as Mackay reported on 26 July in a dispatch published on 9 August, there was a complete reversal of Johnston's strategy:

The whole interest of the war has suddenly shifted from Richmond to Atlanta. Not that people have lost faith in [Lieutenant-] General Grant, for they still believe that he will capture the Confederate capital, some time before Christmas, if he be left alone by Mr Lincoln and Mr Stanton on the one hand, and by Mr Jefferson Davis and General Lee on the other; but because the chances of a great victory achieved or an overwhelming defeat to be suffered by [Major-] General Sherman are more immediate. General Joseph Johnston, the Confederate comman-der, has been superseded in his command, not because his plans were otherwise

John Hood

than skilful or the best that could be adopted with so small an army as that with which he had to confront a formidable antagonist, but because the Southern people and his own subordinates were of opinion that a stand ought to be made for Atlanta, at any risk and any cost. General Hood, appointed to succeed him, lost not a day, it appears, in carrying out the new policy, and attacked the Federals in their intrenchments between the city and the Chattahoochie. The contest was a stubborn one – as all the battles of the Americans are – and according to the latest accounts had lasted for three days with varying fortunes, but without desired results. The Federal Government, through Mr Stanton, though without official dispatches from General Sherman, continued to assert on Saturday last [23 July], as well as on the previous day, that the Confederates had been driven out of Atlanta with great loss, and had retreated towards Macon.

Inheriting a force of some 70,000 men compared to the almost 90,000 immediately available to Sherman, Hood had indeed attacked at once and continued to do so. In three assaults spread over the period from 20 to 28 July, Hood lost 15,000 casualties compared to but 6,000 for Sherman, although McPherson was killed in the second engagement on 22 July. Nevertheless, Sherman was forced to pause before Atlanta and it was only at the end of August that he felt able to swing round to the west of the city to cut the rail link to Macon, leaving Hood no alternative but to abandon the city on 31 August.

Initially it had appeared that Sherman might be drawn into a prolonged siege at Atlanta similar to that at Petersburg. At the latter, Grant had continued to probe the Confederate defences but on 30 July failed to break into them after the explosion of a

A Confederate Battery at Peach Tree Station, Atlanta defences

large mine dug by Pennsylvanian miners unkder the Confederate works. Burnside, who had been in command of the attack, had been compelled to replace a specially trained negro assault division with a white unit in the first wave, for fear of losses among black troops leading to political repercussions. With no clear idea of their mission, three white divisions simply pressed into the crater formed by the explosion rather than exploiting the considerable psychological dislocation it had effected in the Confederate defence. The defenders rallied and inflicted some 4,000 casualties on the white troops and the negro division, which was subsequently committed to the 'Battle of the Crater' to no great purpose, simply milling about below them. Lawley described the débâcle in a dispatch of 5 August which appeared on 9 September:

The explosion of the mine took place before 5 o'clock in the morning, and, within a quarter of an hour of its occurrence, the salient was occupied by from 12,000 to 15,000 Federal troops. But from that moment forward until the work was regained by the Confederates, about 2 o'clock, [Lieutenant-] General Grant found himself unable to reinforce his troops. Such was the fire of the Confederate artillery issuing from the lines leading up to the captured salient that it swept away every formation of men which emerged from the Federal earthworks. The body of Federals, had they been suffered to remain until night, would undoubtedly have been largely reinforced above ground or below by the following morning. But at about 2 o'clock, General Lee, after one unsuccessful attack upon the aggressors about noon, ordered [Brigadier-] General [William] Mahone to make short work with them. There are few names more deserving of European notice than that of Mahone. He is, as an executive officer, conspicuously the hero of the Campaign in

Inside the Confederate lines at Petersburg, 15 June 1864

Virginia of 1864. Advancing along the line of earthworks which led up to the Federal right, Mahone flung a brigade of Alabamians upon them, and the struggle was almost instantly at an end. At the first onset of the Confederates, many of the panic-struck negroes (who numbered 2,200 in all) crowded into the empty crater of the mine, and cowered down in abject terror. As the Confederate soldiers, infuriated by the passions of battle and maddened by being for the first time in their lives engaged hand to hand with negroes, forced their way up to the ghastly hole, into which wounded, dead, and shrinking men had together been thrust, a scene ensued which baffles description. Confederate officers who have witnessed this war from the commencement, and who have seen 'on horror's head horrors accumulate', tell me that their eyes have rested on no such other scene. Here and there, a few white Federals, who did not share the panic of their black associates, kept firing from the edge of the pit, while volley after volley was poured by the Confederates into the writhing, quivering conglomeration of black and white humanity which struggled and died in this hole of horror. Out of 2,200 negroes carried into the Confederate salient at 5 o'clock in the morning the Federals are said to have regained only 900. 300 were taken, and are now held prisoners by the Confederates; the rest, that is to say 1,000 perished in and about the Cave of Despair which I have attempted to describe.

No further mining operations were attempted and this fiasco coupled with Sherman's temporary halt before Atlanta hurt the Lincoln administration at a sensitive time, since the Democratic convention to choose their presidential candidate began at Chicago on 29 August. The fall of Atlanta at once undermined any lingering challenge to Lincoln's own renomination by the Republicans, which had been effected at the Republican convention at Baltimore in May, and immeasurably strengthened his electoral appeal *vis-à-vis* his Democratic opponent. As Mackay reported on 2 September in a dispatch printed on 17 September, that opponent, as widely anticipated, was McClellan:

General [Major-General] M'Clellan developed greater strength in the Chicago Convention than his warmest friends anticipated. On the first ballot he received nine votes more than a two-thirds majority, and as the Democrat party, warned by the experience of the feuds of 1860, which led to the triumph of Mr Lincoln, and, consequently, to civil war, resolved that this time at least there should be no schism in the doctrine and no mutiny in the ranks, the ultra-peace section, and all those to whom the General for various reasons was personally or politically objectionable, accepted the decision of the majority without a murmur, and consented to make the nomination unanimous. New York has received the tidings with immense delight, if enthusiastic public meetings, jubilant speeches, fireworks, transparencies, bonfires, music and the expenditure of gunpowder can be accepted as testimony of the joy and approbation of the people. Mr [George] Pendleton, of Ohio, the nominee for the Vice-Presidency, is a well-known lawyer of Cincinnati, a very effective public speaker, and a 'gentleman' in the European sense of a word not very accurately understood in America. He has always been opposed to the war, and shares with Mr Benjamin Wood, Mr [Alexander] Long, Mr [Daniel] Voorhees, Mr Vallandigham, and others of the small but illustrious Peace phalanx in the present Congress, the honour of never having supported by vote or speech the slightest infringement of the law or Constitution on the plea of military or any other necessity. Both candidates are under 40 years of age, General M'Clellan having been born in 1826, and Mr Pendleton in 1825. Their friends claim for them that if they may thus lack some of the wisdom of age the defect, if it be one, is likely to be more than compensated by youthful vigour of purpose, aptitude to receive new impressions, and comparative freedom from deep-rooted prejudice.

The 'platform' of the Convention conforms in its main principles to the outline which I was enabled to draw of it at Niagara Falls [in an earlier dispatch from there dated 15 August]. It demands an Armistice and a Convention of the States, to debate on the restoration of the Union; affirms the sanctity of the Constitution, and pledges the united Democracy to resist by force any attempt on the part of the Administration to interfere by military coercion with the freedom of election. It is clear, succinct, and emphatic, and conceals under its love for the Union a tacit admission that, if reason cannot restore it, the attempt to impose it by violence must prove a failure. What the party will do, or proposes to do, should the Southern people make conditions of Armistice that the North could not accept without humiliation, or should the Southern States refuse to send delegates for any other purpose than the discussion of separation, the platform very judiciously refuses to prescribe. Sufficient for the day is the evil thereof. The War Democrats will not renounce the idea of Union until it shall have been driven out of the minds of the people by Southern success in the field. When that time comes, if come it must, they will succumb to necessity, as democracies, like kings and emperors, must do, and make the best arrangements they can to repair past and avert future evil.

The platform Mackay described was a compromise between Peace and War Democrats, which effectively put the granting of an immediate armistice before the ideal of the Union and balanced the 'ticket' of a War Democrat in McClellan with a Peace Democrat in Pendleton. McClellan, however, being conscious of the need to avoid appearing to award complete victory to the South at the moment that Atlanta had fallen to the North, effectively reversed the policy by making it known that preservation of the Union was the condition for armistice. It did little to bring wider support for the Democrats, while later in September Lincoln achieved a greater unity in his own party by sacrificing Montgomery Blair to the radicals. Back at the Republican convention in May, Lincoln had also acted to widen his national appeal by dropping the vice-president of his first term, the virtually unknown Hannibal Hamlin, and choosing a War Democrat in the person of the Governor of Tennessee, Andrew Johnson.

With Sherman contemplating his next move and with few developments on either side of the lines at Petersburg, the focus of military action turned to the Shenandoah where Sheridan had now gathered some 50,000 men opposed to but 25,000 under Early. Not only did Sheridan intend to eliminate any threat posed by Early's forces but also to lay waste the rich agricultural resource of the valley so that, as Grant put it in his orders to Sheridan, 'crows flying over it for the balance of this season will have to carry their provender with them'. The initial engagements fought at Winchester and Fisher's Hill on 19 and 22 September respectively pushed Early back, as Lawley, writing from a visit to Wilmington on 24 September, reported in a dispatch published on 15 November:

S ince the above letter was written [the first part of the dispatch, dated 22 September] information has been received that a disaster, occasioned apparently by [Lieutenant-] General Early's contemptuous estimate of his enemy, has overtaken his army, which will long be numbered as having cost the Confederacy one of its most valuable lives. It appears that Early, having been weakened by the withdrawal from his ranks of that portion of Anderson's (late Longstreet's) corps which had been sent two months ago to the Valley, continued, with very inferior forces as compared to Sheridan's, to occupy his old lines between Winchester and Berryville, instead of falling back to the very strong position some 20 miles in the rear, which has long been regarded as the key to the Valley, and which is at a place called Fisher's-hill, in the neighbourhood of Strasburg. Upon the 19th inst. Sheridan, inspirited, as it is here believed, by a visit from Grant, who was with him on the preceding day, attacked Early in very heavy force, and after flanking the little Confederate army with a large body of cavalry compelled Early to retreat to Strasburg. The action, of which I have received no details, appears to have been one of the sharpest of the war, and is to be bewailed principally in connexion with the death of [Major-] General [Robert E.] Rodes, one of the most promising Major-Generals in the Confederate service. It will be

Jubal Early

found, I think, that Early will be strong enough to hold his ground at Strasburg until winter makes further operations in the Valley impossible.

Lawley, of course, overestimated Early's capacity to hold even the entrenched position at Fisher's Hill and the Confederate retreat enabled Sheridan to complete his work of destruction, which by 7 October he reported had included over 70 mills and 2,000 barns, all of which had been filled with grain. In addition, Sheridan estimated that he had carried off 4,000 head of stock and slaughtered a further 3,000 sheep to feed his troops. Reinforced from Lee's army, Early made a surprise dawn attack upon Sheridan's forces at Cedar Creek on 19 October while Sheridan himself was absent in Washington. Initially the Confederates were successful but, returning from Washington at the critical moment, Sheridan was able to rally his forces and deal Early such a counter-blow that the Confederates were never again in a position to contest control of what had once been such a vital strategic asset. This was not immediately apparent at the time Lawley filed his thoughts on the affair on 27 October, taking the opportunity to refute Federal claims that Longstreet had been in command rather than Early: recovered from his wound, Longstreet had actually resumed command of the Confederate I Corps at Petersburg on the day of Early's attack. The report appeared on 13 December:

The Confederate army in the Valley upon the 19th inst. was the same force which was sent there in June, which menaced Washington early in July, and was commanded from the commencement by the same leader, [Lieutenant-] General Early. The only augmentation which it had received was the division of

Philip Sheridan

[Major-] General Kershaw, which left the neighbourhood of Richmond early in August. The Northern public has again and again been assured that 'the rebel army in the Valley has ceased to exist'. Yet upon the 19th inst. this same shadowy army assumed the initiative, utterly routed two Federal corps, which in their flight annihilated a third corps of their associates, and at 1 in the afternoon of that day the Confederates had captured 18 pieces of cannon, and inflicted upon their enemy a loss of 5,000 men in killed, wounded, and prisoners. Unfortunately, at this stage the want of discipline in General Early's force proved its ruin. They took to plundering their enemy's camps, and, making no preparation against the possibility of another attack from an army which they conceived to be utterly routed, they laid themselves open, as easy victims, to the reprisals which [Major-] General Sheridan, who had come late upon the field, vigorously initiated. The artillery, caissons, and ambulances, all huddled together in inextricable confusion, fell an easy prey to some 25 Federal horsemen who were adventurous enough to dash in among them and to shoot down the horses attached to the guns. Mr Lincoln is unquestionably greatly indebted to General Sheridan, who did more, by arresting what would otherwise have been to the Federals one of the most disgraceful defeats of the war, to insure his re-election, than all the orators who have taken the stump in his favour from Maine to California. But, although the Federal General regained his lost 18 pieces, and took from General Early 23 Confederate pieces in addition, it is indisputable that the Federal loss in men far outweighs that of the Confederates. The Valley is further than ever from being in the Federal grasp; and although General Sheridan has taken pride in applying the torch to private property with a recklessness of cruelty which is unsurpassed even in the annals of this ruthless war, it is not in his power sensibly to diminish the abundant wealth of this favoured region after one of the most lavish harvests which the Valley has ever seen. It is more than ever necessary for Mr Lincoln to keep a large army, and more especially, a considerable force of cavalry, in the Valley to protect Washington, and I see little prospect of Grant being able to withdraw from Sheridan that fine body of cavalry which was so active in the neighbourhood of Richmond during the months of May, June, and July, and without which Grant's operations against Richmond and Petersburg promise to yield but little fruit.

Sheridan's success was yet another fillip for Lincoln's re-election campaign and a further blow to Confederate hopes that a Democratic victory at the polls would bring an atmosphere of political compromise in Washington. There had been some expectations among Democrats that McClellan's name would win the army's votes but this was not to prove the case. The military vote had less effect than contemporaries anticipated and probably at most made a difference only in New York, Connecticut and Indiana. In any case, Lincoln had an overwhelming victory on polling day – 8 November – with a popular vote of 2.2 million to McClellan's 1.8 million, only three states falling to the Democrats (Delaware, Kentucky and New Jersey) although the Republican majority was narrow in some others such as New York and Connecticut, and an enormous 212–21 majority in the electoral college. Mackay reported the first polling indications on 11 November in a report which appeared on 28 November:

The complete returns of the Presidential and local elections in the States have not yet been received, but sufficient is known to make it absolutely certain that Mr Lincoln has a popular majority of a quarter of a million, or it may be half a million, over General M'Clellan, and that his majority in the Electoral College will be so large as to render it unnecessary to count the votes of Tennessee, Louisiana, or Florida, or any other State where illegal test oaths have been employed as a means of intimidation. In the State elections the Republicans have been considerable gainers, and the next Congress will contain a fully two-thirds majority of the members of that party. [Democrat] Governor Seymour's re-election in New York is asserted by his friends and denied by his opponents, each party making up returns to prove its point. As yet the returns prove nothing but that they must be fraudulent on the one side or the other. The contest all over the country has been very close, and has been conducted with such good feeling, propriety, and order, as to be in the highest degree honourable to the American people. That frauds have been committed there is every reason to believe. Frauds are difficult to detect or prevent under a system of universal suffrage, and there has never perhaps been a Presidential or any other election in this country in which they have not occurred. But the frauds have usually borne so slight a proportion to the vast volume of legitimate votes as to have been of no more account than straws upon a strong current. Unfair votes may have been cast for Mr Lincoln, and undue means may have been employed on his behalf in the army and in districts under military control, but the results prove that he needed neither to be successful, and that it was the firm determination of a decisive though not very large majority of the Northern people to intrust him for a second term with the destinies of the Republic.

Mackay was uncharacteristically positive in his view of the election and also correct in that undoubted fraud in some areas, notably Indiana, did not affect the overall result. Republican organization had been far superior and had been able to capitalize effectively upon any issues or events which could be turned to electoral advantage. Alleged conspiracies by Confederate agents based in Canada had been one such issue, particularly coupled to the raid from across the Canadian frontier on St Albans, Vermont by twenty-one Confederates led by Lieutenant Bennett H. Young on 19 October. Having robbed the town's banks of $201,522, the raiders were pursued across the frontier and detained, although subsequently handed over to the Canadian authorities. When the latter released the raiders on a technicality there was renewed Anglo-American tension, which was defused by British pressure on the Canadian legislature to enact new controls on any attempt to conduct hostilities from Canada. Mackay reported on continuing rumours of plots on 29 November in an article printed on 12 December:

When, nearly a month ago, Mr Seward announced to his astonished countrymen the existence of a plot concocted by Southern refugees in Canada to burn to the ground the principal cities of the North on the night of the Presidential election, the revelation was received with a burst of derision. One-half of the public considered the Secretary either to be indiscreet in making such a statement, or foolishly credulous in believing it; while the other half, more complimentary to his *savoir faire* was of opinion that he had either invented the report or given it authoritative currency, as a pretext for the appointment of [Major-] General Butler to the military command of New York. It appears that on Friday [23 November] rooms were taken in 16 of the New York hotels by 16 mysterious strangers, none of whom had more luggage than was contained in a small bag, carried in the hand; that the 16 strangers, having obtained possession, piled the bedding upon chairs and tables, placed a bottle of phosphorus, and in some cases of turpentine, underneath; ignited a lucifer match, set fire to the clothes, which were previously saturated with the turpentine, or some other liquid; locked the doors, and then withdrew, to be seen no more. Some of these persons are said to have been dressed in the uniform of officers in the Federal army, the better to avoid suspicion. A very singular part of the business is, that not one of these 16 attempts was successful; that the fire so kindled created much smoke, but no flame, and that it was in every instance extinguished with little or no damage, except that produced by water and breakage. The circumstances are certainly remarkable, and now that the first alarm has begun to subside, the invention of the people has gone busily to work to account for them. Some believe, and these form by far the largest number, that the 16 conspirators, if there were so many, were Southern agents. Others contend that they were thieves, who intended to create such confusion, by the simultaneous outbreak of so many conflagrations, as to leave ampler scope for professional plunder than was ever enjoyed by the fraternity in any city of the world. A third section of observers – so cynical is the spirit of the time and people – assert that it was never intended to set fire to the city, or to the hotels; that the beds and bedding were saturated with a solution of sulphate of soda, which rendered them uninflammable, though not incombustible; that the object was to alarm the people for the safety of their lives and property, and to take advantage of the public terror to reinstate General Butler as military Dictator, if not to 'fire the Northern heart' to such a pitch of fury against the South as to render a conscription unnecessary. There are others, again, who know not what to believe, who have formed no theory to explain the mystery, but, who, in default of any other object on which to vent their ill-will, fall foul of Mr Seward, and declare that his announcement first put the idea into the heads of the conspirators, whoever they may have been, and that if it had not been for his over-zealous babbling, no such wicked act would have recommended itself to any one outside of Bedlam. But these latter critics do Mr Seward injustice. The idea did not originate with him, but in a Richmond newspaper, edited by John Mitchell, the Irish exile, which, before Mr Seward said a word upon the subject, openly advocated the incendiarism of New York and Boston, in retaliation for the devastation of the Shenandoah Valley by [Major-] General Sheridan.

Mackay went on to intimate that the rumours had diverted attention from the 'most daring as well as most perilous movements' of Sherman in Georgia. With his lines of communication under attack from the Confederate cavalry of Forrest and Wheeler, Sherman had resolved to cut loose altogether from his communications and march to the sea, at the same time both emphasizing the South's vulnerability and also bringing home to the population of the deep South the consequences of continuing to sustain the war effort. In a situation in which it had become as important to out-produce as to out-fight an opponent, the civilian population assisting in war production in its broadest sense became a legitimate target for attack. Cutting his force down to some 60,000 men, Sherman left Atlanta on the night of 15/16 November, leaving in his wake uncontrolled fires that spread rapidly from factories and other war-related installations to domestic housing. He was to cut a corridor of destruction some 50 miles wide across the 250 miles that separated him from Savannah on the coast.

At the same time that Sherman was marching south-eastwards, Hood was marching northwards and westwards in the expectation of severing Sherman's lines of communications and disrupting Union strategy as a whole by an invasion of Tennessee and even Kentucky. However, Thomas had been sent back to defend Nashville. Hood launched a disastrous and costly attack on an advanced Union force commanded by Schofield at Franklin on 30 November, and was then sent into headlong retreat from Nashville, which he had attempted to besiege, in a two-day battle on 15 and 16 December which comprehensively destroyed the Army of Tennessee as an effective fighting force. Sherman, meanwhile, was meeting little opposition in an advance upon which Lawley reported on 27 November, in a dispatch eventually printed on 6 January 1865:

Intense interest continues to be expressed here in regard to Sherman's progress in Georgia. Your readers have long been aware that upon the 12th inst. [actually the 15th] Sherman cut loose from Atlanta, setting fire, as is alleged to the city, and darting with five army corps, and a large cavalry force, into the heart of Georgia. It is difficult to estimate each army corps as containing less than from 6,000 to 7,000 men, and thus, with a cavalry force estimated at 9,000, Sherman must have with him at least 40,000 men. His force is probably the finest army which the Federals have ever had in the field. He is said to carry with him everything necessary for success in his hazardous expedition, such as indiarubber pontoons and all that science has invented to facilitate rapidity of movement in an army advancing in light marching order. Nevertheless, it must be confessed that he has done hitherto wonderfully little harm, and effected almost nothing during the 15 days which have elapsed since he started. It is, of course, difficult to know where the whole of Sherman's army is, but it is believed that up to last night he was on the line of the Oconee River. The bridge which carries the Georgia Central Railroad (connecting Macon with Savannah) over the Oconee River is long, and adjoining it there are five or six miles of high wooden trestlework, which carry the railroad over a vast cypress swamp to the west of the Oconee. The bridge and trestlework were attacked by a part of Sherman's forces on the 24th, 25th, and 26th, but up to the latest advices the Federals had been drawn off by the Georgia troops and by [Major-] General Wheeler, who is believed to be in the neighbourhood of Sandersville with 10,000 cavalry. It is believed that Sherman's main force was yesterday near Milledgeville, where it is presumed that the State-house and other public buildings were burnt. And here I may remark that already the earnestness and zeal of the Georgians as Confederates have been wonderfully stimulated by the savage and ruthless spirit which Sherman and his men have everywhere exhibited. If there were much truth in the alleged disloyalty to President Davis of Governor [Joseph E.] Brown and Vice-President [Alexander H.] Stephens, it would have been easy for Sherman by applying to Georgia an antiphlogistic treatment to cultivate and encourage the Union sentiment of Georgians. But, with the fatuity which everywhere attends Mr Lincoln's emissaries, Sherman has left nothing but embittered rebels in his track. Men are not to be coaxed back into the Union by burning their barns and houses, stealing their horses, cattle, poultry, hogs, slaves, provisions, and waggons. It is already seen in Richmond that there will be little occasion hereafter to complain of Georgian lukewarmness. In the interest of the Confederates, nothing could be more desirable than the destruction of Governor Brown's house and barns in the neighbourhood of Canton, by Sherman.

Sherman's purpose, of course, was hardly to 'coax' Georgians back into the Union, but Lawley's report is more significant for being one of the few occasions on which he addressed the divisions which were as much a feature of the South as of the North. It was not just a case of those areas such as the western part of North Carolina and the eastern part of Tennessee, where there had never been support for the idea of the Confederacy – those parts of Virginia which had most opposed secession had been occupied by the Union in 1861 and admitted as the new State of West Virginia in April 1863 – but of the difficulties in reconciling the principle of states' rights with the Confederacy's need for centralized control in order to wage the war effectively. Taken to extremes as it was by Governor Brown of Georgia and Governor Zebulon B. Vance, states' rights could only harm the Confederate cause. Brown, for example, had not only opposed conscription and exempted Georgia's militia from service in the Confederate army, but actually withdrew the militia from co-operation with the army after the fall of Atlanta. His fellow Georgian, Stephens, had been an opponent of the administration in which he was supposedly vice-president from at least 1862 and was increasingly an advocate of peace. Brown, too, was moving towards the idea of making a separate peace and, in this regard at least, Sherman's activities were unlikely to be the unifying factor Lawley claimed.

What Mackay referred to in one dispatch as Sherman's 'retreat' culminated in his emergence, after bypassing for the time being the defences of Savannah, at Fort McAllister on Ossibaw Sound at the mouth of the Ogeechee river on 13 December, where he linked with Federal warships. Mackay had news of Sherman's arrival on the coast on 17 December, his report being published on 29 December:

The public anxiety for news of [Major-] General Sherman has been relieved by the announcement, on Confederate, and, therefore, unimpeachable authority, that he has reached the seacoast and taken by assault Fort M'Allister, commanding the entrance to Ossibaw Sound, and forming one of the main defences of Savannah [it was 15 miles south of the city]. The announcement is simultaneously made that he has captured Savannah itself and 11,000 prisoners, after a fight which lasted eight hours [not true, of course]. This news, though generally credited by the Federal press, is not official, and rests entirely upon statements made by steamboat passengers from Charleston Bar, who allege that it was received by flag of truce just prior to their departure. Mr Lincoln states, as a fact within his own knowledge, that General Sherman has reached the Atlantic with 40,000 men, black

David Porter

and white, more than he started with; and, as the Confederates admit, and the Federals assert, that he has suffered but little loss, and met with but little real impediment, in his hazardous march, it may be assumed as certain, if he have not already taken Savannah, that he has commenced the siege. Important, if not decisive, news may therefore be hourly expected from that quarter. In Tennessee both the news and the rumours are equally unfavourable to the Confederate cause. General Hood, besieging Nashville with a force not equal to that opposed to him, has been attacked and defeated with severe loss, and forced back, according to the testimony of [Major-] General Thomas, in a dispatch to Mr Stanton, no less than eight miles. At Petersburg and Richmond all is quiet, [Lieutenant-] General Grant having attempted no further movements since the repulse of [Major-] General [Gouverneur K.] Warren on the Weldon Railway [actually Warren's V Corps had seized the vital Weldon line running into Petersburg from the south in an operation from 18 to 21 August]. The expedition of [Rear] Admiral Porter, the same that was destined for Wilmington more than six weeks ago, and that was ordered to 'go in and win' at any cost before the day of the Presidential election, and that appears to have been detained in consequence of the sudden determination of General Sherman to abandon Atlanta and march through Georgia to the sea, received final instructions on Tuesday last, and in the forenoon of that day the Admiral with his whole fleet sailed under sealed orders to the southward. Whether the point at which he aims is Charleston, Savannah, or Wilmington, is not known to the public; but the popular theory fixes upon Charleston as the most likely place, and presupposes, moreover, that the attack upon that peccant city – 'the cradle of rebellion' – is to be simultaneous with Sherman's assault upon Savannah.

In fact, Porter's 150 vessels including transports carrying 6,500 troops commanded by Butler were bound for the original target of Wilmington – the last major port open to blockade runners since the effective closing of Mobile by Farragut on 5 August – and it was from that city that Lawley reported on Porter's attack of 24 and 25 December upon Fort Fisher. Dated 27 December, the report was published on 7 February 1865:

At about noon of the 24th the lunette of Federal ships was arrayed; and never since the 20th of July, 1588, when Lord Howard of Effingham first came in sight of the Spanish Armada, stretching in a crescent of seven miles from horn to horn, did a 'navy more irresistable and disdaining prevention' (to borrow the words of Sir Francis Drake) ride the waves. Commencing shortly after noon, there burst simultaneously upon a given signal from the throats of hundreds of guns such a storm of shells as has never before been rained upon any fort or work of human construction. It was in vain that [Brigadier-] General [William H.C.] Whiting or Colonel [William] Lamb attempted to make an accurate calculation how many guns were thundering at the fort, how many jets of flame issued from the infuriated ships, or how many shells were discharged in each minute. Suffice it to say that the reports of the artillery, usually as distinct as the strokes of a bell, swelled up to heaven in a diapason as continuous and uninterrupted as the roar of Niagara; and that three miles of the horizon were checkered with puffs or wreaths of white smoke, which showed against the sky as though Jupiter was pelting the earth with gigantic snowballs. For five weary hours upon the 24th the iron hail-storm, without one instant's cessation, descended upon or around the fort, tore great rents in the pallisades which protect the land face, set fire to the wooden quarters of the garrison, swept away every vestige of flag or flagstaff, howled above Lamb's Mound without injuring a hair of the head of its defenders, scattered iron splinters broadcast over the beach, bored great holes and chasms into the sides of the mound, the slopes of the fort, and the barren waste of sand that surround them, and occasionally, flying wildly inwards, lashed the water of the Cape Fear River into lofty columns of spray. From 5 in the afternoon of the 24th until about 10 in the morning of Christmas-day there was a lull in the firing, followed by its resumption for seven hours with unabated fury and ferocity upon the latter day. The burning buildings in the interior of the fort, when darkness closed in, cast a lurid glare over the scene, as the men, wild with excitement, but calm and pale and with set teeth, issued from the bomb proofs, and looked in wonder at their comrades, to see so many unwounded survivors after a bombardment such as mortal ear never heard before, and of which the reality seemed, even now, but an unsubstantial dream.

What, it will be asked, was the damage effected by the tons upon tons of iron which now lie buried in the sand of North Carolina? Briefly summed up, two or three guns were dismounted, three men were killed, and 55 wounded. As for the damage done to the mounds of sand which constitute Fort Fisher, it was scarcely visible yesterday, and will be wholly invisible within a week from this time. Upon the first day of the bombardment the fort responded more excitedly than upon the second, firing 660 shots during the five hours' bombardment of the 24th, and rather less than 600 shots during the seven hours' bombardment of the 25th. Two English guns especially distinguished themselves – an 8-inch, or 150-pounder, Armstrong shunt gun, and an 8-inch Blakeley. It is believed that upon each occasion when the Armstrong gun was discharged (it was only fired thrice) a Federal ship shifted its position, or hauled out of action. The Blakeley gun was fired much more frequently, and with excellent effect. The value of these guns, as compared with the Brook gun, which gained such credit for sinking the [USS] *Keokuk* off Charleston in April, 1863, is now satisfactorily settled, according to the judgement of the defenders of Fort Fisher, in favour of the English pieces. In regard to the minor incidents of the action it is worthy of record that upon the afternoon of the 25th several boats or barges were lowered from the Federal frigates on the extreme left of the arc, which boats approached the rip at the mouth of the river, under the guns of Fort Buchanan, and were believed to have been feeling for torpedoes [mines]. A gun from Fort Buchanan opened upon them, and at its fourth discharge a shot cut a Federal barge in two, scattering its crew upon the water. The men were picked up by their comrades in the other barges, which immediately proceeded to withdraw from action.

It remains for me to narrate the fortunes of that portion of the Federal forces which disembarked upon the beach. About 4 in the afternoon of Sunday, the 25th, several surf boats were lowered from the transports and ferryboats, which were anchored off shore in the deep water, about three miles to the north of Fort Fisher. It is believed that, availing themselves of leading lines warped to the shore, these boats landed three brigades of Federal troops under the command of [Brigadier-] General [Adelbert] Ames. The woods and beach in the neighbourhood of their landing-place had been swept previous to their debarcation by a storm of shell and shrapnel, which drove off [Brigadier-] General [William W.] Kirkland and his brigade of Confederates, who would otherwise have prevented the landing of any Federal troops. Immediately after landing, the Federals possessed themselves of a redoubt upon the beach, named Battery Anderson, and threw a strong line of pickets across the tongue of land upon which Fort Fisher stands. Just before sunset a strong demonstration (assault it could hardly be called) was made, chiefly against the land face of Fort Fisher, and it will readily be believed that this was the most anxious moment experienced by its gallant defenders. It seems to have been the impression of the Federals that after such a bombardment as the fort had sustained the resistance to an attack could not have been otherwise than feeble. It is probable that at no moment during the last 18 months had Colonel Lamb so small a garrison available for the defence of his cherished fort. But, calling upon his gallant little band of about 900 men, half of them tried and seasoned troops, and half consisting of Governor Vance's junior reserves, Colonel Lamb rushed down to man the pallisades, and his efforts were nobly responded to by his men. Immediately that the Federals saw the defenders of Fort Fisher swarming over the parapet, and rushing forward with undiminished heart and in unabated numbers to the defence of its pallisades, all vigour and hope departed from the assailants and the fort was saved. All night the Federal pickets lay upon their arms, and in the dim dawn of the 26th the fog of early morning momentarily lifted and revealed a strong line of soldiers standing almost elbow to elbow, and stretching from the sea to the river. Again the fog fell and obscured the view, but when it once more lifted and cleared off for the day the assailants had disappeared. Upon the night of the 26th and during the early morning of the 27th they took to their boats, and this attack upon Fort Fisher, either by land or sea, was at an end.

With the failure of the operation, which had also involved an attempt to explode an old vessel loaded with 215 tons of gunpowder and disguised as a blockade runner close to the fort on the night of 23 December – it went off but failed to do any damage – Porter and Butler withdrew to Fort Monroe in Virginia. The débâcle finally ended Butler's active military career and in January 1865 he would be replaced in a renewed attempt on Wilmington by Major-General Alfred H. Terry. However, the repulse in North Carolina was readily balanced by the fall of Savannah to Sherman, the Confederates being forced to abandon the city on 21 December once it became apparent that they would be encircled to no purpose if they remained. Mackay's account of 28 December appeared in *The Times* on 9 January 1865:

General [Major-General] Hardee having but 15,000 men to defend Savannah against the attack of 50,000, under [Major-] General Sherman, and by a co-operating fleet, crossed over the Savannah river on the 20th inst. at the only side on which the city was uninvested, taking with him his whole force. He destroyed a large quantity of stores and ammunition – all military stores, in fact, that could be made available or useful to the enemy, and on the following day General Sherman took possession. Sherman found in the city, according to his own report to Mr Stanton, no less than 25,000 bales of cotton – or, according to the report of

William Sherman

[Brigadier-] General [John G.] Foster, 33,000 – all of which, with the city of Savannah itself, he presented as a 'Christmas gift' to the Yankee nation. The Yankee nation has received it with shouts of joy and gratitude, and for the second, if not the third time has proclaimed General Sherman to be the true and only hero of the war, and the predestined saviour of the nation. The value of Savannah to the Confederacy was greater in point of honour and prestige than in solid help to the cause, and its loss will doubtless be deplored in the South and its gain exulted over in the North in a degree incommensurate with its military importance. Some of the Northern journals seem to consider the capture of the 25,000 or 33,000 bales of cotton as of more account than the possession of the city, and go the length of calculating what it is worth in gold or greenbacks, and what sum it would fetch in Liverpool if immediately sent across the Atlantic to feed the hungry mills of Lancashire. Possibly (and most probably) the calculation is utterly idle. The cotton may be worth two millions sterling, as some of these journals estimate, but it may be reasonably supposed that General Hardee in evacuating the city would not have left such a splendid prize to the enemy, and that he refrained from destroying the cotton solely because it was the bona fide property of English or other foreign owners. This view of the case, however, has not yet been publicly suggested in New York, though in private society the explanation is freely offered to account for what would otherwise be an unpardonable neglect or oversight on the part of the Confederate General.

Without doubt the year had been one of almost unmitigated disaster for the Confederacy in strategic terms, and as it closed there could be little real expectation that the South would long survive complete defeat.

1865

Having seen the old year out at one city under attack – Wilmington – Francis Lawley opened the new with a report from another that had been under constant threat for eighteen months, namely Charleston. Even such a staunch champion of the South as Lawley was compelled to speculate that the fourth anniversary of the beginning of the bombardment of Fort Sumter in April 1865 might see the Union flag once more flying over the 'crumbling historical ruin'. In a report dated 14 January but which did not appear in *The Times* until 7 March, he described a visit to Sumter:

Yesterday evening, immediately after sunset, I visited the irregularly-outlined mass of dark red-gray ruin, which, crumbling bit by bit and inch by inch under such a storm as fort never yet sustained upon earth, remains as unsubdued as on the days when [Rear Admirals] Dupont and Dahlgren recoiled before its guns, and [Major-General Quincy A.] Gillmore and a host of his brother engineers exhausted their illimitable resources against it in vain [in 1863]. 'Cold, indeed, must be the nature of that man' who can at this moment approach Fort Sumter without that swelling of the heart which is felt when one looks on such scenes as the Plains of Marathon, or the Rock of Gibraltar for the first time. Famous passages of history, such as [Sir Robert] Sale's defence of Jellalabad [in 1842 during the First Afghan War] against the Affghans [*sic*], or [Sir Henry] Havelock standing at bay in the Residency of Lucknow [in 1857 during the Indian Mutiny], pale their ineffectual fires when matched with the resistance at Fort Sumter. Neither to Havelock nor to Sale was retreat or submission a possibility; whereas the garrison of Fort Sumter has never been cut off from communication with the mainland, and has always been fighting a civilized enemy and not a savage brood of human wolves. The artillery brought against Sale was insignificant, and against Havelock there was employed no gun larger than the 42-pounder smooth-bore. The visitor to Fort Sumter this day sees lying unexploded in the centre of its old parade-ground 300-pounder Parrott and 15-inch spherical shells, a few dozen of which are equal in weight to the whole amount of metal which was rained upon Jellalabad or Lucknow. Such has been the mass of these gigantic globes and barrel-shaped projectiles of iron which have been thrown into Fort Sumter that the mind shrinks from the effort to compute the tons upon tons of metal launched from mortars, smooth-bore or rifled guns, into a space not exceeding three and a half acres in area, and hitherto launched in vain.

While Charleston still held out, however, Wilmington's Fort Fisher, from which Lawley had so recently reported, fell on 15 January to a renewed assault commanded by Terry. Lawley was still at Charleston when he reported on the closing of the last major port open to Southern blockade runners. Dated 23 January, it appeared just one day later than his earlier report, on 8 March:

The four ironsided vessels which I have mentioned kept up a steady fire on the land face of Fort Fisher during the whole of the 13th, and about half-past 4 in the afternoon of the same day the entire Federal fleet steamed very leisurely and slowly past the sea face of the Fort, and threw a *feu d'enfer* for about an hour into its open embrasures. In the meantime the Federal infantry was being landed, during the whole of the 13th, about Gatlin's Battery, or about five miles to the north of Fort Fisher. No opposition or molestation was offered, as they slowly effected a landing under circumstances singularly favourable to them, and with the sea as smooth as a mill-dam. During the whole night of the 13th and 14th the Monitors kept up a steady though not rapid fire on the land face, which was continued with more spirit on the morning of the 14th, and in which two large frigates, stationed off the sea face, took part upon this day. Upon Sunday, the 15th, the whole fleet resumed the lunette attitude which they wore on Christmas-day, and pelted the Fort mercilessly until about 2 o'clock, when the troops which the Federals had now thrown across from the sea to the river drew near along the river bank. At this point the Fort is entered by a road or causeway, leading from Colonel Lamb's house. There is a proverb in this country to the effect that no earthwork is ever completely finished, and long as the preparations for defending Fort Fisher have been continued, there was no defensive work, or *tête de pont*, at the spot where this causeway enters the Fort. The Federals threw about 2,500 men upon the Fort at this point, and effected an entrance there about 3 o'clock. It was in vain that [Brigadier-] General Whiting and Colonel Lamb threw themselves at the head of such troops as they could rally with the most determined gallantry against the assailants. General Whiting with his own hand, as I am informed, tore down the Federal flag several times until he was severely wounded. By his side fell Colonel Lamb, after displaying the valour which all who are acquainted with him and witnessed his exertions at the close of last month, would have expected him to exhibit. I understand that the wounds of both are serious, but not dangerous [Whiting died of his wounds in March]. After their fall the resistance seems to have assumed no organized shape. The Federals advanced along the inside of the land face until they had possessed themselves of eight merlons, or the embrasures in which eight guns were mounted. Here they halted for the rest of the afternoon, and did not proceed to accomplish their task until after darkness had fallen. Then they advanced once more, and driving the garrison of the Fort beyond Lamb's Mound, they took the survivors prisoners at the extreme end of Confederate Point. I believe that there were inside the Fort about 2,200 men when the 2,500 Federals advanced upon it [in fact it was a combined assault by some 4,500 infantrymen on the land face and 2,000 seamen and marines on the sea face]. I am also under the impression that the Federal attack was made without artillery, and that their soldiers gallantly approached a work which mounted not only some 50 heavy guns, but was also defended by several 12-pounder howitzers and light field pieces, with nothing but muskets in their hands. The result might have been different if General Whiting and Colonel Lamb had not been wounded at the outset, but it must be confessed that the general sensation here is that the fight was not one which is creditable to the Confederate arms. It must be remembered that most of the garrison had never been under a serious fire before last Christmas-day, and that they were for the first time under a heavy musketry fire upon the 15th inst. The reinforcements hastily thrown into the Fort when the attack commenced were, for the most part, raw troops; the aggregate was composed of heterogeneous bodies of men without concert; the only two commanding officers of mark and character who were well acquainted with the locale were wounded at an early stage of the fight. Public opinion, which is in America more censorious than anywhere upon earth, and which invariably selects one individual as the mark for its shafts, has in this instance fixed upon General Bragg, and animadverted severely upon his want of enterprise in not attacking the Federals as they landed at Battery Gatlin, and as they approached to take the Fort *en revers*. I am unable, from want of full and accurate information, to say whether General Bragg, who had previously done much to regain public favour, is deserving of censure or not. But it must be confessed that General Bragg has hitherto, to an extraordinary extent, been a lightning conductor for bad luck.

Lawley had underestimated the strength of the assault force on Fort Fisher, which had been backed by another 8,000 troops not brought into action, and in fact the Confederates had inflicted some 1,300 casualties on their attackers for the loss of some 500 themselves, excluding prisoners. Nonetheless it was a powerful blow to the Confederacy, forcing the resignation of the Secretary of War, James A. Seddon, and the appointment of Lee as General-in-Chief, although far too late to make any difference to the ultimate result of the war. As Mackay reported on 27 January in a report published on 11 February, it also put increasing pressure on Jefferson Davis:

The political dissensions in the Southern capital, as reported both in the journals that support and in those that oppose the Administration of Mr Davis, also attract unusual attention. Some observers see nothing in the attacks made upon Mr Davis but a proof that the Southern people are so weary of the war that they are anxious to make peace upon no other terms than those of a general amnesty and a repeal of the Confiscation Acts [of August 1861 and July 1862, by which the property – including slaves – of those in rebellion could be deemed forfeit to the Union upon capture]; while others, better informed, or drawing more correct conclusions from the study of human nature and of the lessons of history, see in the animosities expressed against Mr Davis and in the forthcoming appointment of General Lee [it took effect on 6 February] to the supreme control of the armies of the Republic nothing but a determination on the part of the South to carry on the war with renewed vigour, to centralize power for the better organization of victory, and to allow no man, however great and able, or however eminent in character and previous service, to stand in the way of the accomplishment of the national purpose, if, from any cause, real or imaginary, he have forfeited the once implicit confidence of the people. The restoration of General Joseph E. Johnston to the command of the Army of the Tennessee [Hood having resigned on 15 January], contrary to the advice and wish of the President, marks not alone the diminished respect of the Confederate Congress for the military judgement of Mr Davis, but shows to what cause the public opinion of the South attributes the recent reverses which have befallen their arms. In like manner, the resignation of several members of the Cabinet [only Seddon resigned although the Secretary of State, Judah Benjamin, had also come under pressure to do so] is to be accepted as proof, not of discouragement, but of the inauguration of a more vigorous or, at all events, of a more popular system; and if, as the indications seem to prefigure, Mr Davis will cordially accept the position in which a temporary want of success – if not an error of judgement in the removal of General Johnston – has, perhaps, undeservedly, but not unnaturally, placed him, and act in thorough military subordination to General Lee, it is probable that such energy will be infused into the heart of the Southern people as will speedily enable them to achieve a victory sufficient to overbalance their late losses, and bring upon the North a renewal of the cold fit of despondency which it suffered in the early days of the Chicago Convention, when the war was pronounced to be a failure, and the whole tendency of Northern opinion was towards peace and conciliation.

In fact there was an increasing mood for peace in the South and, when Francis Preston Blair initiated the idea of negotiations, Davis nominated his Vice-President, Stephens, and two others to meet Lincoln's Secretary of State, Seward. Davis clearly expected little compromise on the part of the North at this stage of the war and appears to have decided to exploit the harsh terms likely to be offered to revive popular commitment to the necessity of fighting on. At the same time, such a well-known peace advocate as Stephens would be discredited by the process. In the event, when it seemed to Lincoln that Stephens and his fellow negotiators were serious in their intent to talk terms, he joined Seward on the steamer, *River Queen*, lying off Hampton Roads, Virginia on 3 February. Mackay reported that same day on this dramatic development in a dispatch printed on 20 February:

This city [New York], if not the whole of Federal America, was taken by surprise yesterday morning by learning that no less a person than Mr Seward had left Washington for Fortress Monroe [which overlooked Hampton Roads] to receive and confer with Vice-President Stephens of the Southern Confederacy and two other prominent Southern gentlemen dispatched from Richmond on an informal mission to the Federal Government. Last night the surprise was augmented by the announcement that Mr Seward had no sooner reached his destination than he had telegraphed to Mr Lincoln to follow him without delay, and that Mr Lincoln had packed his small effects in a carpet bag, and, attended by one servant, had departed by special express to Annapolis within less than an hour after the receipt of the message. Most people were incredulous, but the assertion came from so many and such independent sources in Washington that none who saw the telegrams could remain in doubt that the facts were substantially as stated, and that, waiving all considerations of his official or personal dignity, Mr Lincoln, in the sacred interest and the firm hope of peace, had determined, remote from the intrigues, the cabals, and the passions of the capital, to hear with his own ears what proposals the Confederate emissaries had to convey, and to learn whether submission to the ancient constitution without further struggle or bloodshed were or were not in the heart of the Southern people. Of course, under such extraordinary circumstances, the whole talk of the public in every circle, society, and place of resort, as well as in the newspapers, is of PEACE. To cite all the rumours that are afloat would serve no good purpose, for they are not only contradictory and absurd, but evanescent, and live one moment but to fade away the next.

Lincoln's terms were indeed uncompromising in demanding effective unconditional surrender and no reversal of emancipation as it now stood. There was an indication, however, that the thirteenth amendment to the constitution abolishing slavery recently passed in the House of Representatives might not be ratified in the immediate future. Moreover, Lincoln was not insistent on the application of the Confiscation Acts or other sanctions against prominent Confederates and there was even suggestion of compensation for slave owners. Despite being empowered to negotiate only on the basis of independence, Stephens and his colleagues explored a wide range of alternative options in response to Lincoln's proposals but, of course, with Southern independence never on offer, the talks could yield no result. The South could have expected little else but, as Lawley reported on 16 February in a piece appearing on 20 March, the reaction to the Union terms went some way to give Davis hope that his intentions with regard to the negotiations had been met:

Never in any community have I witnessed such a revolution of public feeling as has been wrought in Virginia by the contemptuous terms offered to the three Southern Commissioners who have lately returned hither from their informal interview with President Lincoln and Mr Seward at Fortress Monroe. It is idle to pretend that previous to that interview the general heart of the Confederates had not reached a lower pitch of dejection than was ever observable at any earlier stage of this rueful war. It is true that the Confederate army around Richmond has never participated in the despondency of the Gulf States, and has hardly realized the amount of depression prevalent in half-hearted Georgia; but, in addition to the fall of Fort Fisher and the triumphal march of Sherman to Savannah, there was much to abate the characteristic hopefulness of Richmond and Virginia. For more than 100 days the Southern Houses of Congress have been in session in this city, and anxious spectators have awaited some exhibition of valour and vigour from Legislative Bodies called to deliberate upon the most momentous and appalling crisis that ever engaged the attention of a representative Assembly. I know of no parallel to the feebleness and imbecility of the results attained in the Southern Congress, unless it can be found in the simultaneous deliberations of the Federal Congress, or in the war of words which [Edward] Gibbon has held up to undying scorn, and which raged at Constantinople among the Greeks of the Lower [Roman] Empire while the battering ram thundered at the city's gates.

There is at this moment a lull, a breathing place, a new *point de depart* for these sorely tried Southerners. In the first place, Wilmington has been sealed as a port of entry, and all the sharks and Shylocks who there congregated and shirked duty in the ranks have lost their occupation. The demand for gold, now that the chief port through which it lately flowed has been closed, has already sensibly diminished, and the spirit of speculation has received in the loss of Wilmington a staggering blow, from which all who wish well to Secessia cannot but pray that it will be slow to recover. Secondly, there is a prospect that the Southern Congress will shortly adjourn, that the 'action of Congress' will no longer be invoked as a mysterious Abracadabra, destined to neutralize the debasing influences of disaffection and corruption, and that the finance of the country will be committed to the far more capable hands of Mr [George A.] Trenholm [Memminger's replacement as Secretary of the Treasury in June 1864], while military affairs are left to the mature wisdom of General Lee. Thirdly, the exchange of prisoners, so long delayed, so long disingenuously eluded by the North, has been resumed, under the inexorable pressure of the relatives of Northern prisoners, and will, if honestly carried out (and we have General Grant's word that it will be honestly carried out), give to the Southern armies some 30,000 or 40,000 men, many of whom still breathe the spirit of 1862, and carry back to their comrades, now sadly shrunk in numbers, voices that speak of Gaines' Mill, of Chancellorsville, or of Antietam. Fourthly, the question of putting negroes into the ranks, long and vehemently debated and combated, not only within the walls of Congress, but also at the corner of every street and round every fireside in the South, is gaining manifestly in public opinion, and seems likely to lead to immediate and energetic action, with a view to opposing to Mr Lincoln's 200,000 African soldiers, when the great collision of next spring shall arrive, at least a very considerable body of their dusky brethren. Fifthly, the appointment of [Major-] General Breckinridge to the important office of Secretary of War [in succession to Seddon] and the vigour which he has already exhibited in discharging the onerous functions of that bureau have given elastic confidence to men's minds, since it is recognized that, perhaps, the most important office of the State is now held by one who more than any other man in the South possesses simultaneously the qualifications of the soldier and the statesman, and that the Bureau of War and the Bureau of Finance are now administered by unquestionably the two fittest heads for the purpose that Secessia affords. But, lastly, and most important of all, the strong revulsion of feeling occasioned by the fruitless errand which carried Vice-President Stephens, Judge [John A.] Campbell [Assistant Secretary of War], and Mr [Robert M.T.] Hunter [President of the Senate] to Fortress Monroe, and exposed them to the indignity of listening to terms very different from those shadowed forth by Mr Blair, has revived, at least in Virginia, the fervid passion which glowed in every Virginian heart when Mr Lincoln's proclamation of 1861 roused the Old Dominion to flame. Upon the 6th and 9th inst., the two greatest and most excited popular assemblies which this city has ever witnessed listened on the former day to President Davis and on the latter to Mr Benjamin. In words weighty from the intensity of feeling with which they were uttered, and which dropped like solid shot among the listening thousands, President Davis told his audience that they might have peace if they would accept a Yankee satrap in every State, a Yankee emissary in every Southern Post-office, and if the soldiers among them would pluck off their uniforms and hand over the individual who was then speaking to them, and General Lee, and a thousand other soldiers whose names are engraven on every Southern heart to the well-known clemency and liberality of President Lincoln. But it was reserved for Mr Benjamin to demonstrate upon the 9th inst. that the reputation which he has long enjoyed as one of the greatest orators of this continent is not in jeopardy because for nearly four years his voice has been hushed in public. Boldly grappling with the question of negro enlistment, Mr Benjamin demanded what the South would have done had she known three years ago that at the end of 1864 Mr Lincoln would announce that he could not carry on the war without 200,000 negro soldiers stolen from Southern plantations. You have to decide, he said, between admitting emancipated negroes to the ranks, or the evacuation of Richmond. He deprecated the notion of negroes being forced to fight as slaves, as a sure method of recruiting the ranks of the enemy. Give them, he argued, the option of volunteering and fighting as freemen for their own homes and the soil where they have been raised, or of being abducted by the Federals as the country is overrun, and fighting, according to the new fashion of Northern emancipation, whether they like it or notes as freemen for the North. For 100 years and more Richmond has been renowned for her orators, but never in the history of this proud old State has the public heart so leapt up to meet a speaker, so responded to his every utterance and sentiment, as when upon the 6th and 9th of February cheer after cheer greeted President Davis and Mr Benjamin, and hurled back in fierce renunciation the contemptuous overtures of Mr Lincoln. For the moment the war spirit of 1861 has driven speculators, money-grabbers, and extortioners into the shade. At no previous stage of the war have I felt so painfully impressed by the dark uncertainty of the future; but I never had less hesitation than at this moment in assuring the North that their work is not more than half done, and that they are counting upon a victory as already secured which it will yet cost them thousands of lives to consummate.

In reality, of course, while the Southern Congress was relatively more accommodating than had been customary in the past and embraced so difficult a decision as to arm slaves, the South was being increasingly strangled by Union advances. Its main ports were all now closed and, having initially contemplated bringing Sherman's army back from Savannah to Virginia by sea, Grant was persuaded by Sherman to let him loose in the Carolinas. Accordingly Sherman left Savannah on 1 February and seventeen days later had reached Columbia which, like Atlanta before it, was largely destroyed by fire although in this case perhaps more through the action of retreating Confederates than Sherman's own forces. Mackay reported the loss of Columbia and the Confederate decision to evacuate Charleston – now effectively outflanked by Sherman – that same day, on 21 February in a communication printed on 6 March:

The retreat of Beauregard before the steadily advancing columns of Sherman, the evacuation of the line of the Congaree River without a battle, Sherman's unopposed entry into Columbia, his forward march upon Charlotteville, with the supposed intention of effecting a junction with Grant, and the sudden, though by no means unexpected, evacuation of Charleston, are events that have followed too rapidly upon each other to permit of a due appreciation of their actual importance or their probable influence upon the future fortunes of war. The sanguine people who habitually look upon every victory as final, who 'break the backbone of the rebellion' with every little or great success of Federal strategy or valour, are more sanguine than ever that the cause of the South is hopeless, and that on the day of his second inauguration Mr Lincoln will be able to announce that he is President *de facto* and *de jure* of the whole Union, and that the 'stars and stripes' float not only over all the sea-board cities of the South, but over rebellious Richmond. This roseate anticipation, however, finds more countenance from the sensational press than from the public; and military critics, so far from lending the weight of their knowledge and character to support such expectations, assert that Beauregard's tactics in retreating before Sherman are sound, that a junction between his forces and those of Lee can be sooner effected than a junction between Sherman and Grant, and that Sherman's army is in imminent peril of being suddenly attacked and defeated by the combined armies of Beauregard, Hardee, and Lee before Grant or any portion of his force can come to the rescue. Whether the South will win its Austerlitz [Napoleon's victory against Austria and Russia in December 1805] or suffer its Waterloo within the next ten days is a question that is everywhere discussed, and almost invariably decided by the political bias of the critic rather than by cool calculation and dispassionate judgement of events and probabilities. It is evident, however, that great events are at hand, and that neither the slaves of the South, nor the new and as yet unenlisted levies of the North, can be brought into the field in time to take part in the spring campaign – that will, in all human probability, decide the fortunes of the Confederacy.

The evacuation of Charleston will be celebrated to all future time as among the grandest and gloomiest events of the war. It appears to have been determined upon by General Lee immediately after his assumption of the supreme military power conferred upon him by the President and the Legislature, and heartily approved by the people of the South. There are indications that the first movements to this end commenced fully three weeks ago, and it is positively known that the principal citizens and the bulk of the army had withdrawn four days before the Federal commanders had any suspicion of the fact; and when the Northern forces entered the almost abandoned city, they found that the Confederates had determined to make a Moscow of it, and that the arrival of the foe was to be the signal for its destruction. Six thousand bales of cotton and two ironclads were ruthlessly destroyed lest they fall into the hands of the enemy; the arsenals, containing large quantities of arms and ammunition, the quarter-master's stores, the railroad station and bridges, the vessels in the building yards, and fully two-thirds of the once beautiful and flourishing city were reduced to ashes; the other third, fronting the sea, having been so riddled by the shot and shell of the besiegers during the last six or eight months as to be virtually uninhabitable. None but the poorest portion of the population, chiefly negroes, were left behind. All the rest had departed, bearing with them, there can be no reason to doubt, a spirit of vengeance which will yet blaze forth in new and fiercer struggles.

Despite bad weather, Sherman continued to make rapid progress as he turned to the north-east and headed for Fayetteville in North Carolina to link with forces under

Schofield advancing westwards from Wilmington, Schofield's corps having been detached from Thomas in Tennessee especially for the purpose. Lawley, who now advocated Lee's assumption of some form of military dictatorship in Richmond, wrote about Sherman's latest advance on 4 March in a report which appeared on 31 March:

Your readers will have followed Sherman's course since he captured Columbia and flanked his enemy out of Charleston and Wilmington. In the first instance it seemed to be Sherman's design to advance along the railroad which connects Columbia with Charlotte in North Carolina; but whether he was checked by Beauregard's firm attitude (previous to the assumption of command by Johnston) on the Catawba River to the south of Charlotte, or whether he was baffled by the difficulty of moving supplies and artillery through the miry swamps of the Carolinas, Sherman, shortly after capturing Columbia, struck eastward towards the sea coast with the apparent design of making a fresh sea base at Fayetteville, which is connected with Wilmington by the Cape Fear River. Simultaneously a strong force of Federals, probably 20,000 strong, under [Major-] General Schofield, is striking inwards from the coast at Newbern [New Bern], with a view to effecting a junction with Sherman near to Goldsborough – an important station on the Wilmington and Weldon Railroad, and distant not more than 40 miles from Fayetteville. It seems probable that the coming battle will be fought on the line between Goldsborough and Fayetteville, unless Johnston elects to give up Raleigh to his enemy with a view to getting him deeper into the heart of North Carolina before he ventures upon battle. Meanwhile the old lesson of the war about the immensity of Southern distances is again likely to be taught to Sherman. In order to gain a new base at Wilmington he has been compelled to set free the main artery of General Lee's army from the South – the railroad from Columbia to Richmond, via Charlotte, Greensborough [Greensboro], and Danville. It is my belief that the impossibility of starving out the Confederate armies while Johnston's army derives supplies from South Carolina and Georgia, and the abundant resources of Virginia and North Carolina are available for Lee, will be learnt before many weeks have flown. The obvious danger which menaces Secessia is that, in order to defeat Sherman, Lee may be compelled so to weaken his army as to be unable to hold the lines around Petersburg and Richmond. But it will, I think, be found that in the coming battles the Confederates will fight with the old elan and impetuosity which carried against superior numbers the heights of Chancellorsville, and bracketed with Albuera [where British and Portuguese forces advancing up a hill defeated the French in a particularly bloody battle in the Peninsular War in May 1811] the recent name of Gaines' Mill.

The continuing Federal successes against scattered Confederate forces in the Carolinas, whom Lee had placed under the command of Johnston on 22 February, were a perfect backdrop for Lincoln's second inauguration on 4 March. Mackay filed his report on the inauguration from Washington three days later, it being published in *The Times* on 20 March:

Four years ago Abraham Lincoln, elected by a majority of the States, but by a minority of the American people, took the oath of office administered to him by the Chief Justice of the Supreme Court, an ardent pro-slavery politician and friend of the Southern cause [Roger B. Taney]. Washington was more than half rebellious, and it was at the risk of his life that the new President – whose personal character and ability were then little known or appreciated – ventured to show himself in public. Very different were the circumstances of his re-installation yesterday. Though fully one-third of the States took no part in his re-election and considered him a foreigner, and the bitter enemy of their liberty and independence, the other two-thirds re-appointed him to office by a majority so triumphant as to prove that in spite of many errors, shortcomings, and failures he was their deliberate choice for the highest honour they could confer, and the only man who, in their judgement, was fit to carry to its close the fearful war of which his first election had been the signal. On this second occasion, Washington, which was crammed to overflowing with visitors from all parts of the country, instead of receiving Mr Lincoln with distrust, or even with scant courtesy, was ardent in the expression of its joy. If he had an enemy in the capital none such dared to show himself. He drove unprotected through the streets in an open carriage, receiving at every pace the vociferous plaudits of the multitude, and when at last he arrived in the Senate Chamber and walked to the platform, where in the presence of the people the oath was to be administered, he took it from the lips of a Chief Justice of his own appointment [Salmon P. Chase, appointed on Taney's death in December 1864], a man whose opinions on the great questions which agitate the country and underlie its mighty struggle for existence are identical with his own.

The night previous to the inauguration was cold and rainy. The Senate and House of Representatives, both of which sat till daylight of the 4th to dispatch the vast arrears of business which they had suffered to accumulate, were startled at short intervals by sharp gusts of wind and hail which battered on the skylights, and which on one occasion, in the dim grey of the early dawn, suddenly burst with such fury as to suggest the idea of an explosion within the building. Many of the members rose affrighted from their seats and rushed towards the door. The deliberations were for a while suspended in the general alarm, until the Speaker, rising from his chair, begged the representatives to resume their places, announcing that the noise 'was only a storm'. When day broke the rain was falling in torrents, and scarcely ceased until 10 o'clock. Washington, never free from horrible mud in wet weather and from still more horrible dust in the dry, was more than ankle-deep in the middle of the streets and ankle-deep at least in the footpaths. Every one predicted that the ceremonial of the day would take place undercover, in the Senate Chamber, and that the unprivileged multitude would lose their share of the spectacle. At 11 o'clock, however, the storm began to moderate, and a streak of light in the far horizon gave promise of fair weather. The processions speedily began to form, including regiments of soldiers in their shabby blue uniforms – horse, foot, and artillery – white men as well as black – deputations of firemen from Baltimore, Philadelphia, and other cities, Masonic Lodges, Friendly Societies, all with bands of music and banners, amid which the 'green flag of Erin' was next in conspicuousness to the all-pervading stars and stripes. From the White House, down the wide and pretentious but mean-looking thoroughfare called Pennsylvania-avenue, the Broadway and High-street of Washington, which connects the Presidential mansion with the Capitol, all was life and bustle. In spite of the mire and the weather the streets swarmed with people. The women trailed their long garments through the slush, as if silks were of no value, and the men trampled on heedlessly in long boots worn over their trousers, through mud and filth of a consistency and depth which no European who did not know the contrary from his American experience could believe to be compatible with the government of a civilized city. It was remarked by everybody, strangers as well as natives, that there never had been seen such crowds of negroes in the streets of the capital. At least one-half of the multitude were coloured people, pouring in from far and near to 'assist' in the ceremonial of a day which to them and to many wiser people seemed the triumph of their race over a fast fading social prejudice and political injustice. The negresses, 'dressed all in their best', flaunted in red, blue, yellow, and every variety of brilliant and gaudy colour, and looked as buoyantly happy as servant girls usually do when out for a holyday. The negroes held their heads high, as if they thoroughly understood that, under the beneficent sway of Abraham Lincoln, 'a man was a man for a' that'; if even he were not something better than a man – if his skin happened to be of the Ethiopian and not of the Caucasian colour.

Mackay was unimpressed with Lincoln's 'singular but pathetic address' and reported rather more fully upon the extraordinary performance of the new vice-president, Andrew Johnson, who was all too clearly drunk. Nevertheless, Lincoln's short speech was highly significant in its allusions to the magnanimity which must follow victory in the interests of reforging national unity.

Andrew Johnson

The opportunity for Lincoln to exercise that magnanimity came ever closer as Sherman, although temporarily checked by Hardee at Averasboro on 16 March, brushed aside Johnston's forces at Bentonville and joined Schofield on 23 March. Meanwhile at Petersburg the long winter months had taken an increasing toll of Lee's strength and he even made a tentative approach to Grant for terms in early March. He then planned a diversionary effort eastwards out of the Petersburg lines which might enable his army to march quickly to link with Johnston and defeat Sherman. On 25 March, however, the diversionary assault on Fort Stedman failed and six days later Grant began his own spring offensive with Sheridan's forces, now freed from the Shenandoah, able to co-operate from the west. When Sheridan cut the South Side Railroad to the west of the city on 1 April and Grant's forces overran the defences to the south on the following day, the defences of Petersburg became untenable. In turn that meant that Richmond, too, must be abandoned, Lee's message to that effect reaching Davis as the Confederate President worshipped in Richmond's St Paul's church. Mackay's hasty dispatch of 4 April was printed on 15 April:

General [Lieutenant-General] Grant's dispatches to Mr Lincoln state that the struggle which commenced to the south-west of Petersburg on Friday [31 March] continued with great fury and varying results until Saturday afternoon, when Sheridan turned the Confederate right at Five Forks Station on the South Side Railway, 15 miles west of Petersburg, and drove it back upon the centre, capturing several thousand prisoners and many cannon.

Early on Sunday morning Grant ordered a general advance, while Sheridan continued to press upon the Confederate flank, and after desperate fighting, lasting throughout the day, they succeeded in breaking through the Confederate lines at different points, and seizing the South Side Railway. The Confederates then retired to their intrenchments immediately about Petersburg. During the night they evacuated the city, though the movement was not discovered by Grant until yesterday morning, when he dispatched the bulk of his army in pursuit.

At about the same time [Major-] General [Godfrey] Weitzel, commanding the troops left by [Major-] General [Edward O.C.] Ord to hold the Federal works north of the James, discovered that Richmond had also been evacuated, and at 8.15 announced to the War Department that he had occupied the city, capturing many cannon and a large quantity of railway rolling stock. He also stated that the citizens received him with enthusiastic expressions of joy.

A fire which broke out in the city was speedily extinguished.

Non-official accounts state that the abandonment of the city commenced on the 26th, and that on Sunday night the Confederate rams on the James, and the fortifications on the banks of that river, were blown up.

Grant reports this morning from Sutherland, 10 miles west of Petersburg, that his forces were occupied yesterday in collecting Confederate soldiers, who, together with abandoned rams and other war materials were scattered about the country.

No trustworthy accounts of the losses in killed and wounded have yet been received, but they are stated to be very heavy on both sides and include many General and Staff officers. The Federals claim the capture of 12,000 prisoners.

A dead Confederate soldier lies in Fort Mahone, Petersburg, after its capture, 3 April 1865

There have been great rejoicings throughout the country in consequence of this success. In this city [New York] the courts adjourned, and business was almost entirely suspended. Congratulatory meetings were held, church bells rung, and salutes fired in Washington; the different departments of the Government were closed, and the employers granted a holyday.

Lawley was in a rather closer position to observe the fall of Richmond, although his account of its final hours was not written until he had reached New York on 11 April, and appeared only on 25 April:

Upon the afternoon of Saturday, the 1st of April, Richmond, long familiar with the sights and sounds of war, wore its usual look of unconscious security, and there were but few persons acquainted with the fact that Sheridan, with some 6,000 or 8,000 cavalry, supported by Warren's corps of infantry and artillery, was at work upon General Lee's right, that he was opposed only by a handful of

Union forces in Fort Sedgwick, Petersburg, 18 April 1865

Confederate cavalry, and that momentous events were probably at hand. It should be mentioned that for some days prior to the opening of April Grant had been massing troops on his extreme left, near Hatcher's Run, and that Lee had been compelled to mass correspondingly on his own extreme right. But, in addition to massing on his left, Grant had withdrawn all his troops, save two small divisions, from the north of the James River and from the Bermuda Hundred lines, and had placed them opposite to [Lieutenant-] General A.P. Hill's corps, at a spot where, in the immediate neighbourhood of Petersburg, it was known that the Confederate lines were weakly manned. It was not until Saturday, the 1st, that General Lee discovered that [Major-] General Ord and his troops had been withdrawn from the north side, and that he set to work also to bring [Lieutenant-] General Longstreet and most of his men across the river to the south side. My impression is that before Longstreet had taken position near Petersburg, the Federal attack of Sunday morning, conducted by [Major-] Generals [Horatio G.] Wright and Ord, had been successfully delivered. Be that as it may, at 5 upon the morning of Sunday, the 2nd, the Federals swept forward in a fine broad front, and ran fairly over A.P. Hill's weak lines of defence [Hill himself being killed]. Onward, right onward, the Federals eagerly pressed, until they got into the immediate neighbourhood of General Lee's head-quarters. I believe that in one or two spots the Confederates, and especially Mahone and [Major-General John B.] Gordon, succeeded in re-establishing their lines, but the fact remained that a broad belt of the Confederate earthworks, including four or five important forts, was in Grant's possession and General Lee immediately saw that the evacuation of Petersburg, and consequently of Richmond, was inevitable. He telegraphed at once to Richmond, desiring that everything necessary for its instant evacuation should be done (your readers will have gathered that the first steps towards its evacuation were taken two months ago), and announcing that the enemy would probably enter and take possession the following morning at daybreak. Upon the arrival of General Lee's dispatch in Richmond President Davis was occupying his accustomed seat during morning service in the Church of St Paul's, in which church, served by the same clergy-man, the Prince of Wales attended divine service upon the occasion of his visit to Richmond, and the President was surrounded by a congregation, of which the fairer portion was, as usual, arrayed with an elegance which has long been an unfailing source of wonder to those who reflect upon Richmond's four years of blockade. Suddenly the sexton, approaching President Davis, handed to him a paper, which was slowly perused. Rising from his seat with singular gravity and deliberation, Mr Davis left the church, and immediately afterwards several promi-nent citizens were by the same sexton summoned to follow him. It will be believed that the excitement among those who remained was at its highest, but it was remarked by sly observers that the excellent clergyman, who has endeared himself to his congregation by four years of brave and hearty sympathy with their trials, did not omit to make the usual collection – possibly with the design of impressing upon his congregation that nothing unusual had happened, possibly to give credit to a currency from which all felt that every semblance of value was passing away. The congregation was not slow to disperse, and quickly from mouth to mouth flew the sad tidings that in a few hours Richmond's long and gallant resistance would be over. The scene that followed baffles description. During the long afternoon and throughout the feverish night, on horseback, in every descrip-tion of cart, carriage, and vehicle, in every hurried train that left the city, on canal barges, skiffs, and boats, the exodus of officials and prominent citizens was unin-termitted. About 8 in the evening President Davis, accompanied by all the mem-bers of his Cabinet, except [Major-] General Breckenridge [Breckinridge], started by an express train for Danville, with a view to await further tidings there, and thence to proceed and form, if possible, the nucleus of a fresh Government at Charlotte, in North Carolina. Up to the hour of their departure from Richmond I can testify that Mr Davis and the three most prominent members of his Cabinet went undaunted forth to meet the future, not without hope that General Lee would be able to hold together a substantial remnant of his army, and to effect a junction with General Johnston. That hope, your readers are aware, has been disappointed, nor shall I now attempt to gauge the future history of those 10 or 11 vast provinces which are still at heart as rebellious as ever, but of which the organized resistance seems for the moment beaten down.

It will be believed that during that memorable night there was no sleep in Richmond. In front of every Government bureau, of every auditor's office, around the Capitol, and upon each side of Capitol-square, the glare of vast piles of burn-ing papers turned night into day. As the night wore away the tramp of Kershaw's division and of Custis Lee's local Militia was heard in the streets, and it was felt

The ruins of the Tredegar Iron Works at Richmond

that as the last men were now withdrawn from the north side there was no longer anything to interpose between Richmond and the enemy. As the first streak of dawn heralded the approach of day, several tremendous explosions seemed to shake every building in Richmond to its foundations. As I walked up between 5 and 6 in the morning of Monday, the 3rd, to catch the early train upon the Fredericksburg Railroad, a vast column of dense black smoke shot into the air, a huge, rumbling, earthquake-like reverberation rent the ground, and the store of gunpowder garnered in the city magazine passed out of existence. As the eye ranged backwards along the James River, several bright jets of flame in the region of Pearl and Cary streets augured the breaking forth of that terrible conflagration which subsequently swept across the heart of the city. As the train moved off from the Fredericksburg depot about 6 o'clock I parted with Mr Conolly, the member for Donegal, who had passed a month in Richmond, and was upon this eventful morning still undecided whether to follow General Lee's army or to strike north-wards like myself. About half an hour after my departure General Breckenridge, one of the last passengers who traversed the already blazing railroad bridge over the James River, started to rejoin his colleagues. About two hours after my eyes rested for the last time upon the dingy old Capitol under whose shadow I have

More devastation in Richmond after its capture

passed so many hours, the Stars and Stripes floated in triumph from its rebellious roof. The scene which upon that Monday morning greeted the incoming Federals will not soon, I imagine, be obliterated from their memory. Upon the edge of the roaring crackling flames, larcenous negroes, crazy Irishwomen, in a word, all the dangerous classes of Richmond (many of them infuriated and made reckless by whisky, of which hundreds of barrels had been emptied into the streets), danced, and dived into cellars and into the open and undefended doors of warehouses, plying their search after plunder, with the howls of demoniacs. Thousands of hogsheads of tobacco, and among them, I believe, the warehouses which contained the French tobacco, which has so long been a subject of diplomatic discussion between Mr Seward, Mr Benjamin, and the Emperor's Government [Napoleon III of France], added to the volume of the flames. Never might Prospero's words, 'Hell is empty, and all the devils are here', have been more appositely spoken. It was a scene unparalleled, I believe, even among the ghastly revelations of this war.

Subsequently Lawley decided to turn back to find Lee's army but his account of the final days of the Army of Northern Virginia, of which he seems to have been the only journalistic witness, was to be published in the *Fortnightly Review* rather than *The Times*. That army itself, its numbers dwindled to some 30,000 men, had moved westwards to Amelia Court House where Lee had anticipated finding supplies. None materialized, however, and Lee was forced to halt to scour the countryside. All the time the Union net was closing in and on 6 April the Confederate rearguard of 8,000 men was destroyed at Sayler's Creek. Blocked from reaching Danville, Lee struck off for Lynchburg but by 8 April was all but surrounded at Appomattox. When a last attempt to break out failed in the early morning of 9 April, Lee, who had already had some contact with Grant went to meet his opposite number. They met at the home of Wilmer McLean, who had moved from his former residence on the battlefield of Manassas to escape the war. Mackay reported on Lee's surrender on 11 April in an account published alongside Lawley's dispatch on the fall of Richmond:

It must have been with a heavy heart that General Lee surrendered to his grim and successful opponent the brave and for four long years the victorious army of Northern Virginia. Oppressed alike with private and with public sorrows, for he had lost one son by death and another by captivity in the series of unavailing struggles against superior force which ended on Saturday last [actually none of Lee's sons had been killed although Custis had been captured at Sayler's Creek], he resolved to prevent the further effusion of blood, and to descend from the lofty position of hero and patriot, in which he formerly stood, and accept from his countrymen, and perhaps from the world, the lower but not in his case the disgraceful place of discomfited rebel. With the small remnant of force at his command there

The McLean House at Appomattox Court House

was no alternative that it would not have been foolish, perhaps criminal, to adopt. Whatever may be thought by the Americans, it is difficult for a foreign spectator of the great event to decide to which of the two Generals the highest meed of praise should be accorded for true nobility of character, in circumstances that might well have filled the mind of the conqueror with elation, or depressed that of the conquered with a feeling akin to humiliation. But the truly brave man is bravest in adversity, and even in our prosaic time, when heroism is rarely exhibited and still more rarely recognized, there are few, whatever their political opinions may be, who will withhold from General Lee their sympathy and respect, or who will not indulge in the hope, if the American Republic is to be reconstituted on the basis of true liberty for all men, that the services of such a patriot and statesman as he should not be lost to his country.

In surrendering the Army of Northern Virginia General Lee seems to have guarded himself against the assumption of any powers that he may still consider as rightfully vested in Mr Jefferson Davis, as President of the Confederacy. Though Commander-in-Chief of all the armies of the South, he surrendered to the enemy only the one army under his immediate control, leaving to his superior to hold aloft the banner of the Confederacy, if still able or disposed to do so, and to the other armies in the field under Johnston, Kirby Smith, or Forrest, to make or refuse such terms as the fortune of war might present. There are few, however, in this city and throughout the North who do not believe that the Confederacy is a thing of the past; that the 'rebellion' is at an end, and the Union re-established beyond the power of man to destroy or shatter it. There has been a vast amount of very natural rejoicing over the result; but, as in the commercial parlance of this city, the surrender of Lee was 'discounted' as soon as the news arrived of the evacuation of Richmond, there has been much less 'buncombe' and fewer fireworks than were let off a week ago. The Doxology has again been sung in the streets, in the Corn-market, and even in the 'Gold-room'; the guns have been fired in the Park and on the Battery, and orators have hurled the usual amount of invectives against European Powers, especially against England; but as yet all these celebrations have been but a comparatively faint echo of the sturdier and heartier jubilation which burst forth with irrepressible energy on Monday last.

Lincoln had visited Richmond on 4 April and, in speaking to Campbell whom he had met in the abortive talks off Hampton Roads, again indicated a willingness to treat the South with some leniency. Back in Washington he went to Ford's Theatre on the night of 14 April, Good Friday, in the company of his wife and Major Henry Rathbone and his fiancée – Grant and his wife had been unable to attend – to see a production of the English comedy, *Our American Cousin*. As is well known, a minor actor with Southern sympathies, John Wilkes Booth, had gathered together an ill-assorted group of followers with the intention of kidnapping Lincoln, but the plot had turned to murder with Lincoln, Seward and Andrew Johnson as the intended victims. In the event the conspirator tasked with Johnson's elimination lost his nerve at the last minute while Lewis Paine only managed to wound Seward, who was ill in bed. Booth, however, was to enjoy more success as Lawley reported on 15 April in a dispatch printed on 29 April:

A thousand American cities, linked together by a network of lightning [i.e. the electric telegraph], have this morning awakened to the simultaneous knowledge that he who 12 hours ago was their first citizen, the chief architect of their fabric of a resuscitated Union, the figure-head round which clustered their hopes and pride, is numbered with the dead. Already over hundreds of thousands of square miles is every particular and detail of the rash and bloody deed of last night scrutinized by millions of eager eyes. It is believed that precisely at the same hour two ruffians, manifestly in concert with each other, lifted their hands against the two most valued lives of the Republican party – that upon the night of Good Friday Abraham Lincoln was stricken with his death-wound [he died at about 7.30 a.m. on the Saturday morning] in his private box at Ford's Theatre; that the small pocket pistol which launched the fatal bullet was found, still smoking, on the floor of the box; that the undaunted assassin, having entered from the rear, stretched his hand over Mrs Lincoln's shoulder until the muzzle of his pistol almost touched the President's head; that the bullet, designedly (as it would seem) propelled by a small charge of powder, did not pass through the head, but lodged in the brain about three inches from its point of entrance; that the ruffian who fired it, rescuing himself without difficulty from Colonel Parker, of [Lieutenant-] General Grant's Staff, who was in the box with Mr and Mrs Lincoln [Lawley confuses Major Rathbone with Lincoln's police bodyguard, John F. Parker, who had already absented himself from his post earlier in the evening to visit a saloon and had then gone into the theatre to get a better look at the play just before Booth's arrival outside Lincoln's box], calmly stepped [actually jumped and broke his leg] from the private box upon the stage; that, brandishing with melodramatic gesture a naked

John Wilkes Booth

dagger in his hand, he pronounced the well-known motto of the State of Virginia, 'Sic semper tyrannis', in apparent justification of a deed against the atrocity of which all that is noble and manly in that proud old State will recoil with indignant execration; that, turning with unruffled imperturbability, he left the stage and made his exit from the theatre by one of the side scenes with which he seemed familiar, and, mounting a horse which was attached to a tree in the immediate neighbourhood of the theatre, galloped swiftly into the night, and was lost.

The conspiracy theories in the wake of Lincoln's assassination even extended in some imaginations to embrace Stanton and Johnson, who, of course, immediately succeeded to the Presidency. However, Booth and his small group had acted alone and, indeed, only eight individuals were to be tried subsequently for complicity, including the hapless Dr Samuel Mudd, who treated Booth's leg without knowing the identity of his patient. Mackay, reporting on 21 April in a piece appearing on 5 May, rightly discounted most of the wilder rumours:

Though many arrests have been made, Booth has so far succeeded in eluding all pursuers, and there is as yet but scanty and unsatisfactory evidence to prove that any of the real conspirators are in custody, or that there were any conspirators at all, except Booth and the cowardly ruffian who stabbed the helpless Secretary of State and crushed the skull of Mr Frederick Seward, when endeavouring to protect his father. Rewards amounting in the aggregate to upwards of $100,000, have been offered for the apprehension of both or either of the wretches, and unless they evade justice by the commission of suicide America and Europe will be too small to conceal them. Booth's face and person are well known to thousands of playgoers in most of the cities of America, and not the most ingenious of theatrical disguises, in all of which he is a proficient, will be enough to screen him from the prying eyes which even without the incentive of a large reward would be sharpened to detect so heinous a criminal. If in the madness of his diseased imagination he relied upon the sympathy or approval of the South, and has made his way into Virginia, whose motto he has infernalized by adopting it as his vindication, he will find that the South as well as the North revolts with horror at his deed, and that the evil passions which the war has excited are not so evil as to make him other than what he is – the vilest assassin known to history, and one to meet the enormity of whose crime no punishment that man can inflict is adequate. Death is the utmost, and death to such a desperado, especially if it be made sufficiently solemn to afford him an opportunity of ending with a theatrical flourish and a display of stage heroism, may be the very fate he craves to hand him down to that immortality of infamy which seems to have had such a frightful charm to his perverted intellect.

Booth was hunted down at Bowling Green in Virginia on 26 April and died from a wound (although possibly self-inflicted) following a firefight with his pursuers. Four of those tried were hanged including Paine and Mrs Mary Surratt, in whose house the plot had been allegedly hatched.

Meanwhile, other Confederate forces were also surrendering. On 18 April Johnston

The execution of the Booth conspirators

had sought terms from Sherman, now at Raleigh in North Carolina. Sherman not only offered broadly the same terms Grant had given Lee – a virtual amnesty and parole allowing all to go home and to take horses they owned with them – but went even further in guaranteeing that existing state administrations would be recognized if they took an oath of loyalty and also promising full political rights. Grant had actually exceeded his instructions in the terms offered Lee but, with Lincoln now dead, Sherman's terms were totally unacceptable to Congress. Accordingly only those terms accepted by Lee were now offered but, unable to continue, Johnston accepted them on 25 April. During the negotiations Johnston had been in contact with Davis, who was maintaining the semblance of an administration at Greensboro. Now, however, Davis fled further south and was eventually apprehended at Irwinville, Georgia on 10 May, upon which Mackay's successor, L.J. Jennings, reported on 16 May in a dispatch published on 29 May:

> The capture of Mr Jefferson Davis must be regarded as a serious misfortune to the Northern people. His escape to Europe was the solution of the difficulty which above all others the Government ought to have prayed for, if it had not covertly endeavoured to facilitate. Even his escape across the Mississippi into Texas would have been less of a calamity to the North than his trial and execution for the crime of failure in an attempt, which only required success to elevate him

into the position of one of the world's heroes. The manner in which the 'sensation' journals gloat over his capture creates a feeling of horror, such as that which came over the hearts of most men when they heard of the assassination of Mr Lincoln. Though there is not a particle of evidence, and probably never will be, except that suggested to or extorted from the lips of perjured villains, to connect him in the remotest manner with the murder, his complicity with the assassins is assumed, and every base and vile epithet is hurled against him by men who would have licked his boots had he been successful in founding a Southern nationality, if by so doing they could have secured his favour or received the promise of a place. An immediate trial before the military commission now sitting at Washington to unravel the tangled skein of Booth's conspiracy is suggested by the most violent as the speediest means of deciding his fate, and the best mode of degrading him to the level of a common felon. Others, with equal vindictiveness, but with more sense of the dignities and proprieties of the case, recommend his trial on the charge of treason before the Supreme Court – a trial which is certain to end in his conviction, and in which conviction is equally certain to be followed by sentence of death. It begins to be conceded by all moderate men, friends as well as opponents of the Administration, that Mr Johnson was misled by false information, placed before him by an over-zealous, passionate, and too credulous public functionary, when he issued his proclamation against Mr Davis and the five Southern refugees in Canada; and to be apparent as the trial proceeds that there is no valid evidence against them individually or collectively. Mr Johnson, with a promptitude that does him credit, when he saw for the first time how all but unanimous public opinion was in denouncing the secrecy observed by the military tribunal in the trial of [David] Harrold [actually Herold, who had been captured at the time Booth had died], Mrs Surratt, and their accomplices, gave orders that the reporters for the public press should be admitted. He has thus done much to set himself right with the country, and to throw the disgrace of unconstitutional and illegal action upon the violent men whom he found in office. Were he to go a step further, recall his ill-judged proclamation, direct Mr Davis to be tried in open court before a jury for the treason which, by fact of his failure, that unhappy gentleman has undoubtedly committed; and, after sentence of death duly pronounced and recorded against him, magnanimously exercise his prerogative of pardon, or commute the sentence into banishment for life from the North American continent, President Johnson might not only rescue his Government and his country from a great and fruitful peril, but surround his 'plebeian' name – and as he is proud of being a 'plebeian' there ought to be no offence in the word – with a halo of true glory and mercy, which any patrician or aristocrat in the world might envy.

Even the arrest of Jefferson Davis did not necessarily mean the end of the war since Confederate forces remained in being. Major-General Richard Taylor had surrendered most of those still east of the Mississippi at Citronelle, Alabama on 4 May and others in Arkansas and Florida shortly followed suit. To the west of the Mississippi, however, General Edmund Kirby Smith still commanded a substantial army and, indeed, in presiding over the Trans-Mississippi Department since February 1863 had ruled a virtually autonomous state – 'Kirbysmithdom' – with some success. Jennings speculated on the immediate future in an article of 23 May, published on 6 June:

At this moment of triumph the exultation of the people is such that any one who ventures to hint that the war is not positively ended, and that on the west of the Mississippi there still remains a large country claiming to be a part of the Confederacy, and that it is held by a large army and a capable leader, is pronounced to be either a lunatic or a traitor; or, if he be a foreigner, a decided enemy of Republican institutions. Nevertheless, it may be of interest to Europe, and possibly to America, to know what force is actually under the command of General Kirby Smith, in the Trans-Mississippi region, and what spirit animates the leader and the army at a time when all other portions of the Confederacy yield enforced obedience to the Federal authority. It is possible that General Kirby Smith may be convinced of the uselessness of any further struggle. It is also possible that he may be in his heart a Unionist, and equally possible that if he have the desire to carry on his back the burden of the Southern cause, and hold aloft in his hands its banner in this day of its humiliation, he may not possess either the energy, the genius, or the good fortune necessary to insure success. Without speculating in this respect one way or the other, or asking what will or can be done by the Federal Government to trample out the last embers of the Civil War in that region, I proceed to place before your readers some facts in relation to Texas which are not publicly known, and which, if not sufficiently grave to embarrass the Federal Government in its domestic policy, are serious enough to impose the utmost caution upon it in reference to Mexico, and, above all, in its attitude towards the Emperor of the French [Napoleon III having used the excuse of Mexico's bad international debts to retain French troops there in an attempt to conquer the country after Britain and Spain had withdrawn from the venture in 1862]. I learn from an intelligent English gentleman, who has just arrived in this city from Texas and Louisiana, where he passed two months, part of the time in the camp and tent of General Kirby Smith, whose friendship and hospitality he enjoyed, that the Trans-Mississippi army has 150,000 men upon its muster rolls, and that its effective force is fully 85,000, to which number rations are daily issued. In this number are included 30,000 cavalry, well mounted on good Texan horses. Were it desirable, he says, to convert the whole force of 85,000 into cavalry the want of horses would be no impediment to the realization of the project. So great has been the quantity of clothing, ammunition, material of war, and other supplies from Europe run into Texas, via the Rio Grande, that General Kirby Smith calculates on unmistakable data that if not another ship were to run the blockade he would have sufficient stores of all kinds to supply all the wants of his army for two years. The vast plains of Texas swarm with herds of cattle, but, in consequence of the vigilant patrol of the Mississippi night and day by the agile and numerous gunboats of the Federal army, he was not able during a whole twelvemonth to transport more than 700 head across the river to the relief of the famishing armies of Lee, Hood, and Johnston. For the same reason, although he made four several attempts to throw reinforcements into Tennessee and Mississippi he was utterly unable to aid Mr Jefferson Davis with the 30,000 or 40,000 men whom he could well have spared from Texas, and whose timely assistance might have retrieved the falling fortunes of the Confederacy. Texas, he added, is not only much more prosperous, but more populous than it was at the commencement of the war. There has been a large immigration of planters and landed proprietors from the Gulf States, bringing their negroes with them. One of these gentlemen brought 600 negroes, and has purchased a large estate, in which he is successfully cultivating cotton. Another, from the eastern bank of the Mississippi, got over nearly 1,000 slaves, and has produced by their labour during the last year a highly profitable crop of sugar. Altogether, about 250,000 slaves and their masters have been thus located in Texas, since the fortunes of the war began to turn against the Confederates, and have greatly aided in developing the resources of the country. Last year the cotton crop was partially destroyed by the worm, and only about 50,000 bales were secured. This year the crop is healthy, and will yield on a fair estimate 250,000 bales. The Germans – a numerous body in Texas – were at one time inclined more or less to favour the abolition of slavery, but have modified or renounced their opinion in this respect, in consequence of the great immigration of rich planters and their negroes, and the immensely profitable cultivation of the soil by their agency.

As it happened, just three days after this report, Kirby Smith, whose army was by no means as strong as implied, chose to surrender, an event recorded for *The Times* by 'a correspondent' writing from Philadelphia on 30 May. He also reported on the first real indications of Johnson's proposals for the reconstruction of the South, his article appearing on 13 June:

On the 26th of May all the Confederate armies west of the Mississippi were surrendered by their commander, General E. Kirby Smith, to the Federal [Major-] General [Edward R.S.] Canby at New Orleans. The terms of surrender were similar to those given General Lee's army in Virginia; all the officers and men are to give their paroles not to bear arms against the United States, and are to go home and engage in peaceful pursuits. The faith of the United States is guaranteed that they will not be molested so long as they obey their paroles. The number of men surrendered by Kirby Smith was about 25,000. Forty general officers were surrendered; among them Lieutenant-Generals S.B. Buckner, J.B. Hood [actually a full General], and Sterling Price; Major-Generals [John B.] Clark, [Thomas C.] Hindman, and [John B.] Magruder; and Brigadier-Generals [Hamilton] Bee, [Albert] Pike, [James E.] Slaughter, and [Camille A.J.M.] Prince [de] Polignac. There is now no armed force of the Confederates east or west of the Mississippi, and the war is ended. The last battle of the war was one at El Paso del Chico, near Brownsville, Texas [13 May], between a Federal foraging party 300 strong and some Texan cavalry. The foragers were driven into Brownsville with a loss of 70, mostly prisoners.

The war being thus officially and really ended [the very last Confederates to surrender were actually the Indian forces of Brigadier-General Stand Watie, a Cherokee, on 23 June 1865], the Federal Government is busily engaged upon the great questions involved in the reconstruction of the Union. The effect of Mr Lincoln's assassination upon the public mind is entirely spent. The desire among Northern people for reconciliation with the South is universal. The friendly spirit so prevalent before Lincoln's death has returned. Orders have been issued for the unconditional pardon and release of all political prisoners confined in various parts of the country upon sentences by court-martial of imprisonment during the war. This is to be followed by an order for the release of all other political prisoners whose offences were not of a criminal nature. It is generally believed that by the middle of June there will be scarcely any State prisoners in confinement. By various orders issued during the past month nearly 50,000 Confederate prisoners of war, confined in various parts of the North have been released. Almost all have been sent to their homes in the South.

Yesterday, 29 May, President Johnson issued his great amnesty proclamation. He grants to all persons who have directly or indirectly participated in the rebellion, excepting such as are hereafter specified, amnesty and pardon, with the restoration of all rights of property, except as to slaves, and except where legal proceedings for confiscation have begun, on condition that such persons take an oath. The oath is that the person who takes it will support, protect, and defend the Constitution and the Union of the States, and abide by all laws and proclamations made during the war to secure emancipation. The various classes of persons excepted from the benefits of the amnesty are the following – All civil and diplomatic officers of the Confederacy; all who left judicial stations under the United States to aid the rebellion; Confederate military officers above the rank of Colonel; naval officers of higher grade than lieutenant; all below those grades who resigned commissions in the United States' army or navy to aid the rebellion, or were educated at West Point or the Naval Academy; all persons who left seats in the Federal Congress, or left their homes in the North, to aid the rebellion; all persons who treated Northern prisoners unlawfully, or engaged in privateering, or made raids from Canada; all persons who have been or are absentees from the United States for the purpose of aiding the rebellion; all Governors of Southern States; all who at the time they ask to take the amnesty oath are in custody, and all who participated in the rebellion and have taxable property worth more than $20,000. It is provided, however, that any one in these excepted classes may make special application for pardon to the President, 'and such clemency will be liberally extended as may be consistent with the facts of the case and the peace and dignity of the United States'. The great number of exceptions to the pardon is considered harsh, but the proviso somewhat mitigates this. The proclamation itself is considered as evidence that Johnson wishes to restore the Union as perfectly as it can be done, excepting slavery, so that the States may have the same rights as they enjoyed before the war. Many of the persons excepted will no doubt apply for pardon, but as every one, North and South, now seems anxious to restore the Union and return to peaceful pursuits, the proclamation will soon become a dead letter. The exception of all persons whose property amounts to $20,000 savours a little of Johnson's 'plebeian' ideas. The proclamation shows the triumph of the Conservatives, in the fact that no provision is made for negro suffrage in the South. A division in the Cabinet upon this point delayed its promulgation for over a week.

Johnson's proclamation of amnesty was, indeed, accompanied by increasing numbers of individual pardons and only Jefferson Davis really suffered, being incarcerated in often unpleasant conditions in Fortress Monroe for two years. A second proclamation on the same date as the first had reorganized the government of North Carolina and was soon applied to the other states, with provisional governors proceeding to elect conventions based on a franchise of pre-war voters who had taken the oath of loyalty. Almost invariably, as the unknown correspondent from Philadelphia recognized, such a franchise excluded negroes and large numbers of former Confederates returned to power, a process eventually resulting in a confrontation between Johnson and Congress in 1866, the effective imposition of military rule over the South by the Reconstruction Act in 1867 and the laying down of the principle of civil rights under the fourteenth and fifteenth amendments of the constitution in 1866 and 1869 respectively. Ultimately, however, if reconstruction was less radical than it appeared, yet none could doubt that the war did leave a profound legacy in the United States, not least the knowledge that Americans had fought each other and that over 620,000 soldiers and perhaps 50,000 civilians had died.

SELECT
BIBLIOGRAPHY

GENERAL

McPherson, J.M., *Battle Cry of Freedom: The American Civil War* (Oxford, 1988)

Paludan, P.S., *A People's Contest: The Union and Civil War, 1861–65* (New York, 1988)

Parish, P.J., *The American Civil War* (London, 1975)

Thomas, E.M., *The Confederate Nation, 1861–65* (New York, 1979)

ANGLO-AMERICAN RELATIONS DURING THE CIVIL WAR

Bourne, K., *Britain and the Balance of Power in North America, 1815–1908* (London, 1967)

Cook, A., *The Alabama Claims* (Ithaca, 1975)

Crook, D.P., *The North, the South and the Powers, 1861–65* (New York, 1974)

Ellison, Mary, *Support for Secession: Lancashire and the American Civil War* (Chicago, 1973)

Ferris, N.B., *The* Trent *Affair: A Diplomatic Crisis* (Knoxville, 1977)

Foner, P.S., *British Labour and the American Civil War* (New York, 1981)

Jenkins, B., *Britain and the War for the Union*, 2 vols (Montreal, 1974, 1980)

Lester, R.I., *Confederate Finance and Purchasing in Great Britain* (Charlottesville, 1975)

Merli, F.J., *Great Britain and the Confederate Navy, 1861–65* (Bloomington, 1970)

Owsley, F.L., *King Cotton Diplomacy* (2nd edition, Chicago, 1959)

Warren, G.H., *Fountain of Discontent: The* Trent *Affair and Freedom of the Seas* (Boston, 1981)

THE TIMES AND ITS CORRESPONDENTS

Brogan (ed.), H., The Times *Reports the American Civil War* (London, 1975)

Crawford, M., *The Anglo-American Crisis of the Mid-Nineteenth Century*: The Times *and America, 1850–62* (Athens, GA, 1987)

Hankinson, A., *Man of Wars: W.H. Russell of* The Times (London, 1982)

Hoole, W.M.S., *Lawley Covers the Confederacy* (Tuscaloosa, 1964)

Jenkins, B., 'Frank Lawley and the Confederacy', *Civil War History*, 23. 2 (1977), pp. 144–60

Russell, W.H., *My Civil War Diary* (London, 1954) edited by F. Pratt with an introduction by H. Brogan

Stephen, L., The Times *on the American War: A Historical Study* (London, 1865, reprinted New York, 1915)

The Times, The History of The Times: *The Tradition Established, 1841–84* (London, 1939)

INDEX